The Mortal Hero

An Introduction
to Homer's *Iliad*

Seth L. Schein

UNIVERSITY OF CALIFORNIA PRESS

Berkeley / Los Angeles / London

University of California Press
Berkeley and Los Angeles, California

University of California Press, Ltd.
London, England

Printed in the United States of America

1   2   3   4   5   6   7   8   9

Library of Congress Cataloging in Publication Data

Schein, Seth L.
   The mortal hero.

   Bibliography: p.
   Includes index.
   l. Homer. Iliad.   2. Heroes in literature.   I. Title.
PA4037.S394   1984   883'.01   83–5096
ISBN 0–520–05128–9

The Mortal Hero

For Sherry, with gratitude and love

Contents

Preface

This book is addressed mainly to non-specialist readers who do not know Greek and who read, study, or teach the *Iliad* in translation; it also is meant for classical scholars whose professional specialization has prevented them from keeping abreast of recent work on Homer. It is grounded in technical scholarship, to which it constantly refers and is intended to contribute, and I hope that even Homeric specialists will find ideas and interpretations to interest them. I have tried to present clearly what seem to me the most valuable results of modern research and criticism of the *Iliad* while setting forth my own views. My goal has been to interpret the poem as much as possible on its own mythological, religious, ethical, and artistic terms. The topics and problems I focus on are those that have arisen most often and most insistently when I have taught the poem, in translation and in the original, as I have done every year since 1968.

This book is a literary study of the *Iliad*. I have not discussed historical, archaeologoical, or even linguistic questions except where they are directly relevant to literary interpretation. Throughout I have emphasized what is thematically, ethically, and artistically distinctive in the *Iliad* in contrast to the conventions of the poetic tradition of which it is an end product. For example, I try to show how the *Iliad* transforms conventional attitudes toward the gods, heroism, and immortality in accordance with its own thematic emphasis on mortality and on the limitations and opportunities of the human condition. Sometimes it is clear that the poem alludes to traditional mythology and heroic values, with which it is not itself primarily concerned, in order to bring out by contrast its own characteristic themes. Often it invites readers to consider ironically and critically contradictions in the traditional heroism and heroic world which it depicts. In most cases what is distinctive about the poem in relation to its own tradition is also what has always seemed to its readers especially moving and stimulating. For this reason I have been able to write both for scholars and for non-specialist readers.

No one is likely to read all that has been written about the *Iliad*. Every Homeric scholar finds some books and articles more helpful and more to his or her taste than others. This is partly a matter of training and influence by one's teachers, but also a question of individual temperament and susceptibility to the approaches to literature that are current when one is thinking and writing. I have been most strongly influenced by and have tried to combine the approaches of the two most fruitful "schools" of modern Homeric scholarship: the (chiefly Anglo-American) study of Homer as a traditional oral poet, which began with the work of Milman Parry, and the "Neo-Analysis" originated by Johannes Th. Kakridis and exemplified by the work of such German students of the poem as Karl Reinhardt and Wolfgang Schadewaldt. The *Iliad* books of E. T. Owen and of Cedric Whitman, which I read when I first studied the *Iliad* in Greek, have been abiding influences. I have learned a great deal, as well, from the more recent books by Michael Nagler, James Redfield, and Gregory Nagy, although it will be obvious that my approach and interpretations are significantly different from theirs. I have cited frequently these and other works of Homeric scholarship in order both to acknowledge my intellectual debts and to suggest to readers where they can learn more about particular topics or lines of interpretation. I have not, however, aimed for and make no claim of bibliographical completeness. I feel fortunate to have studied Homer with Professors Charles Kahn and Howard Porter at Columbia University and with Bruno Snell in his term as Sather Professor at the University of California at Berkeley. I am especially indebted to Professor Porter, whose courses on the *Iliad* and *Odyssey* I attended for three years as an undergraduate and graduate student: he first taught me to read and think about the *Iliad* as literature and opened up for me the world of Homeric scholarship. I also have been privileged to know and to benefit from conversation and correspondence with Professor Johannes Th. Kakridis, whose work and personality have been inspiring.

The *Iliàd* can be a difficult poem—far more difficult than the *Odyssey*—for non-specialists who approach it simply as the earliest work of Western literature and have no knowledge of its place in its own poetic tradition or of how to appreciate its distinctive themes, values, and artistry. It can be equally difficult for classical scholars whose professional training often leads them to ask detailed philological or historical questions of the text without proceeding on to its broader structures and meanings. I hope that this book will help both groups of readers to appreciate the poem on its own terms with greater pleasure and understanding.

In order to make my work accessible to as many readers as possible, I have used no Greek apart from a few transliterated words and phrases which seemed helpful or necessary to make particular points and which I have always translated. I give my own line-by-line translations of the text, which are more accurate and more literal than existing translations, so that readers who do not know Greek can control textual detail and nuance and follow the interpretations I suggest. Where necessary, I have sacrificed normal English style and word order to my desire to bring out as much as I could of what I see in the Greek. The line numbers of my translations and textual citations refer to the Oxford Classical Text edited by D. B. Monro and T. W. Allen. These numbers never differ by more than one line from the numeration in the line-by-line translation of Richmond Lattimore.

I would like to thank the many friends and colleagues who helped me to write this book. My earliest efforts were encouraged and criticized by Caesar Adams, Penelope Adams, Helen Bacon, Harry Berger, Jr., James Coulter, John DeWind, Muriel Dimen, Helene Moglen, Julius Novick, Howard Porter, and Penelope Robbins. At later stages, one or more chapters benefited from the criticism and suggestions of Sara Bershtel, Norman O. Brown, Laurie Cosgriff, Carola Greengard, Mark

Griffith, Katherine King, John Lynch, Stephen Marx, Garry Miles, Michael Nagler, Gregory Nagy, Norman Rabkin, Peter Rose, and Charles Segal. I am especially grateful to Laura Slatkin, who read and discussed with me drafts of each chapter, helped me to clarify my ideas about the *Iliad*, and suggested numerous improvements in substance, style, and organization, as well as my title. I am conscious of my debts to all these readers, but in some instances I decided not to follow their advice, so I wish to state emphatically that they should not be held responsible for any of the idiosyncrasies or shortcomings of this book.

I am grateful to Wallie Romig for typing the final manuscript quickly and accurately, and to Cassandra Cleghorn for checking line references and helping to eliminate a number of stylistic blemishes.

I also am grateful to the State University of New York, College at Purchase, and the University of California at Santa Cruz for leaves of absence during which most of this book was written; to the National Endowment for the Humanities for a Fellowship in 1980 that helped support my work; and to the Academic Senate of the University of California at Santa Cruz for Research Grants in 1980/81 and 1982/83 that likewise assisted my efforts.

I am indebted to the editors of *Eranos*, in particular to Dr. Stig Rudberg, for permission to use parts of two articles on the *Iliad* published in volumes 74 (1976) and 78 (1980) of that journal.

I would like to thank Doris Kretschmer, Mary Lamprech, and Richard Holway of the University of California Press for their editorial care and helpfulness, and Paul Psoinos for his exceptionally detailed, salutary copyediting. Working with them has been both pleasant and instructive.

I am grateful to my parents, Albert Schein and Sylvia Orlikoff Schein, whose copy of the Samuel Butler translation of the *Iliad* first introduced me to the poem, for their continuing encouragement of my work.

Most of all, I am grateful to Sherry Crandon, my wife, for the support, criticism, and confidence in me that made it possible for me to write this book. I dedicate it to her with gratitude and love.

1

The Poetic Tradition

The *Iliad* is read today as the earliest example of Western literature, the first work in a long tradition of heroic narrative. Yet to a modern reader the poem, while emotionally and intellectually affecting, can seem simple and naive in its repetitive style and difficult to appreciate. Actually, the *Iliad* is not a "first work"; rather it is an end product of a poetic tradition that may have been as much as a thousand years old by the time this epic was composed, probably in the final quarter of the eighth century B.C. Its style, mythological content, and heroic themes and values are traditional, but it generates its distinctive meanings as an ironic meditation on these traditional themes and values. Through parallels, contrasts, and juxtapositions of characters and actions, a dramatic structure is created that forces us to consider critically the traditional heroic world depicted in the poem and the contradictions inherent in this kind of heroism.[1] The overwhelming fact of life for the heroes of the *Iliad* is their mortality, which stands in contrast to the immortality of the gods. We see the central hero of the poem, Achilles, move toward disillusionment and death to reach a new clarity about human existence in the wider context of the eventual destruction of Troy and in an environment consisting almost entirely of war and death. This environment offers scope for various kinds and degrees of heroic achievement, but only at the cost of self-destruction and the destruction of others who live in the same environment and share the same values.[2]

Homer generates the characteristic themes and ideas of his poem by fulfilling the traditional expectations of his audience at the same time that he innovatively plays against them. At every level—language, style, themes, portrayal of gods and humans—the *Iliad* expresses its distinctive vision of reality through a strictly traditional artistic medium. In the past half-century scholars have come to understand more accurately the formal organization and the mythological content of this medium. Today, readers of the poem, building on this understanding, can approach the poem on its own terms and appreciate both its distinctive vision and the poetic structure through which Homer expressed it.

1

The traditional medium, we know today, was one of oral poetry. In it a poet created a poem anew each time he said (or, rather, sang) it, for there was no established, written text. At the same time, the poems he sang were *formulaic*: the language, meter, and style, as well as the kinds of events and even many of the specific events in the story, were traditional and common to all poets who learned to work with the basic building blocks of the genre—fixed formulas, consisting of words, phrases, and lines, and typical scenes, episodes, and sequences. These building blocks changed somewhat from poet to poet, usually through small innovations that may sometimes have been unconsciously introduced by the poets and that, to judge from studies of modern oral poets, they would sometimes have denied making. A poet in command of his medium could manipulate these building blocks to say whatever he wished: a poor, unimaginative poet would produce poor, unimaginative songs, as would such a poet writing, for example, in English iambic pentameters; a great, imaginative poet like Homer would produce correspondingly great, imaginative poetry, as would Shakespeare. In other words, the fact that the *Iliad* is composed in formulaic language and meter and according to strict narrative conventions does not mean that it is therefore unoriginal or inartistic.

The preceding statement may seem unnecessary or ridiculous to any reader who has felt, even in translation, the poetic power of the *Iliad*. I make it because one result of the discovery that the Homeric poems are composed in a traditional style, which enabled illiterate singers to create and perform heroic poetry, has been the conviction among some Homeric scholars that it is impossible to speak of the artistry or originality of any particular poet, including Homer, who composed in this style, and that it is equally impossible to speak of the meaning of the *Iliad* as a whole or even of many of the individual words in the fixed formulaic phrases of which the poetry largely or entirely consists. In other words, these scholars argue, the traditional oral style and its concomitant heroic values and mood are what count; since these were uniform and belonged equally to all singers in the tradition, and since the innovations of any particular poet must have been relatively slight, Homer's "responsibility for [the] *Iliad* was incidental" and cannot be specified.[3]

In order to see how scholars, including some of those philologists who have studied the text of the *Iliad* most closely, can have come to such apparently strange conclusions about a poem that has universally been considered one of the creative masterpieces of the human imagination, it is necessary to understand just what is meant by a traditional oral, formulaic style. That the *Iliad*, like the *Odyssey*, is composed in such a style was the discovery of the great American classical scholar Milman Parry. Parry first demonstrated his discovery in a series of publications in French and in English in the late 1920s and early 1930s.[4] Then he seemed to confirm it between 1933 and 1935 by his field studies of a still-living oral poetic tradition in Yugoslavia.

Parry began from two phenomena which are obvious to anyone who reads Homer in Greek: the metrical form of the dactylic hexameter, the meter in which the *Iliad* and *Odyssey* are composed, and the fact that certain words and phrases, often in combination with other specific words and phrases, recur frequently in the poems, usually in the same metrical positions in the line. Parry paid particular attention to repetitions of nouns, especially proper nouns, and of the adjectives that modify them—a distinctive kind of repetition everywhere apparent to anyone reading a faithful translation such as Richmond Lattimore's.[5]

Like all Greek meters, the dactylic hexameter is based on the patterned occurrence of "heavy" and "light" syllables (more usually but less accurately called "long" and "short" syllables). The line, or hexameter, is the main metrical unit; there are from 12 to 17 syllables per line arranged according to the following pattern of heavy (–) and light (⌣) syllables:

$$-\overline{\smile\smile}-\overline{\smile\smile}-\overline{\smile\smile}-\overline{\smile\smile}-\overline{\smile\smile}--$$

Thus, the first, third, fifth, seventh, ninth, eleventh, and twelfth elements are always heavy, and the other elements consist either of one heavy or two light syllables. Each line is further delineated into (usually) four metrical subunits called *cola*; a *colon* is a sequence of syllables, often consisting of a distinct semantic unit—a word, word group, or phrase—that ends regularly at a particular position in the line. It is as if each individual hexameter were a small stanza consisting of four *cola*.

The numerous repeated words and phrases tend to recur at the same metrical positions in the line, that is, in the same *cola*, because in this way they were functionally useful to a performing singer composing a heroic song. Such a singer, for whom composition and performance were identical, would use these metrically fixed words and phrases as naturally as anyone might use ordinary language (though the mixture of dialects in the traditional poetic language indicates clearly that it never was anyone's ordinary language). As a performer he could not think over his next words or revise what he had just said at leisure in the manner of a literate poet. The highly complex system of repeated words and phrases made it possible for him to continue the flow of metrically correct verse without hesitation and to express any idea whatsoever that the subject matter of the traditional epic might make it necessary or desirable for him to express.

Parry called "a group of words which is regularly employed under the same metrical conditions to express a given essential idea" a "formula."[6] An "essential idea" he defined as "that which remains after one has counted out everything in the expression which is purely for the sake of the style," that is, for the sake of achieving a metrically correct hexameter verse by filling a specific sequence of heavy and light syllables in a particular place in the line.[7] Parry cites as an example of a formula and its essential idea the formulaic phrase, "the goddess grey-eyed Athene." These words occur 19 times in the *Iliad* and 31 times in the *Odyssey*, filling the metrical sequence ⌣−−−⌣⌣−− at the end of the line; the words "grey-eyed Athene" alone occur another 9 times in the *Iliad* and 19 times in the *Odyssey*, also at the end of the line. Parry says that Homer uses these words to express in this metrical position the essential idea "Athene"; presumably neither the poet nor his audience would have been conscious of the separate, specific meanings of "goddess" and "grey-eyed." Parry similarly cites the recurrent line "But when the young Dawn showed again with her rosy fingers" (2 times in the *Iliad*, 20 times in the *Odyssey*) as expressing the essential idea "When it was morning."

If we look at one of the repeated combinations of proper names and epithets, which Parry studied in the fullest detail, we can begin to get some idea of how the traditional formulas worked. When the name Odysseus occurs in the nominative case, as the subject of a finite verb, it almost always (49 out of 53 times in the *Iliad*) is the final word in the line. In 38 of these 49 instances, the proper name is accompanied by an adjective or combination of adjectives or an adjectival appositional phrase: "brilliant," "resourceful," "sacker of cities," "long-suffering brilliant" Odysseus. What governs the choice of adjective or adjectives in each instance is not what Odysseus is saying or doing but rather what sequence of heavy and light syllables is required to complete the line with metrical correctness. The Greek word for "brilliant" is *dios*; combined with Odysseus, it gives a metrical sequence of −⌣⌣−− (*dĭŏs Ŏdŭsseūs*). Both "resourceful" (*pŏlŭmētĭs*, 13 times) and "sacker of cities" (*ptŏlĭpōrthŏs*, 2 times) combined with Odysseus yield a sequence of ⌣⌣−⌣⌣−−. "Long-suffering brilliant Odysseus" (*pŏlŭtlās dĭŏs Ŏdŭsseūs*) fills ⌣−−−⌣⌣−−. Whichever epithet is used, the same essential idea, "Odysseus," is expressed. In two of these three combinations of epithet and noun, there is only one adjective or combination of adjectives to fill a given metrical sequence. In the third instance, one of the adjectives is much more common than the other. This illustrates what

Parry called the "thrift" or the "economy" of the Homeric systems (groups) of formulas: "The thrift of a system lies in the degree in which it is free of phrases which, having the same metrical value and expressing the same idea, could replace one another."[8] The system I have been describing is thrifty but does allow some variation. A clear indication of the degree of thrift in the traditional style generally is the fact, determined by Parry, that of the 37 characters in the *Iliad* and *Odyssey* who have noun-epithet formulas in the nominative case filling the metrical sequence ⌣−−−⌣⌣−− at the end of the line there are only three names having a second formula that could replace the first![9] Obviously, without such thrift, the formulas would have been far less useful for a performing poet because he then would have had to take time to decide which of several possible, that is, metrically correct, words or phrases to use.

Parry emphasized that "when the element of usefulness is lacking, one does not have a formula but a repeated phrase which has been knowingly brought into the verse for some special effect."[10] This, he argued, is a procedure of literate poets who write down their poems. An oral (by definition, illiterate) singer, on the other hand, follows a fixed pattern of words and does not consciously decide to repeat a phrase. He denies himself, and the traditional style denies him, any other way of expressing his essential idea. He thinks in terms of the formulas, so there is an unbroken flow; this is the utility of the formulaic style. And Parry claims that "because at no time is he seeking words for an idea which has never before found expression, . . . the question of originality in style means nothing to him."[11]

The systems of formulas discovered by Parry, like the one I have described for Odysseus in the nominative case at the end of the line, exist not only for all the proper names and epithets in the *Iliad* and *Odyssey* in all their possible grammatical cases, but also for most, perhaps all, of the words and phrases in the poem in all their forms and relationships with one another. (If more material were extant, words and phrases that seem to us unique and nonformulaic might be recognizable as formulaic.) All these systems are characterized by the same extraordinary thrift. For example, "Homer uses for the five grammatical cases of Achilles, 46 different noun-epithet formulas representing the same number of different metrical values."[12] In other words, no two grammatically synonymous noun-epithet formulas for Achilles fill the same sequence of heavy and light syllables in the same position in the line. As astonishing as the thrift of the traditional formulaic language is its complexity. "Each formula is . . . made in view of the other formulas with which it is to be joined; and the formulas taken all together make up a diction which is the material for a completely unified technique of verse-making."[13]

Since Parry set forth what might be called an ideal definition and description of the Homeric formula, students of the Homeric poems have modified and extended his findings in various ways. Resemblances in sound—especially important when one is considering oral performance and composition—and in grammatical and syntactical relationships between words or parts of speech recurring in the same metrical positions have been interpreted as criteria for "formularity." M. N. Nagler has defined a formula not in terms of the actual words and phrases we find in our texts but as a "central Gestalt" existing "on a preverbal level in the poet's mind"; each phrase that actually does occur in the texts is considered an "allomorph" of this central Gestalt, "which is the real mental template underlying the production of all such phrases."[14]

Even more important than the suggested changes in Parry's definition of a formula has been the realization by some scholars that while Parry undoubtedly was correct in his demonstration and elucidation of the traditional nature and function of the formulaic style, he went too far in his reduction of formulas to essential ideas and his assumption that the epithets in noun-epithet formulas are metrically convenient but otherwise merely "ornamental"—meaningless, that is, apart from their evocation of traditional, general heroic qualities, moods, or values. It has been suggested, for instance, that many of the adjectives and adjectival phrases describing particular heroes in the *Iliad*, in addition to being metrically useful, are in some way associated with those heroes' chief functions or with especially memorable and significant scenes or activities in which they take part.[15] For example, "lord of men" (*anax andrōn*) is particularly appropriate to Agamemnon; "of the shining helmet" (*koruthaiolos*), frequently used of Hektor, recalls the scene with Hektor, Andromache, and Astyanax in Book 6 where Hektor's helmet plays such a significant role; "swift-footed" (*podas ōkus, podas tachus*), often used of Achilles, may suggest, among other scenes, his climactic pursuit of Hektor around the walls of Troy in Book 22. Obviously, not all epithets of heroes will have such relevance, and not every potentially relevant epithet will be felt as relevant each time it occurs; nevertheless, these and many other such epithets may have originated or may have persisted in the tradition because they were or could be especially distinctive and thus meaningful, not merely because they were useful.

Parry's theory has also been modified by the recognition that where thrift is not absolute, considerations of context or dramatic effect may govern the poet's choice of which of two possible epithets to use. Thus, Hektor in the genitive case at the end of the line can be either "tamer of horses" (*hippodamoio*) or "manslaughtering" (*androphonoio*), which are metrically equivalent. But by "tamer of horses," an epithet suggestive of the domination of nature by human culture, Hektor is associated with Troy as a *polis*, a social community, and with Apollo, who in the *Iliad* is a protecting deity of this particular community.[16] But it is noteworthy that no Greek ever calls him "tamer of horses": that is not how they perceive him. Furthermore, Homer's narrative refers to him as "manslaughtering" at several poignant moments, such as at 6.498, when after the moving family scene at the Skaian gate Andromache returns to the "well-settled household of manslaughtering Hektor," or at 24.724, when she laments, "holding in her hands the head of manslaughtering Hektor." At these moments Homer's use of the adjective seems to call attention to the destructive and, in the end, self-destructive quality of Hektor's heroism. It has similarly been argued that the adjective *phaidimos*, "shining," used to describe Hektor in the nominative case in the metrical sequence $-\cup\cup--$ at the end of the line (*phāidĭmŏs Hēktōr*), is associated almost everywhere in the *Iliad* with defeat and accordingly points to Hektor's essential role in the poem as "loser" of his own life and (symbolically) of his city.[17]

There are other ways in which the traditional formulas are manipulated in the *Iliad* to produce meanings beyond what Parry, at least in his published work, seems to have considered possible. Sometimes they are used at other metrical positions in the line than those at which they usually occur, playing against the normal expectancy in the minds of the audience or reader and thus calling attention to themselves and gaining in emphasis. Sometimes a word or phrase normally used only of a god or of a personified abstract noun such as Fate or Death is applied to a person, thus making him an impersonal force. For example, *oloös*, "destructive," is used of Achilles at 24.39, and *mēnis*, "anger," is used for his wrath throughout the poem.[18] Sometimes certain formulas are used together with certain other formulas, or in specific narrative contexts, that momentarily actualize a latent poetic signification, as when the word *krēdemna*, denoting the "battlements" of a city whose destruction someone is envisioning, calls to mind another meaning of *krēdemna*, a woman's "veil," which is an emblem of her chastity.[19] Thus the sack of the city is associated with sexual violation, an association made almost explicit at 22.466–72, when Andromache faints at the sight of Hektor's corpse being dragged away by Achilles' horses and, in the process, throws away the veil which Aphrodite had given her on her wedding day. This occurs shortly after we learn that the wailing and lamentation that arose in the city when Hektor was killed "was most like what would have happened if all / beetling Ilion had been burning top to bottom in fire" (22.410–11). The death of Hektor means both the destruction of Troy and the destruction of the married chastity of Andromache—in short, the destruction of the domestic, civilized life of which Hektor is the poem's main male exemplar and for which he falls fighting.

Few scholars have tried to consider the formula both as a useful tool of oral composition and as meaningful in its own right and contributing to the meaning of the entire poem.[20] Yet only such an attempt can do justice both to the uniformity of the formulaic style and to that individuality of the speeches, actions, and attitudes of the various characters in the *Iliad*, which any reader cannot help but recognize. Traditional heroic values are presented in a traditional heroic style, but these values are not all that is presented in the poem. Emphasis on what is traditional in the style common to all poets has led scholars to ignore what is distinctive, at times almost counter-traditional, in the *Iliad* of Homer. Yet any conception of a traditional oral style is inadequate if it does not allow one to recognize and critically analyze both the particular dramatic, thematic, and ironic structures of the *Iliad* and the meanings it generates through the poet's unique organization of traditional material and individual use of the traditional style. Such a conception does not account for the emotional and intellectual impact the poem has always made and still makes on its readers: though this conception may help us to understand the history of the form in which the *Iliad* was created and to account for and appreciate many of its poetic techniques, it does not by itself contribute to literary criticism and an understanding of the poem.

There are, I think, two main reasons why the discoveries of Milman Parry and his successors led so many classical scholars, and through them a wider reading audience, to deny originality and distinctive artistry to Homer and to miss so much of the meaning in the *Iliad*. In the first place, these discoveries seemed to solve the so-called Homeric Question that had occupied scholars through the late eighteenth, nineteenth, and early twentieth centuries; secondly, the conclusions arrived at by Parry through detailed examination of the texts were apparently confirmed by his later study of Serbocroatian oral poetry, and much that was true of the Yugoslav poets was too simplistically projected back onto Homer and the *Iliad*.

In essence the Homeric Question may be stated as follows: is the *Iliad* (leaving aside the *Odyssey*, for the sake of convenience) that we read today the work of a single artist, or is it the result of a number of separate poems by different poets having been grouped together into a composite with no overall artistic design? Those scholars who held the first view were known as Unitarians, those who held the second as Analysts. By the 1920s the Analysts were in the vast majority among professional scholars, though probably not among the general reading public. The characteristic aims of their work were to distinguish various "early" and "late" layers and "short epics" in the poem and also to trace historically the process by which these layers and poems were combined to form our *Iliad*. Not the least indication of their futility was the number of highly arbitrary, mutually contradictory analyses and historical developments that various Analysts posited. Parry's demonstration of the uniformity of the traditional, formulaic style made the Homeric Question meaningless by showing that it was in fact impossible to distinguish, within this uniformity, either chronological layers or the work of particular poets, including Homer. The demonstration that all poets working in the tradition of oral composition relied totally on the traditional style that, as it were, sang through them seemed to make questions of originality or individuality unanswerable and irrelevant. And the same features of Parry's theory that resolved these questions seemed also to indicate the impossibility of genuine literary criticism of the *Iliad*.[21]

As I have said, Parry's field studies of Serbocroatian oral poetry seemed to him, and have seemed to many others, to confirm the conclusions to which the intensive study of the Homeric texts themselves had previously led him. In effect, Parry had analyzed the style of the *Iliad* and *Odyssey* and decided that such a style could only have evolved because it was functional for a certain type of poet—an illiterate, oral poet for whom composition and performance were one—in a particular kind of society. When he learned that such poets still flourished in rural Yugoslavia, he went to study them. His premature death cut short his work, which Professor A. B. Lord has continued both in the field and in publications.

Parry and Lord argued that both Homer and the Slavic *guslars*, who sang oral heroic poetry in a formulaic style functionally like that of the *Iliad*, performed a similar role in similar societies and that their "primitive," "popular," "natural," "heroic" style actually depended on their being oral and illiterate (and therefore traditional) "singers of tales." Parry did not live long enough to develop fully or test the validity of his analogy between the Homeric and Yugoslav poems in regard to their quality. All he was able to do was to confirm in his own mind and "prove" to others the conclusions he had already drawn about the oral tradition that ultimately produced the *Iliad* and *Odyssey*, and to stress the differences between this kind of tradition and traditions of literate, sophisticated poets. There still is no general agreement about the extent and validity of the analogy between the Homeric and Yugoslav material or even about the artistic merit of the latter. Lord concedes the greater excellence of the Homeric poems but argues, or rather, assumes, that the two bodies of poetry are wholly comparable in terms of traditional style and compositional techniques.[22]

In particular, Lord has pointed out and analyzed similarities in "composition by theme." He defines a "theme" as "a recurrent element of narration or description," for example, of a feast, an assembly, a ship beginning or ending a voyage with the crew embarking or disembarking, or a warrior putting on his armor.[23] Such "typical scenes" had previously been studied in a pioneering work by W. Arend as a special feature of the *Iliad* and *Odyssey*; Lord, following Arend and Parry, showed that they are distinctive constituent elements of oral poetry, almost as formulaic in their function as the repeated words and phrases Parry had studied.[24] Other scholars have extended the concept of "theme" beyond these "typical scenes" with fruitful results. For example, as B. Fenik has shown, the battle scenes in the *Iliad* consist of a finite repertoire of "repeated details and action-sequences which undergo numerous and repeated combinations. The poet put together his battle description in much the same way as he constructed his verses and sentences, namely out of smaller, relatively unchanging 'building blocks'—phrases and sentence formulae at one level, typical descriptive details and action-sequences at another."[25] One of Fenik's examples of such an action sequence is: 1) A throws at B and misses, 2) B strikes A's shield or body armor but fails to pierce it, 3) A slays B. Another is: 1) A strikes B but fails to pierce his armor, 2) A tries to withdraw to safety, 3) he is wounded or slain by a third party, C.[26] (In the latter sequence, A is always a Trojan, never a Greek.) But descriptions of fighting in the *Iliad* are thematic to a far greater degree than is indicated by these sequences: the main compositional unit of battle narrative, the *aristeia*, consists normally of a combination of five typical sections, and the poet could rely on his audience to appreciate both the fulfillment of the norm and artful variations on it.[27] Nor is "composition by theme" limited to battle scenes: D. Lohmann has demonstrated the care with which speeches are constructed out of typical units so as to correspond significantly to one another even when they occur in different parts of the poem.[28]

The study of composition by formula and theme is part of the study of the *Iliad* as traditional oral poetry. Yet it is important to recognize that while the *Iliad* is stylistically an end product of an oral poetic tradition of the kind demonstrated by Parry, it is equally the first work in Greek literature, that is, in writing. Evidence indicates that the Phoenician alphabet was introduced into Greece sometime about 725 B.C., and it is reasonable to suppose, though not demonstrable, that the poem as we have it was written down, or perhaps dictated to a scribe or amanuensis, by a poet trained in the oral tradition who took advantage of the new linguistic medium to create something special. This would account both for the traditional formulaic style—with slight narrative inconsistencies and slips, such as the same man being killed twice, that are common to all oral poetry—and for the overall unity, profundity, and artistic excellence found neither in the Yugoslav material nor anywhere else in oral compositions of comparable length. It has even been suggested by one scholar that the alphabet may have been introduced specifically to create the Homeric poems.[29] While this may seem unlikely, it does call attention to the significance of literacy for creating our *Iliad*: through writing the text has been fixed in a way that is impossible in oral composition. In an illiterate tradition each singing, even by the same poet, yields a new and different poem produced from the basic building blocks in the poet's memory, and within a few generations, to judge from the Yugoslav evidence, even a work as large as the *Iliad* would become so drastically altered as to be no longer the same poem.[30] Undoubtedly, as Parry and Lord discovered in the case of the *guslars,* the introduction of writing brought the oral poetic tradition to an end. While some of the earliest extant elegiac and lyric poets, like the seventh-century Archilochos, may well have been trained as oral singers, the enormous influence of Homer on later Greek (and Western) literature and civilization was the influence of a more or less fixed text into which lines might be interpolated or from which lines might be omitted by any given reciter, but which, as an artistic whole, was unchanging.

2

So far I have been describing what might be called the formal tradition behind the *Iliad*, that of meter, formulaic diction, and oral composition. But just as important for a proper understanding of the poem as recognition of the traditional style is appreciation of the traditional content. There was a mythological tradition, or as G. Nagy has said, "a plethora of various different traditions,"[31] a repertoire of stories, story patterns, and smaller narrative motifs, some about or attached to particular characters and some free-floating, that were familiar to the poet and his audience. We see this, for example, in the way Homer invokes the muse to tell the story of the wrath of Achilles from the point at which he and Agamemnon "first stood in division of conflict" (1.6–7), thus implying that there were other points known to poet and audience from which the muse might have begun. We also see it in the way he sometimes first mentions a character (for instance, Patroklos at 1.307) merely by his patronymic, that is, by calling him "son of X" and assuming in the listeners sufficient familiarity with the traditional figures to know who X is, who his son is, and why he should be doing what he is described as doing. Indeed, in reading the *Iliad* we are repeatedly aware that Homer's audience must have known the whole story of the Trojan War and other stories of the deeds of many characters on both sides. As we shall see, there is good reason to suspect that Homer made some heroes and events more important in the *Iliad* than they were traditionally, just as he reduced the importance of or entirely suppressed others. We should not, however, conceive of him as creating out of whole cloth either plot or characters; the mythological tradition provided him with the material to express his ideas and vision of reality, just as the stylistic tradition provided him with the medium in which to express them.

One of the special features of Homer's artistic "personality," to borrow Nietzsche's term,[32] is the way he not only assumes but also takes poetic advantage of the familiarity with the mythology he and his audience shared. Homer fulfills and thus satisfies listeners' expectations by telling the traditional stories in the traditional ways; but sometimes he plays against these expectations by transferring a traditional speech or episode from one heroic character or setting to another. At other times he alludes to such an episode or event, thus calling it to the audience's attention without actually including it in his poem. At still other times (more often in the *Odyssey* than in the *Iliad*) he incorporates not only traditional heroic stories but also traditional folktales, with whatever modifications are necessary to make them thematically or dramatically relevant. In some cases Homer reinforces the themes and ideas of the *Iliad* by suggesting analogous mythological material. Often an indirectly suggested episode from elsewhere in the mythological tradition sets what happens in the poem in an ironic perspective or otherwise comments on it. Homer thus manages to generate additional meanings behind or beneath or in addition to the literal meaning of his text. His handling of the traditional mythology is as skillful, sophisticated, and distinctive as his wielding of the traditional formulaic style.

It is impossible to say just when the mythology behind the *Iliad* originated. It is at least as old as the formulaic style, which a combination of linguistic and archaeological evidence has shown to be perhaps as much as a thousand years older than the *Iliad* itself. Undoubtedly the great Swedish scholar Martin P. Nilsson was correct when he spoke of "the Mycenaean origin of Greek mythology."[33] The *Iliad*, though composed in the late eighth century B.C., takes place in a remembered, long-past heroic age. This heroic age corresponds in general with what we might loosely call the Late Bronze Age, the era of the final stages of the Minoan civilization on Crete and of the Mycenaean civilization on the Greek mainland, from whose remains so much has been learned by archaeologists during the past century. The end of this era, toward the final decades of the thirteenth century B.C., is close in time to 1184 B.C., the date accepted later by Greek chronographers for the fall of Troy. It also coincides with the date, as determined by archaeologists, of the destruction of one of the cities whose remains have been found superimposed in layers at the historical site of Troy, near the Hellespont in northwestern Turkey.

That the heroic age depicted in the *Iliad* corresponds to the Late Bronze Age of Mycenaean civilization is shown, for example, by the fact that most weapons and armor in the poem are bronze, not iron as must have been the case in the poet's own lifetime. Of course there are inconsistencies in this respect, as there are in descriptions of military formations, tactics, and weaponry, of social and political organization, and of religious practices and ideas. Generally speaking, however, these inconsistencies are few and unimportant. Whether in detail they derive from the late eighth century or from the so-called "Dark Age" between the Mycenaean period and the end of the eighth century, they do not leave seriously in doubt that Homer is depicting an era that we know was at least five hundred years earlier than his own, whose memory had been preserved in the heroic mythology transmitted as the subject matter of the oral poetic tradition.[34] One of the clearest signs of the great antiquity of this tradition, of its origin in the Bronze Age, is the fact that although the poet, Homer, who sang of the Olympian gods, lived in the later, historical era of the emerging city-state, the conception and the social and political organization of these gods is anachronistically modeled on the Mycenaean society as portrayed in the *Iliad* and as evidenced by the archaeological record.[35]

Even while we recognize the Mycenaean origin of the mythology of the *Iliad* and of the poetic tradition, we should realize, too, that the origin of some of the story patterns in the poem may be much older. The earliest poetry extant in several major Indo-European language families—poetry which presumably reflects earlier, originally oral traditions—includes stories of the exploits of warrior-heroes who fight both for the benefit of their people and for their own glory. It has been shown that there are etymologically cognate, metrically identical formulaic phrases in Greek and Indic by which the poets designated both their "own medium, when it serves the function of glorifying the deeds of heroes," and the imperishable glory attained by heroes through poetry when they have performed virtuous, victorious deeds.[36] These Greek and Indic phrases presumably are derived from an earlier formula in the old, undifferentiated Indo-European poetic language; they imply that even long before the heroic age portrayed in the *Iliad* there was a tradition of heroic mythology narrated in epic song.

Homer's epic may have been influenced by Mesopotamian

heroic poetry as well as by this common Indo-European background. The Sumerian *Epic of Gilgamesh*, probably as old as the
middle of the third millennium B.C., and extant in Babylonian
and other Mesopotamian texts dating from about 1750 B.C.
down to about 550 B.C., includes a number of motifs found in
the *Iliad* and *Odyssey*. Its hero, Gilgamesh, is a great warrior-
king, of partly divine and partly human parentage but defi-
nitely mortal; he experiences profound grief at the death (due
in part to his own desire for glory) of his beloved warrior-com-
panion, Enkidu. Gilgamesh strives to achieve immortality for
Enkidu and himself, but in the end learns that heroic deeds and
the memory of them are the only immortality possible for human beings, however great. At what may be its opening and its
close, this fragmentary poem refers to the "walls of Uruk," Gilgamesh's city, thus placing Gilgamesh's individual achievements in a social setting. While it would be simplistic to claim
that Homer must have been directly influenced by the *Epic of
Gilgamesh*, which in any case is a far shorter and less organic
work than the *Iliad* or *Odyssey*, the Greek and Sumerian epics
obviously have certain themes in common. Archaeologists
have discovered eighth-century B.C. sites on the coast of Asia
Minor, such as Al Mina in present-day Syria, where Greeks
and Mesopotamians seem to have been in contact at least com-
mercially.[37] It is not hard to imagine that either at these or at
earlier settlements, the story of Gilgamesh and other heroic
mythology were transmitted from East to West. This is not at
all surprising, since we have abundant evidence that Hesiod's
Theogony (probably contemporary with Homer) and, thereafter, early Greek philosophy were influenced by Babylonian
mythopoetic accounts of the origin and order of the universe.[38]

The mythological tradition behind the *Iliad* emphasized the
achievements of great warriors who were of mixed divine and
human heritage but nonetheless mortal. They fought individ-
ually for their own glory and socially for their comrades and
community. However great their deeds, these heroes could not
transcend death, the limit of the human condition, except
through celebration in song by poets, who thus conferred on
them undying glory, and through worship in hero cults by later
generations, who thus acknowledged their godlike, though
not divine, status.[39]

Long before Homer sang of it, the mythology about Troy and the various Greek and Trojan heroes of the war took shape along with stories about other Mycenaean figures such as Herakles, the seven warriors who led a doomed expedition from Argos against Thebes in the generation before the Trojan War, and Jason and the Argonauts, whose ship is referred to at *Odyssey* 12.69–72 as "in the minds of all men."[40] Many generations of oral poets had sung of these heroes before Homer. After he gave definitive poetic expression in the *Iliad* and *Odyssey* to the stories of certain episodes during and after the Trojan War, a series of epics filling in all the rest of the story of the war and its aftermath was composed. This Epic Cycle was constructed around the *Iliad* and *Odyssey*. We know of its contents chiefly through plot summaries in portions of the *Chrestomatheia*, or *Summary of Useful Knowledge*, by the second-century A.D. grammarian Proclus, which are preserved partly in the *Bibliotheca* of the ninth-century A.D. scholar Photius and partly in some manuscripts of the *Iliad*.[41] The Epic Cycle included the *Kypria*, on the causes of the war, including the abduction of Helen, and its conduct up to the beginning of the *Iliad*; the *Aithiopis*, which took up where the *Iliad* leaves off and told of the death of Achilles and the dispute for his arms between Odysseus and the greater Ajax; the *Little Iliad*, on the story of the war from Odysseus' being awarded the arms of Achilles to the fall of Troy; the *Sack of Ilium*, on the story of the wooden horse and the fall of Troy, apparently overlapping with the *Little Iliad*; the *Returns*, about the homecomings of various Greek heroes; the *Telegony*, continuing the story of Odysseus from where the *Odyssey* leaves off through his death. Although the different poems of this Cycle were attributed to different post-Homeric poets, these other epics, like the *Iliad* and *Odyssey*, drew on the mythological tradition for their subject matter. The major difference between the two Homeric epics and the others was one of quality. According to Aristotle (*Poetics* 23.1459b1) the authors of these other poems simply narrated in chronological order all the events that were supposed to have happened in the time that they covered; their works lacked the organic unity of the *Iliad* and *Odyssey*, which are organized around the wrath of Achilles and the man Odysseus, respectively.

While Aristotle's observation is undoubtedly true, never-

theless one of the most striking features of the *Iliad* is the way
Homer uses the techniques of allusion and indirect suggestion
that I have already mentioned to refer to numerous incidents
in the Trojan War that traditionally took place before or after the
events narrated in the *Iliad*. It is not going too far to say that
Homer manages to work the story of the entire war into his
poem. Much of this story is known to us from sources later
than the *Iliad*—fragments and summaries of the Epic Cycle and
archaic and classical vase paintings—but in fact it is pre-Iliadic
in its general features. Audiences schooled in the oral poetic
tradition would have recognized Homer's constant reflections
of this traditional mythology in his poem; they would have
understood his exploitation and transformations of it even
while they appreciated the form and thought of the new poem
he created from it. The closer we ourselves can come to such
recognition and understanding, the better we can see not only
how the *Iliad* works artistically but also, in some detail, how
Homer created it from the traditional mythological building
blocks with which he worked. In this way we can appreciate
both how the plot of the poem is, as it were, a digression in the
story of the entire war, which in a sense it interrupts, and how
Homer is able to include within this digression the greater narrative whole.[42]

After Achilles' quarrel with Agamemnon and the outbreak
of his wrath in Book 1, Books 2–4 recall in numerous details the
beginning of the war. In these books the linear plot of the poem
progresses from episode to episode, but at the same time these
episodes evoke events which took place nine years earlier.
Thus, as many scholars have pointed out, the Catalogue of
Ships (2.494–760) really belongs to, and probably derives from,
a traditional description of the Greek army assembling at the
port of Aulis before sailing to Troy. Homer adapts this description to the circumstances of his poem; for instance, when he
mentions Protesilaos (2.698–709) and Philoctetes (2.718–25),
the former killed "as he leapt from his ships, far the first of the
Achaians" (2.701), the latter "languishing on the island, suffering overwhelming pains, / on sacred Lemnos, where the sons
of the Achaians left him" (2.721–22), he says that although their
men longed for these leaders, they were not leaderless, because Podarkes and Medon commanded their respective con-

tingents. Both Protesilaos and Philoctetes, of course, would have been included in a catalogue of the army gathering at Aulis, and Homer does what is necessary to account for their absence in the *Iliad*.[43] In a more general way, he adapts the traditional description to the circumstances of his poem by specifying the number of ships in each contingent only as a kind of addendum, and instead emphasizing the number of men, the names of the leaders, and their ancestry, homelands, and special qualities.[44] That Homer is transforming a traditional catalogue of the army assembling at Aulis is made more likely by Odysseus' recalling the omens they saw there and how Calchas interpreted them (2.299–330) and by Nestor's recollection of the favorable lightning from Zeus when the Greeks set sail for Troy (2.350–53).

Homer also suggests the beginning of the war in his contrast between the silent Greeks and the noisy Trojans marching to battle, and in his simile about the dense cloud of dust they raised as they were crossing the plain (3.1–14). It is significant that the Trojans are compared to cranes who aggressively initiate battle,

> bringing slaughter and death to the Pugmaian men,
> and at daybreak they bring on the evil conflict,
>
> (3.6–7)

while the Greeks are described in terms of their defensive intent,

> eager in their hearts to protect one another.
>
> (3.9)

At first glance this is strange: the Greeks are attacking Troy and the Trojans are defending their city, so one would expect the Trojans to be described in terms of defense and the Greeks as aggressors. But this opening contrast between the armies begins a consistent pattern in which Homer makes the Trojans initiators not only of battle but of the war, not merely aggressors but transgressors, who are morally responsible for their own ruin. This moral responsibility is emphasized in Book 4

when Athene, at Hera's urging and Zeus' command, incites
Pandaros to break the truce,

> . . . so that the Trojans might begin first
> to do harm to the highly renowned Achaians in violation of
> their oaths.

$$(4.66–67 = 71–72)$$

In this way the Trojans are made to reenact their guilt in ab-
ducting Helen and violating the religiously sanctioned guest-
host relationship (3.46–51; cf. 13.621–27). Their inevitable destruction for thus breaking their oaths is stressed by Agamemnon (4.270–71) and later by Antenor in the Trojan assembly
(7.351–53). This symbolic reenactment of the original Trojan
guilt, like their description as aggressors, effectively calls to
mind the beginning of the war.

Similarly, the characterization and actions of Paris and Hel-
en in Book 3 contribute to our sense that Homer is retelling the
story of the origin of the war without actually narrating it. In
the first place, a single combat between the two husbands of
Helen to settle the conflict, and the view from the wall where
Helen points out the prominent Greek heroes to Priam as if for
the first time (3.161–242), "belong naturally to the first year of
the war and are out of place in the ninth."[45] The same is true of
the recollection by Antenor of Menelaos' and Odysseus' embassy to Troy to demand Helen's return (3.204–24). Furthermore, Helen and Paris are portrayed as the attractive lovers
whose elopement brought on the war. When Paris, saved from
death by Aphrodite, urges Helen to come to bed with him, he
himself mentions that he desires her even more than when
they made love for the first time after leaving Sparta (3.441–46).

But Helen and Paris, though lovers, are not dramatically or
morally identical. Paris' charm, his apparent willingness (3.59–
75) to accept Hektor's rebuke and fight with Menelaos, his fair-
sounding excuse that "the glorious gifts of the gods are not to
be rejected" (3.65), and, after the duel, his matter-of-fact, witty,
false comment, "Now Menelaos has conquered with the help
of Athene / but next time I shall conquer him; for there are gods
on our side also"(3.439–40)—all this may be felt to disarm our
hostility. Certainly Paris has a unique grace and appeal, a light-

ness in a world of rather heavy heroes, as we would expect of one whose area of excellence is "the lyre and the gifts of Aphrodite, / and combed hair and beauty" (3.54–55). But this lightness is fundamentally trivial. As Hektor says, and as the duel with Menelaos shows, "there is not strength in your heart and there is not any valor" (3.45). In the world of the *Iliad*, these are what count.

Even Paris' apparent acceptance of Hektor's reproaches (3.59–75) is superficial. Hektor has denounced him for his cowardice and for the fact that he is good for nothing but sex, concluding with a bitter pun: "the lyre and the gifts of Aphrodite would not be of use to you, / and your combed hair and beauty, when you mingle in the dust" (3.54–55), that is, when he mingles "in the dust" rather than "in lovemaking and the bed" (cf. 3.445). Paris ignores the content of Hektor's speech, except to assert that the gifts of Aphrodite should not be ridiculed or refused by mortals who could not get them of their own accord (3.60–63). W. Leaf remarks that "Paris . . . speaks partly in anger and partly in admiration of Hector's straightforwardness, which thrusts aside without relenting . . . all conventional obstacles," but this misses Paris' cool irony.[46] What Paris really does is compare Hektor to a tool in the hands of a skilled workman (3.59–63). Paris' praise is in fact no praise—at least not in the mouth of one whose personality and chief virtues and values are totally different from the qualities he claims to approve. Paris only seems to accept his own faults; really he mocks Hektor, and though he does fight, his lack of concern to honor the terms of the duel shows how little he cares for Hektor and the values for which he stands.

Helen is deeper and more complex than Paris. She is portrayed neither as trivial nor as completely selfish in the way he is; she commands sympathy "by her own attitude to her guilt and shame," and by angrily chiding Aphrodite (3.399–412) and mocking Paris (3.428–36).[47] If she goes to bed with him immediately afterward, it must be remembered that she, a Greek woman alone in Troy, is compelled by Aphrodite, on whom she is utterly dependent. When the Trojan elders see her on the wall, they appreciate how her beauty can make men suffer for her sake and remark that she should be returned to the Greeks lest she destroy the Trojans and their city (3.156–60). But they do not return her, and she, unlike Paris, cannot be held responsible for the war or the destruction of Troy. Rather, she too is a victim of the gods, in particular of Aphrodite, who now forces her to go make love with Paris after his defeat by Menelaos, just as she had brought about the elopement that led to the war. In other words, Helen is a victim of the inevitability of her situation, of a compulsion to behave in a way like that in which, for example, Patroklos goes to his doom in Book 16. Both react freely to their circumstances, but their chosen actions are conditioned by what the war and the gods force on them; for both there is that characteristic blend of responsibility and lack of ultimate power that imparts a tragic quality both to their condition and to that of everyone in the *Iliad*.[48]

Helen's outstanding beauty and desirability, like Achilles' supreme prowess, are a distinctive, god-given excellence (*aretē*). In each character's case, individual self-realization and self-actualization through a full expression of this excellence involve the suffering and destruction of social communities—the Greek army and the Trojan city and people. Just as Achilles, though responsible for the destruction of Troy, is not morally blameworthy, so with Helen: she simply is who and what she is, simultaneously more-than-human and all-too-human. Her weaving representations of the battles being fought for her sake (3.125–28) makes her an artist, like Hephaistos creating Achilles' shield (18.478–608) or Homer composing the *Iliad*. Helen's remark to Hektor that Zeus placed upon herself and Paris "an evil doom, so that even in the future / we might be the subject of song for people of future generations" (6.357–58) is a further instance of her distanced, artistic perspective on the events of her own life and of the poem. This perspective is unique among mortals in the *Iliad*. Only Achilles, whom we see at one point "delighting his heart with the clear-sounding lyre" as "he sang the glorious deeds of men" (9.186–89), approaches such a view, when he consoles Priam for the doom the gods have given both of them (24.525–51). But Achilles' detached vision of reality in Book 24 is grounded in suffering and disenchantment; it is not artistic. Like Helen, he stands somehow outside the poem as he speaks, but he does so only temporarily and cannot ever escape the consequences of the war and of his own actions. Helen, on the other hand, really is immune from such consequences. Her destiny, as R. Bespaloff has said, "does not depend on the outcome of the war; Paris or Menelaus may get her, but for her nothing can really change."[49] Her immunity and exemption from the normal human consequences of her behavior, along with the necessity of her situation imposed directly by the gods, set her apart from other humans in the poem and make possible her distinctive, detached view of herself and of the war being fought for her sake.

Homer's characterization of Paris as superficially attractive and worthy of sympathy but morally trivial and responsible for the war, like his more complex depiction of Helen's forced complicity, is part of his strategy in Books 2–4 of telling the story of the cause and outbreak of the war without actually seeming to do so. He evokes their elopement and recounts Pandaros' violation of the truce to make his audience aware of the fundamental guilt that makes it inevitable that the Trojans and their city will perish. Thus he establishes the "historical" and moral background against which Achilles' wrath and the action of the *Iliad* so destructively run their course.

Just as in Books 2–4 Homer recalls the beginning of the war, so in the latter part of the poem he repeatedly suggests events the audience knew took place later (in mythological time) than the action of the poem. Chief among these events is the fall of Troy. In addition to the prophetic words of Agamemnon (4.164–65) and Hektor (6.448–49), and Zeus' announcement at 15.70–71, other references to and predictions of the city's doom are so numerous that it becomes clear that the life of the city is inextricably bound up with that of Hektor.[50] Priam makes this explicit at 22.56–57, where he foresees the fall of the city immediately after anticipating his son's death. When Hektor is slain, Homer tells us that the lamentation and groaning

> was most like what it would have been, if all
> beetling Ilion were being consumed utterly by fire.
>
> (22.410–11)

Finally, Andromache, in her lamentation for her dead husband, says,

> the son whom you and I bore in our ill fortune—I do not
> think he will reach his youthful prime, since sooner this city
>   will be utterly

sacked. For you, its guardian, have perished, who used to save
it, and you protected its careful wives and infant children. . . .
(24.727–30)

By the end of the *Iliad*, the situation for the Trojans is superficially not unlike what it was before Achilles' wrath: they are
penned in their city, afraid to come out of the gates to fight. But
as a result of the action of the poem, with Hektor slain, the city
itself has virtually been sacked, and its ultimate doom is fully
present to the minds of the audience. Although this action is
only a brief episode in the tenth year of the war, within the time
frame of this episode the poem has actually narrated the story
of the entire war from the judgment of Paris to the fall of the
city, and even beyond.[51]

This "beyond" is reflected, for example, in certain details of
the funeral games for Patroklos in Book 23, which foreshadow
traditional mythical events the audience knew took place after
the action of the *Iliad*.[52] The wrestling match between Odysseus and Ajax the son of Telamon mirrors in a harmless way
their fatal conflict over the arms of the dead Achilles, which
was narrated in the *Aithiopis* and the *Little Iliad*. When Athene
causes Ajax the son of Oileus to slip on some dung during the
footrace, the scene anticipates his doom in retribution for his
rape of Kassandra at Athene's altar during the sack of Troy. The
most important later event referred to but not told in the *Iliad* is
the death of Achilles. As will be shown in Chapter Five, Homer
repeatedly makes it clear that Achilles' doom will follow closely
after that of Hektor; he portrays Achilles as virtually dead from
the beginning of Book 18 on. Yet Homer does not and cannot
show the death of Achilles, because, in a mythological innovation fundamental for the structure and meaning of his poem,
he uses the events (and perhaps some of the specific language)
associated in the tradition with the death of Achilles to tell of
the death of Patroklos. This enables him simultaneously to portray Achilles' terrible isolation and self-reproach at his comrade's fall and to evoke in his audience the sense that, with the
death of Patroklos, Achilles himself dies.

The death of Achilles was narrated in the *Aithiopis* on the basis of older mythical traditions. In that lost epic, according to
Proclus' summary, Achilles kills a son of the goddess Eos,

Memnon, the Aithiopian prince and Trojan ally who slew Achilles' dearest friend Antilochos. Before Memnon's death, Eos and Thetis, the mother of Achilles, beseech Zeus each for the victory of her son; and Zeus decides after weighing the heroes' "lives" on his scales that Achilles will conquer. Subsequently, Achilles routs the Trojans and, as he presses on to sack the city, is slain by Paris and Apollo. His corpse is rescued by Odysseus and Telamonian Ajax; then Thetis and the Nereids come with the Muses to mourn the dead hero, whose funeral, with athletic contests in his honor, is followed by a dispute between Ajax and Odysseus over his arms. In the meantime, the body of Memnon has been taken away by Eos, who with Zeus' approval confers on him a posthumous immortality.

It seems clear that Homer has selectively and creatively borrowed for Patroklos this tradition about the death of Achilles. Patroklos slays the son of Zeus and Trojan ally Sarpedon (16.462–505) after Zeus and Hera discuss whether he should intervene to save his son (16.433–57). Zeus sends Death and Sleep to convey the corpse to Sarpedon's native Lykia for burial and worship in a hero cult (16.456–57); this implies an immortality analogous to that of Memnon in the *Aithiopis*.[53] Patroklos presses on, drives the Trojans toward their city, and is killed there by Euphorbos, Hektor, and Apollo. At one point, when he is about to take the city (16.698–99), Apollo beats him back and tells him:

> It is not allotted (*aisa*)
> to sack the city of the mighty Trojans beneath your spear,
> nor beneath that of Achilles, who is far better than you.
> (16.707–9)

Thus, just before his death, Patroklos, who is fighting in Achilles' armor, is linked to the son of Peleus by Apollo's words as well as by the general narrative of his exploits. After his death, his body is rescued by Telamonian Ajax (Odysseus has been wounded and is not fighting) and mourned by Thetis and the Nereids. In Book 23, Homer describes Patroklos' funeral and the games in his honor with constant references to the later death and burial of Achilles.[54]

In thus adapting and transforming the death of Achilles into that of Patroklos, Homer is not merely playing with traditional mythological motifs. Rather, as many scholars have pointed out, for an audience familiar with the tradition Patroklos, with whom Achilles has a uniquely close and tender friendship, becomes a substitute or surrogate for his comrade.[55] On the one hand, this enables Homer to include within the *Iliad* the story of Achilles' death, along with the mythology of the war that was known to have occurred earlier or later than the time frame of the poem. On the other hand, and more importantly, by having Achilles "die" while he is still alive, Homer is able to suggest how far beyond normal human limits his dislocation, isolation, and suffering extend.

Just as Homer gives Patroklos traditional mythological features of Achilles and Antilochos, so he gives aspects of Memnon to Sarpedon and to Hektor.[56] Sarpedon, as noted above, resembles Memnon in that he is a Trojan ally of divine parentage who attains immortality after his death on the Trojan plain. Hektor resembles Memnon in being the slayer of Achilles' dearest comrade and the occasion of Achilles' death; in both poems Achilles knows that his own death must follow soon after his revenge. Both Hektor and Memnon (as we know from the *Aithiopis*) are the last hope of Troy; in each case, then, Achilles' triumph virtually constitutes a sack of the city.

The freedom with which Homer transfers to Patroklos and Hektor mythological motifs and dramatic roles traditionally associated with Achilles and Memnon has suggested to some scholars that these two characters are creations of Homer's.[57] This suggestion gains some support from the fact that Patroklos and Hektor, unlike the other major heroes of the poem, appear to have no significant mythological traditions independent of what is told about them in the *Iliad*. Nothing either in what we know of the Epic Cycle or in visual art suggests that they were important in mythology prior to Homer. It is noteworthy that while both are fierce warriors, each has a gentleness that makes his death especially painful to those who love him, thus contributing to the pathos of the war and of Achilles' wrath. Given the conservatism of oral poetry and the way that the names and epithets of Hektor and Patroklos are fully embedded in the formulaic style, it is unlikely that Homer invented the two heroes. It seems more likely that both were less important figures in the tradition and that Homer for his own artistic purposes made them more significant, one as the dear friend, the other as the hated enemy, of his poem's central hero. In the characters of Hektor and Patroklos one can see more clearly than anywhere else in the poem the creativity of Homer adapting and transforming traditional mythology into what is uniquely Iliadic.

Some scholars have supposed that the *Aithiopis* must have been a direct source or model for the *Iliad*, but this is contradicted by the evidence that the *Aithiopis*, like the other Cyclic Epics, was composed later than the *Iliad*. Since most of the resemblances between the two poems concern the achievements of Achilles and his death and burial, several scholars have hypothesized an *Achilleis* or a *Memnonis* as the source or model, and have thought Homer's creative hand transferred incidents and even speeches from this suppositious earlier poem to new characters and contexts in the *Iliad*.[58]

The image of the creative hand indicates one of the major problems with this theory. It seems to assume that Homer had, as it were, the pages of an earlier epic in front of him and simply quoted or adapted them when he found them artistically useful. It ignores the fact that the poetic tradition of these epics was oral and that hence there was no fixed text of an earlier epic from which Homer could borrow. While there can be no doubt that some of the scenes and speeches in the *Iliad* must resemble those that occurred in the *Aithiopis*, it is best to consider these scenes and speeches of the two epics as variants of the same fluid oral tradition rather than as dependent the one upon the other. We may then acknowledge that certain traditional motifs and perhaps even particular lines were associated with Achilles' death and funeral in the *Aithiopis* and are also associated with Patroklos' in the *Iliad*; furthermore, we may recognize that the scenes and characters we find in the *Iliad* were created for their place in that poem and were not simply transferred *en bloc* from a preexistent source or model.[59] In this way, while appreciating what I have called Homer's artistic "personality" and the way he adapts and exploits the tradition and the audience's awareness of it, we can avoid oversimplifying and conceiving too mechanistically of this adaptation and exploitation.

Homer achieves this result not only by transforming specific mythological episodes into events in his own poem but, as K.

Reinhardt pointed out, by reshaping traditional stories and story patterns into dramatic "situations."[60] For example, in the *Iliad* Homer mentions the story of the "judgment of Paris" only once, in passing, at 24.28–30; it is in no way important for the story told in the poem or the meanings generated. On the other hand, it explains, as it were, a significant "situation" that pervades the *Iliad*: the favor Aphrodite shows the Trojans, especially Paris, in contrast to Athene's and Hera's intense and extreme tred toward them. Neither Apollo on the Trojan side nor Poseidon on the Greek side shows the unconditional and unvarying partisanship repeatedly demonstrated by these goddesses, for which no motive other than Paris' rejection of Athene and Hera and choice of Aphrodite as the most beautiful is anywhere mentioned or can easily be imagined.[61] Yet Homer does not tell this story, which was developed in the *Kypria*, in his poem; as Reinhardt said, it makes sense only as an introduction to the story of the fall of Troy, and since the fall is not the story Homer is telling, he has no direct use for that of the judgment of Paris. But just as the deserved fall of Troy occurs symbolically, or proleptically, within the *Iliad*, so the story of the judgment of Paris is, as it were, assumed throughout the poem in the conflict among the Olympians. The transformation of story into "situation" is exemplified also in the contrasts both between Hektor and Paris in Books 3 and 6 and between Hektor and Poulydamas in Book 18; these reflect dramatically a story not developed in the *Iliad* of the good and bad brothers who were respectively the blessing and bane of their city. Such transformations are frequent in the *Iliad* and are one of Homer's characteristic ways of exploiting the mythological tradition.

As already mentioned, Homer composed the *Iliad* looking back to a heroic age that had vanished and that his audience knew had vanished. The poets of the oral tradition had for generations celebrated the imperishable glories of the heroes of the Trojan War, but it probably was not typical of the tradition that the poets endowed these heroes and their timeless actions with the same quality of transitoriness that informs the *Iliad*. Whether or not Homer was original in this respect, there is in the *Iliad* a tension between the vivid, present immediacy of the narrative and the distance which separates the race of heroes from the poet's (and our) own era. We are made aware of this distance by similes taking us from the world of the poem to that of our daily life, by occasional references to Ajax or Hektor easily hurling a rock so heavy that two men today could barely lift it, by the description of the shield of Achilles at 18.478–608, and most powerfully at 12.10–35: there, in the midst of the fighting, we learn how after the sack of Troy and the Greeks' departure, Poseidon and Apollo restored the shore to its pristine appearance by utterly leveling the wall the Greeks had toiled to build and beneath which both armies had fought and died. Only in this passage does Homer use the word *hēmitheoi*, "demigods," for the characters in his poem—the same word used by Hesiod in the *Works and Days* to distinguish his race of heroes from the men of his own day. The poet looks back at a past heroic age in much the same way as, in Book 18, the description of Achilles' shield refers outside the mythical world the shield itself is part of, setting that world in a "continuity of life" that, we feel, has passed it by.[62] The effect is to set the brilliant deeds of Achilles and the Trojan War as a whole in an ironic perspective that makes them no less beautiful or heroic but much more affecting.[63] Such a perspective infuses Homer's creative transformation of the traditional mythology with added meaning. The result is that meditation on death and on the tragic limitations of the human condition—for even the greatest hero— which is distinctive and characteristic of the *Iliad*.

3

The traditional style and mythology of the *Iliad* and Homer's distinctive exploitation of them for his own poetic ends are reflected in the overall structure of the poem. This structure has seemed obscure not only to Analytical scholars, who deny the artistic integrity of the epic, but to many Unitarian critics as well, who have been frustrated by its apparently loose narrative logic and have therefore been unable to appreciate its formal organization. The *Iliad* is structured according to two complementary principles, one related to its traditional style, the other to its traditional mythological content. The former principle may be called static and symmetrical: its main features are, in Whitman's words, "balance, responsion, contrast, and repetition, in an orderly syntax," and it is, in a sense, independent of the plot of the poem.[64] The second principle is dynamic and linear or progressive: it involves the movement of the poem from beginning to end, and it consists, broadly speaking, of three stages, each of which uses and reuses traditional motifs in ways that gradually accumulate meaning.[65] Of course, neither principle excludes the other: the symmetrical balance and repetition in the poem is, in part, a balance and repetition of elements of the plot, and the linear progress through three stages involves the repetition of specific motifs and diction.

The principle of symmetry can be illustrated by the balance between the first three books of the poem and the last three. In Book 1, Agamemnon rejects the supplication of Chryses and refuses to release his daughter for a ransom; in Book 24, Achilles accepts the supplication of Priam and releases the body of his son for a ransom. In each instance, Apollo is instrumental in setting the action in motion: at 1.43–52 he responds to Chryses' prayer by descending from Olympos and sending a plague against the Greek army; at 24.33–54 he chides the other gods for being willing to assist Achilles in his defilement of Hektor's body, and begins the discussion that ends in Zeus' decision to have Achilles accept a ransom for the body. This scene on Olympos near the beginning of Book 24 corresponds to that at the end of Book 1; each book also includes a meeting between Zeus and Thetis in which they discuss Achilles. Even the pattern of the days in the two books is almost exactly balanced: in Book 1, the day of Chryses' supplication is followed by nine days of plague, one day on which the Greeks appease Apollo after Achilles and Agamemnon quarrel, and a twelve-day break until the gods return from the land of the Aithiopes; in Book 24, after Achilles mistreats Hektor's corpse for twelve days while the gods argue about what to do, there is the day of Iris' message to Priam from Zeus and the old man's ransom of Hektor's corpse, followed by nine days during which the Trojans gather wood to burn the body, its cremation on the tenth day, and its burial on the eleventh.[66] This eleventh day (like the confusion about how long the gods were arguing) disrupts the exact correspondence-in-reverse between the two books, but the two long stretches of time in the opening and closing books, unparalleled elsewhere in the *Iliad*, effectively frame the action of the poem and, as it were, throw into relief the deadly consequences of the wrath of Achilles.

The correspondences between Books 2 and 23 and between Books 3 and 22 are less detailed than those between Books 1 and 24 but equally significant. Books 2 and 23 present descriptions of the Greek army assembled as a large group: the catalogue of ships and men introduces the main leaders of the army, the funeral games are a kind of farewell to them. Furthermore, as I have suggested, the catalogue and the recollections by Odysseus (2.299–322) and Nestor (2.350–56) of the omens and prophecies of ten years past are part of Homer's systematic allusion to the beginning of the war, while the success and failure of particular heroes in the games foreshadows their known mythological destinies beyond the time frame of the *Iliad*. Books 3 and 22 are clearly parallel to one another because of the duels of Paris and Menelaos and of Hektor and Achilles. That between the two husbands of Helen, the first combat in the poem, is appropriate to and recapitulates the beginning of the war; that between Hektor and Achilles, the final combat in the poem, resolves the war, because the death of Hektor is in effect the fall of Troy.

The polar or reverse symmetry evident in Books 1–3 and 22–24 reflects on a large scale a basic technique of poetic composition and organization within the poem, and in early Greek literature generally, known as ring composition. Ring composition means that a topic mentioned at the beginning of a speech or a narrative passage is repeated, sometimes verbatim and sometimes in more or less similar language, at the end of the passage, which thus is framed and set off as a discrete poetic entity.[67] Ring composition is found in the *Iliad* in almost every direct speech that begins and ends with what has been called a "*loquitur*-formula"—an explicit statement or other indication in the text that somebody spoke. It also is illustrated by certain digressive passages, such as, for example, Nestor's recollections of his youth at 1.259–74 and 7.129–60. But ring composition can be a far more subtle and thoroughgoing structural device than such simple frames. Often, a series of topics or ideas mentioned in the first half of a speech or description recurs in reverse order in the second half. For example, when Achilles urges Priam to eat at 24.599–620, he tells him: a) your son is ransomed and tomorrow at dawn you will see him and take him away (24.599–601), b) "now let us be mindful of supper" (24.601), c) even Niobe was mindful of food (24.602), d) the story of Niobe (24.603–12), c), she was mindful of food (24.613), b) so let us two think of food (24.618–19), a) you can weep for your son tomorrow, when you take him back to Troy (24.619–20).[68] There can even be ring-compositional correspondence between two speeches: as M. N. Nagler has shown, that of Achilles at 24.599–620 is "a mirror image" of Priam's speech, itself in ring form, a little earlier in the scene (24.518–51) "in its content, overall structure, in many details."[69] Just as individual speeches and scenes are framed or structured according to the principle of ring composition, so the entire poem, with its corresponding scenes at the beginning and end, is organized according to a principle of balance and polar correspondence. This correspondence may be "logical," as when supplication accepted in Book 24 is contrasted to supplication rejected in Book 1; or it may be merely "analogical," as when a group scene in Book 23 is parallel to one in Book 2, with no significant point of contrast.[70] In either case, Homer's "use of polarities as a structural principle" to articulate and order both individual scenes and his entire poem is clear.[71]

Such artistic organization calls to mind the Geometric designs on Greek painted pottery of the eighth century B.C.[72] The structural analogies between the *Iliad* and Geometric art suggest that the balance and symmetry of the poem are not unique but rather indicative of a contemporary feeling for form which characterizes Homer as an artist of his own particular age.[73] This feeling for form would have enabled the opening of the poem, or of a formal subunit such as a speech or a digression, to create an expectation in the minds of a contemporary audience that the closing of the ring would have satisfied. Thus, the effect of its formal, Geometric symmetry is to impart to the *Iliad* a sense of completion and fulfillment.[74]

On the one hand, the *Iliad* is characterized by this formal symmetry, but its story—its mythological content—moves in a certain direction and is never completed or rounded off by a balance of corresponding parts. The direction of this movement is toward death—the death of Hektor, the death of Achilles, the fall of Troy—and in the mortal world of the *Iliad*, the movement toward death is a one-way movement, an overriding reality which lends the poem much of its power as a description of the tragically urgent and limited human condition.

In general, the first third of the poem, which constitutes its first stage, presents the traditional or normative aspects of the Greeks and Trojans as aggressors against and defenders of Troy, respectively. Diomedes, whose *aristeia* in Books 5 and 6 is the major heroic exploit of this part of the poem, is "the perfect embodiment of the [traditional] heroic values" of courage while fighting in the front ranks for honor and glory and of respect toward his commander Agamemnon (4.401–2) and toward the gods (6.128–31). Although on Athene's instructions and with her direct assistance he wounds both Ares and Aphrodite, he prudently retreats before Ares (5.600–606) and gives way before Apollo (5.439–44), thus acknowledging and remaining within his mortal limits. The *aristeia* of Diomedes shows a conventional type of hero successfully and in a straightforward, morally uncomplicated way being who he is, which, according to the norms and values of the *Iliad*, is the same as who he should be. In Whitman's words, "his is the heroic pattern without thought, victory without implicit defeat."[75]

The second stage of the poem, with its depiction of the alienation of Achilles and its consequences (the success of Hektor and the Trojans and the death of Patroklos), presents moral and intellectual issues that probably go beyond anything traditional: it is distinctively Iliadic. The major heroic exploit of this section of the poem, apart from the Zeus-given, temporary success of Hektor, is the *aristeia* of Patroklos in Book 16. In contrast to that of Diomedes, which is traditional and in character, that of Patroklos is uniquely motivated and reflects an odd dislocation of values. For Patroklos is not fighting for his own honor and glory but "so that we might honor the son of Peleus, who is the best / of the Argives beside the ships" (16.271–72). It is appropriate, then, that he fights in Achilles' armor and deliberately assumes his identity to deceive the Trojans. Yet when Patroklos puts on the armor of his comrade and with it his comrade's triumphant power, he loses his own identity and his characteristic gentleness. Homer refers to him, and makes other characters refer to him, as "amiable" (*enēēs*, 17.204; 21.96; 23.252, 648), a word used of no one else in the poem; but when he assumes Achilles' role and power, his "amiability" (*enēeiē*, 17.670) disappears and Patroklos cannot retain his sense of himself and his mortal limits: when Apollo warns him to retreat, in the same language in which he warns Diomedes (16.706–9 = 5.440–42), Patroklos withdraws temporarily but then presses on against the Trojans "equal in weight to swift Ares" (16.784) until Apollo himself opposes him, strips him of his armor, and stuns him, leaving him an easy target for Euphorbos and Hektor (16.788–821).

The *aristeia* of Achilles in the final stage of the poem is even more dislocated and untraditional than that of Patroklos, and in comparison with Diomedes, Achilles stands out as a deadly and daemonic force of destruction barely acknowledging his human limits. For example, at the beginning of Diomedes' *aristeia*, fire blazes from the hero's helmet and spear "like the star in the late summer, which most / brightly shines, when it has been washed in the Ocean" (5.5–6); the reflection from Achilles' armor is compared to the same star, Sirius, "which is the brightest, and it is made as a sign of evil / and it brings high fever to wretched mortals" (22.30–31).[76] Whereas Diomedes observes his mortal limits in refusing to fight with a god, Achilles, with the aid of Athene, Poseidon, and Hephaistos, successfully opposes the river Skamandros and even says that he would "pay back" Apollo, "if only I had the power" (22.15). With the results of Achilles' *aristeia*—the death of Hektor, Achilles' own impending death, and the inevitable fall of Troy—the *Iliad* returns to the traditional mythology of the Trojan War. The three stages of the poem, marked by the *aristeiai* of Diomedes, of Patroklos, and of Achilles, are progressive stages leading toward this death and destruction.

Each of the three parts of the poem is heralded by a crucial action of Achilles: his quarrel with Agamemnon and withdrawal from combat in Book 1, his refusal to accept Agamemnon's gifts in Book 9, and his decision to die at once if he can avenge Patroklos in Book 18. Other actions and motifs similarly recur in the poem, marking its movement toward death. For example, in Book 1 Zeus promises Thetis he will honor Achilles by granting Hektor and the Trojans victory and destroying many of the Greeks. At 8.473–83, he prophesies to Hera that Hektor will be triumphant until he kills Patroklos and reaches the ships, thus arousing Achilles. At 15.61–77, he goes even further, telling Hera that Hektor will rout the Greeks until Achilles arouses Patroklos to fight; Hektor will kill Patroklos, after Patroklos has killed Sarpedon; Achilles then will kill Hektor in revenge, after which the Trojans will be pushed back toward the city until it is taken; all this will happen in accordance with his promise to Thetis in Book 1 that he will honor Achilles. Zeus' promise and prophecies unfold his plans as the poem unfolds. They set Achilles' actions, and all the human actions of the poem, in a divine perspective that imparts to them an ironic and tragic dignity. Each of Zeus' statements of his developing plans follows an intervention or expression of resentment by Hera in support of the Greeks: at 1.555–59 she voices her fear that Zeus has promised to destroy many of the Greeks; at 8.201–7 she tries to persuade Poseidon to intervene on behalf of the Greeks contrary to Zeus' command; at 8.352–56, after she raises the subject with Athene, the two are on their way to the battlefield when Zeus deters them by his threats (8.402–5, 416–19); in Book 14 Hera deceitfully seduces Zeus so that Poseidon can help the Trojans while Zeus is distracted. In each instance Zeus' plans develop in response to Hera's attempt to aid the Greeks. The repeated motif of their divine quarrel gradually clarifies the movement of the *Iliad* toward its tragic conclusion on the mortal plane.[77] Together the divine and human forces impart to the poem a linear momentum that complements the circular, balanced symmetry of its Geometric form. The result is a dual structure simultaneously harsh and harmonious, incomplete and fulfilled. This structure, arising from the uniquely Homeric combination of two opposed, conventional, structural principles, gives the *Iliad* its distinctive artistic organization.

APPENDIX: On the Relationship of the
Iliad to the *Odyssey*

Even in antiquity there were already Separatists who believed that the *Iliad* and the *Odyssey* were not composed by the same poet, though most writers, including Aristotle and "Longinus," spoke unquestioningly of Homer as the author of both poems. "Longinus" seems to have these Separatists in mind when he remarks (*On the Sublime* 11) that both poems are Homer's, but that the *Iliad* is the work of the poet as a young man and the *Odyssey* of the poet already growing old. "Longinus" compares Homer in the *Iliad* to the sun at its zenith and in the *Odyssey* to the setting sun. In modern times not only the Analysts but also many Unitarians have felt and judged that the two poems are so different in style, date of composition, or characteristic themes, values, and ideas that they could not have sprung from the same source. Nowadays the arguments based on style and date of composition have been refuted or judged unconvincing: there are no significant linguistic, metrical, or formulaic differences between the two epics, and no reason to consider either work as dating from much later than 700 B.C. (though within both poems it is possible to take a diachronic view of the style and to be aware of linguistic developments up to this date). There are, however, many who still feel on aesthetic, intellectual, or spiritual grounds that the two poems cannot be by the same poet.

It is difficult not to be subjective in this respect. I would note, first of all, that the *Odyssey* is no more different from the *Iliad* artistically, intellectually, or spiritually than, say, *The Tempest* is from *King Lear*. Furthermore, it is possible that there is a deeper relationship between the two epics analogous to that between the two Shakespearian plays. *King Lear* is a tragedy, and the storm, its central tragic symbol, takes place at its center (3.1–4). *The Tempest* is a romance beginning with a storm but quickly reversing this tragic movement and ending in harmony and restoration. For Shakespeare, as we may see not only in *The Tempest* but in the other late romances, the movement of romance presupposes tragedy: "Though the seas threaten, they are merciful." Similarly the *Iliad* is tragic, and the *Odyssey*, while it begins in a tragic situation (involving sea, storm, and the aftermath of war), ends in homecoming and restoration. Since we know that *The Tempest* was composed about five years later than *King Lear* and that the romances as a group are later than the tragedies as a group, we can speculate about Shakespeare's development as an artist and thinker.

In the case of the *Iliad* and *Odyssey* we do not know the relative chronology of composition, and so we cannot guess about any poetic development. We can, however, speculate that the *Odyssey*, a post–Trojan War poem of return, presupposes the *Iliad* or at least the mythology of the war. Or we can say, with W. J. Woodhouse, that reflection on the story of the return of Agamemnon gave birth to the romance of Odysseus, and that Agamemnon's return logically presupposes the war from which he returned.[78] However we put it, there is a complementarity between the *Iliad* and the *Odyssey* that may lead one to conclude either that they developed together in the mind of the same poet or that whoever composed the second of them, whether the same or another poet, had the first of them in mind. It has been observed that, except for the general outcome, no episode in the Trojan War that is narrated or mentioned in the *Iliad* is narrated or mentioned in the *Odyssey*, and vice versa.[79] Since it is almost impossible to imagine that two poets composing in the same oral tradition could have done this accidentally,[80] it follows, again, either that the same poet composed both epics or that whoever composed the second of them had the first constantly in mind. The first hypothesis seems far more economical and, I confess, more attractive. I would suggest that the *Iliad* and *Odyssey* are complementary works of one poet who took at different times a tragic and a romantic/comic view of reality. In any event, both are products of the same poetic tradition, both were fixed in writing toward the end of the eighth century B.C., and in this form both together became, as it were, the "bible" of the Greeks of historical times, exercising a decisive artistic and moral influence on their (and our) culture.

Notes to Chapter 1

[1]Cf. A. Parry, "Have We Homer's *Iliad*?" *Yale Classical Studies* 20 (1966), pp. 192–93 = J. Wright, ed., *Essays on the Iliad. Selected Modern Criticism* (Bloomington and London, 1978), pp. 10–11.

[2]On the gods, see Chapter 2; on war and death in the poem, Chapter 3; on Achilles, Chapters 4 and 5.

[3]I borrow this formulation from A. Parry, "Have We Homer's *Iliad*?" p. 180 = Wright, *Essays*, p. 2. Perhaps the leading exponent of such a view in recent years has been D. Page. In *History and the Homeric Iliad* (Berkeley and Los Angeles, 1959), Page gave one of the clearest accounts of the traditional formulaic nature of Homeric poetry (pp. 222–25) and argued for multiplicity of authorship and lack of the overall unity that would have resulted from one poet's shaping artistry. But see the criticism of some of Page's arguments by N. Austin, *Archery at the Dark of the Moon: Poetic Problems in the Odyssey* (Berkeley and Los Angeles, 1975), p. 70.

[4]Milman Parry's publications have been gathered together in *The Making of Homeric Verse: The Collected Papers of Milman Parry*, edited and with an introduction by Adam Parry (Oxford, 1971).

[5]R. Lattimore, *The Iliad of Homer* (Chicago, 1951); *The Odyssey of Homer* (New York, 1965).

[6]M. Parry, *Making of Homeric Verse*, p. 272.

[7]Ibid.

[8]Ibid., p. 276.

[9]Ibid., p. 277.

[10]Ibid., pp. 272–73.

[11]Ibid., p. 324.

[12]Ibid., p. 95.

[13]Ibid., p. 329.

[14]M. N. Nagler, "Towards a Generative View of the Oral Formula," *Transactions of the American Philological Association* 98 (1967), p. 281. See also Nagler's *Spontaneity and Tradition: A Study in the Oral Art of Homer* (Berkeley and Los Angeles, 1974), pp. 13–19.

[15]See W. Whallon, "The Homeric Epithets," *Yale Classical Studies* 17 (1961), pp. 97–142; *Formula, Character, and Context: Studies in Homeric, Old English, and Old Testament Poetry* (Washington, D.C., 1969).

[16]R. Sacks, "*Hupo Keuthesi Gaiēs: Two Studies of the Art of the Phrase in Homer*" (Ph.D. diss., Harvard, 1978), pp. 168–75.

[17]Ibid., pp. 108–15.

[18]On *mēnis* and *oloös*, see Chapter Four, p. 91, and Chapter Five, p. 158 with n. 48.

[19]On *krēdemna* and "latent poetic signification," see Nagler, "Generative View," pp. 298–307.

[20]See especially Nagler, *Spontaneity*; Austin, *Archery*; G. Nagy, *The Best of the Achaeans: Concepts of the Hero in Archaic Greek Poetry* (Baltimore and London, 1979); and three essays by A. Parry: "The Language of Achilles," *Transactions of the American Philological Association* 87 (1956), pp. 1–7 = G. S. Kirk, ed., *The Language and Background of Homer* (Cambridge, 1964), pp. 48–54; "Have We Homer's *Iliad*?" pp. 175–216 = Wright, *Essays*, pp. 1–27, 128–34; and "Language and Characterization in Homer," *Harvard Studies in Classical Philology* 76 (1972), pp. 1–22.

In addition to integrating an appreciation of Homer's formulaic style with a literary interpretation of the *Odyssey*, Austin has called into question the extent of the formularity of this style and the degree to which its *raison d'être* is its functional utility for a performing and composing poet rather than artistic considerations. Austin argues that "metrical compulsion is towards the formula name without epithet," that "the epithet formula is metrically useful only half the time" (pp. 38–39), and after a consideration of the noun-epithet formulas for Odysseus, Penelope, and Telemachos (pp. 26–63), he concludes that there is much more in Homeric poetry than formulaic systems.

For a more radical, anti-Parryist view of the meaning of the epithets, see P. Vivante, *The Epithets in Homer: A Study in Poetic Values* (New Haven and London, 1982).

[21]On the Homeric Question, see M. P. Nilsson, *Homer and Mycenae* (1933; reprint, Philadelphia, 1972), pp. 1–55; J. A. Davison, "The Homeric Question," in A. J. B. Wace and F. Stubbings, eds., *A Companion to Homer* (London, 1962), pp. 234–65; A. Parry, "Introduction," in M. Parry, *Making of Homeric Verse*, pp. ix-xli.

[22]A. B. Lord, *The Singer of Tales* (Cambridge, Mass., 1960; reprint, New York, 1965).

[23]A. B. Lord, "Composition by Theme in Homer and Southslavic Epos," *Transactions of the American Philological Association* 82 (1951), pp. 71–80; cf. *The Singer of Tales*, pp. 68–98.

[24]W. Arend, *Die typische Szenen bei Homer* (Berlin, 1933); M. Parry, *Making of Homeric Verse*, pp. 404–7.

[25]B. Fenik, *Typical Battle Scenes in the Iliad: Studies in the Narrative Technique of Homeric Battle Description*, Hermes Einzelschriften, no. 21 (Wiesbaden, 1968), p. xi.

[26]Ibid., pp. 6–7.

[27]On the *aristeia*, see Chapter Three, pp. 80–82, based on T. Krischer, *Formale Konventionen der homerischen Epik*, Zetemata, no. 56 (Munich, 1971), pp. 13–89.

[28]D. Lohmann, *Die Komposition der Reden in der Ilias*, Untersuchungen zur antiken Literatur und Geschichte, no. 6 (Berlin, 1970).

[29]H. T. Wade-Gery, *The Poet of the Iliad* (Cambridge, 1952), pp. 38–41; cf. G. P. Goold, "Homer and the Alphabet," *Transactions of the American Philological Association* 91 (1960), pp. 272–91.

[30]A. Parry, "Have We Homer's *Iliad*?" p. 189 = Wright, *Essays*, p. 8.

[31]Nagy, *Best of the Achaeans*, p. 6.

[32]F. Nietzsche, "Homer und die klassische Philologie," in *Friedrich Nietzsche. Werke in drei Bände*, ed. K. Schlechta, 3 vols. (Munich, 1966), vol. 3, pp. 155–74.

[33]M. P. Nilsson, *The Mycenaean Origin of Greek Mythology* (1932; reprint, New York, 1963).

[34]M. I. Finley, *The World of Odysseus*, 2d ed. (New York, 1977), sees more than a "few and unimportant" inconsistencies in Homer's version of Mycenaean society. Finley argues that the society depicted in the *Iliad* and *Odyssey* is an unhistorical amalgam of features dating from the Mycenaean Age, the ensuing "Dark Age," and the ninth century (which he takes to be Homer's own era).

[35]M. P. Nilsson, *Homer and Mycenae*, pp. 266–72. Homer's gods also reflect the religious values of the city-state; cf. Chapter Two, p. 49.

[36]See G. Nagy, *Comparative Studies in Greek and Indic Metrics* (Cambridge, Mass., 1974), pp. 229–61. The words quoted appear on p. 261.

[37]See T. B. L. Webster, *From Mycenae to Homer* (1958; reprint, New York, 1964), pp. 9, 27–63, 154.

[38]G. Nagy has suggested to me that the "parallelisms" in Homer and Hesiod to *Gilgamesh* and other Mesopotamian poetry may be "typological" rather than owing to influence. Cf. his comments at *Classical Philology* 77 (1982), p. 72, in a review of W. Burkert, *Griechische Religion der archaischen und klassischen Epoche* (Stuttgart, 1977).

[39]On "hero cult," see Chapter 2, pp. 47–49.

[40]"In the generation before the Trojan War" refers to a time within the myth, not to any actual date in history, e.g., 1225 B.C. Whenever I speak of an event or episode in mythology as occurring earlier or later, before or after another event or episode, I mean in mythological time, not historical time.

[41]This grammarian Proclus is to be distinguished from the fifth-century A.D. Neoplatonic philosopher of the same name.

[42]For such an attempt, see the illuminating essay of A. Heubeck, "Studien zur Struktur der Ilias (Retardation-Motivübertragung)," in *Gymnasium Fridericianum. Festschrift zur Feier des 200-jährigen Bestehens des Hum. Gymnasiums Erlangen, 1745–1945* (Erlangen, 1950), pp. 17–36. The most thoroughgoing study of Homer's adaptation of traditional

mythology is W. Kullmann, *Die Quellen der Ilias* (*Troischer Sagenkreis*), Hermes Einzelschriften, no. 14 (Wiesbaden, 1960). Kullman stresses the "Anpassung der überkommenen Sage an die Thematik der Ilias," the "allgemeinen Tendenz dieses Epos, vorliegende Sagen mehr oder weniger gewaltsam ihrem eigenen Thema anzugleichen" (p. 29), as well as the "symbolic repetition" ("symbolhaft . . . wiederholt") of the whole conflict in the course of the poem (p. 366). Cf. his "Vergangenheit und Zukunft in der Ilias," *Poetica* 2 (1968), pp. 15–37.

[43]Might the detail that Protesilaos' ship is the first to be set on fire by Hektor and the Trojans (16.122–23; cf. 15.704–6, 16.285–86) be a reflection of the story that he had been the first Greek killed in the war? See D. Mülder, *Die Ilias und ihre Quellen* (Berlin, 1910), pp. 176–77, to which Heubeck, "Studien," p. 32, refers.

[44]Heubeck, "Studien," p. 31.

[45]C. H. Whitman, *Homer and the Heroic Tradition* (Cambridge, Mass., 1958), p. 265.

[46]W. Leaf, ed., *The Iliad*, 2d ed., 2 vols. (1900 and 1902; reprint, Amsterdam, 1960), vol. 1, p. 124.

[47]E. T. Owen, *The Story of the Iliad* (1946; reprint, Ann Arbor, 1966), p. 33.

[48]On the combination of human and divine motivation of human behavior, see Chapter 2, pp. 56–60.

[49]R. Bespaloff, *On the Iliad*, trans. M. McCarthy (1947; reprint, New York, 1962), p. 61.

[50]See W. Schadewaldt, *Iliasstudien*, 3d ed. (Darmstadt, 1966), pp. 156–57 n. 4.

[51]Heubeck, "Studien," p. 25.

[52]Whitman, *Homer*, pp. 263–64.

[53]On Sarpedon's hero cult, see Chapter 2, p. 48. On the parallel between his immortality and Memnon's, see Heubeck, "Studien," pp. 27–28.

[54]See Chapter 5, pp. 155–56, with references.

[55]Cf. Heubeck, "Studien," p. 30 with n. 1; Whitman, *Homer*, pp. 200–202.

[56]Heubeck, "Studien," pp. 34–35.

[57]On Patroklos, see especially R. von Scheliha, *Patroklos: Gedanken über Homers Dichtung und Gestalten* (Basel, 1943), pp. 236–51, and J. A. Scott, *The Unity of Homer* (Berkeley, 1921), pp. 235–36; for other references, see Heubeck, "Studien," p. 27 n. 3. On Hektor, see above all Scott, pp. 203–38, and other references in Heubeck, p. 35 n. 2. Cf., too, Schadewaldt, *Iliasstudien*, p. 20 n. 1.

[58]See H. Pestalozzi, *Die Achilleis als Quelle der Ilias* (Erlenbach-Zurich, 1945) and W. Schadewaldt, "Einblick in die Erfindung der Ilias.

Ilias und Memnonis," in *Von Homers Welt und Werk*, 4th ed. (Stuttgart, 1965), pp. 155–202.

[59]Cf. J. Th. Kakridis, *Homeric Researches* (Lund, 1949), pp. 65–95; K. Reinhardt, *Die Ilias und ihr Dichter* (Göttingen, 1961), pp. 349–90; B. Fenik, *Battle Scenes*, pp. 231–40; A. Dihle, *Homer-Probleme* (Opladen, 1970), pp. 9–44.

[60]K. Reinhardt, "Das Parisurteil," in *Tradition und Geist: Gesammelte Essays zur Dichtung* (Göttingen, 1960), pp. 16–36; cf. "Tradition und Geist im homerischen Epos," pp. 5–15 in the same volume.

[61]Aphrodite might be considered simply to be favoring the Trojans for the sake of her son, Aineias, but this does not account for the partisanship of Athene and Hera.

[62]Cf. Reinhardt, *Die Ilias und ihr Dichter*, pp. 405–6.

[63]See C. M. Bowra, "The Meaning of a Heroic Age," in Kirk, *Language and Background of Homer*, pp. 22–47, for other examples of epic poetry describing "events so staggering [that they] can only have been carried out by a superior breed of men" (p. 26), and for discussion of the relation between the society of the poet and his audience and that of his heroes.

[64]Whitman, Homer, p. 101.

[65]G. K. Whitfield, "The Restored Relation: The Supplication Theme in the Iliad" (Ph.D. diss., Columbia, 1967), pp. 15–27, also distinguishes two structural principles, the one "static" and "analogical," the other "dynamic" and "logical."

[66]Whitman, *Homer*, p. 351 n. 18, points out that the gods in Book 24 are roused to action on the twelfth day (24.31) but Zeus later says they have been arguing for nine days (24.107); he suggests that "the confusion over twelve and nine is likely enough in oral composition," and that the main point is that the two long time-gaps in Book 24 correspond to those in Book 1.

[67]Ibid., pp. 252–56; cf. Lohmann, *Reden*, pp. 5–8, who refers to the essay by W. A. A. van Otterlo, *De ringkompositie als opbouwprincipe in de epische Gedichten van Homerus*, Verhandelingen der Koninklijke Nederlandse Akademie van Wetenschappen, Afd. Letterkunde, no. 51.1 (Amsterdam, 1948).

[68]Lohmann, *Reden*, p. 13. The overall ring form of the speech is unmistakable, whether or not, as many scholars since antiquity have thought, lines 24.614–17 were interpolated into the poem at a later date. Cf. Kakridis, *Homeric Researches*, pp. 96–105.

[69]Nagler, *Spontaneity*, p. 191. For a detailed demonstration of the extent and importance of ring composition within and among the speeches in the *Iliad*, see Lohmann, *Reden*, passim.

[70]Perhaps the contrast between an army preparing for battle and

one mourning a hero killed in battle is "logical." Whitfield, "Restored Relation," p. 13, uses the term "analogical" in a slightly different sense, when he speaks of the "analogical coherence between [Books 1 and 24], based on themes and salient features . . . which are common to them both."

[71]Whitman, *Homer*, p. 256. Cf. Schadewaldt, *Welt und Werk*, pp. 51, 95, 214, on the compositional importance of "polarity" and "opposition" in the *Iliad*.

[72]The geometric structure of the *Iliad* was first discussed in detail by J. L. Myres, "The Last Book of the *Iliad*," *Journal of Hellenic Studies* 52 (1932), pp. 264–96, and most fully elaborated by Whitman, *Homer*, pp. 87–101, 249–84. Both Myres and Whitman were influenced by J. T. Sheppard, *The Pattern of the Iliad* (1922; reprint, London and New York, 1969).

[73]For an interesting attempt to situate Homer in his age, the eighth century B.C., see Schadewaldt, *Welt und Werk*, pp. 87–129. Cf., too, Chapter 2, p. 49; Chapter 6, p. 169.

[74]Whitfield, "Restored Relation," p. 26.

[75]Whitman, *Homer*, p. 167.

[76]Ibid.

[77]On the "decisive acts in heaven" which parallel those on earth, see Whitfield, "Restored Relation," pp. 18–21.

Appendix Notes

[78]W. J. Woodhouse, *The Composition of Homer's Odyssey* (1930; reprint, Oxford, 1969), p. 247.

[79]D. B. Monro, ed., *Homer's Odyssey, Books XIII–XXIV* (Oxford, 1901), p. 325; cf. R. Lattimore, trans., *The Odyssey*, pp. 19–20. There is one exception to this observation: the death and burial of Patroklos are narrated in the *Iliad* and referred to at *Odyssey* 24.77, 79.

[80]But this is the argument of D. Page, *The Homeric Odyssey* (Oxford, 1955), pp. 158–59, who, however, conceives of the two poets as belonging to two completely different traditions. Against Page, see Nagy, *Best of the Achaeans*, pp. 20–21.

2

The Gods

One of the most characteristic features of the *Iliad* is the gods "who have their homes on Olympos." The names and epithets of these gods are traditional and formulaic: some of them have been found at various Bronze Age sites in Crete and on the Greek mainland written on tablets in an early form of Greek called Linear B, though it is not always certain that the names on the tablets refer to gods rather than to humans. The epithets and the brief, matter-of-fact way in which Homer describes the gods and their relationships to humans indicate, in the words of Walter Otto, "that each of them possessed clearly defined lineaments, which were well known to all hearers."[1] The stories and representations of the gods in the *Iliad* are consistent with those found elsewhere in poems belonging to the same oral poetic tradition—the *Odyssey*, the poetry of Hesiod, and the so-called Homeric Hymns—and "the poet can assume that every listener has a vivid idea of the being and essence of every god."[2] But the Olympian gods were not the only gods with which Homer's audience would have been familiar. Their centrality in the *Iliad* and the way they are made to clarify by contrast the condition of mortals in the poem reflect the way Homer exploits and transforms the religion of the poetic tradition in accordance with the genre and the distinctive themes of his epic.

1

One important group of gods is almost entirely absent from the *Iliad*: the gods of the Chthonic or Earth religion. It has been shown that long before Homer, this religion, not that of the Olympian sky-gods, was dominant in Greece. The "great realities" of this religion were "Earth, procreation, blood, and death,"[3] and its main divinities were groups of primeval goddesses such as the *Moirai*, "Fates," the *Kēres*, "Death Spirits," and the *Erinues*, "Furies." These goddesses were thought to administer sacred rules that, in effect, were principles of order and limit in society and the cosmos; they angrily punished with vengeance any transgressors of these rules and this order. As Hesiod says of the *Moirai* (*Theogony* 218–22), "[These goddesses] grant / to mortals at their birth both good and evil, / and they follow up the transgressions of both men and gods; / nor do the goddesses ever leave off from their terrible anger / until they pay back an evil vengeance to whoever transgresses."[4] The mechanism by which the Chthonic divinities effect their vengeance and maintain order is magical. A person who has suffered wrong calls on them and curses the wrongdoer; this curse releases the Furies. The most serious transgressions are those committed against persons connected by blood kinship. The Furies specialize in punishing such crimes, which in the Chthonic religion are a threat not only to the victim but to society and the universal order. The punishment is drastic and bloody, exacting, as it were, a sacrificial victim in return for the victim of the previous crime.

Perhaps the most fundamental innovation, the most revolutionary feature, of Homeric religion is that the Earth goddesses are almost entirely absent or subordinated to the Olympian gods. Occasionally in the *Iliad* we hear of a different situation in the past, as when Sleep tells Hera how he once fled to Night, the "subduer of men and gods," when Zeus wished to punish him by hurling him into the sea, and Zeus "stopped, although he was angry. / For he dreaded to act in a way that would be displeasing to swift Night" (14.260–61).[5] But for the most part, the power of the Chthonic deities, the curses, magic, and human sacrifice characteristic of Chthonic religion, are ig-nored or suppressed in the *Iliad*. Homer can even make Achil-les sacrifice twelve Trojan youths on Patroklos' tomb (23.175–76), in order (given the normal standards of the poem) to depict his extreme savagery and utter inhumanity at that point, al-though such a sacrifice would not be abnormal or out of place in a Chthonic world order. We learn in Phoinix's speech to Achilles in Book 9 how, after he had slept with his father's con-cubine, his offended father "called on the hateful Furies," who "accomplished his curses" by making Phoinix sterile (9.452–57). Phoinix also tells the story of Meleagros—how his mother cursed him for the murder of her brother, and the Fury "heard her," that is, granted the prayer in which she cursed her son (9.566–72). The traditional Chthonic vengeance in these blood-kin situations is evident, but in each instance Phoinix says that Hades and Persephone, the rulers of the underworld in the Olympian religion, cooperated with the Furies. Elsewhere in the poem we hear of the Furies maintaining order and limit, as when they stop Achilles' horse Xanthos from speaking to him about his impending death (19.418); but such references are in-frequent. The only major Chthonic residue in the *Iliad* is the repeated personification of *Moira*, "Fate," as a spinner of hu-man portions, its description as "powerful" (*krataiē*) in the con-texts of various warriors' deaths, and the fact that it is the gram-matical subject of a number of active verbs—again, always in a passage leading to a warrior's death.[6] Although, as I have pointed out, Hesiod says that the *Moirai* grant both good and evil to mortals at their birth, *Moira* in the *Iliad* is never respon-sible for good gifts or blessings. What is good or positive in hu-man life comes from the Olympian gods. This restriction of the importance of *Moira*, and the absence of the *Moirai* from the poem (see above, n. 4), along with the concomitant emphasis on the power of the Olympians, are central features of Homer's subordination of the female Chthonic divinities to the patriar-chal Olympian religion.

Another variety of Chthonic religion which is particularly conspicuous by its absence from the *Iliad* is hero cult.[7] From the Bronze Age through the archaic and classical periods, a figure who had been exceptionally great and powerful in his lifetime might be considered to live still after death and to be powerful in the earth at the site of his tomb, as for example Agamemnon in Aeschylus' *Libation Bearers* or Oedipus in Sophocles' *Oedipus at Colonus*. These figures were worshipped at their burial places as "heroes"; the social group the hero protected or whose interest he represented offered tangible tribute to him in the form of sacrifices and celebrated him in song. Probably these hero cults originated as a social development of the traditional family practice of ancestor worship. In historical times a hero usually was worshipped in a particular form by an analogous social group—for example, as a young male by young males who themselves were in the process of being initiated into the responsibilities and prerogatives of adulthood.

Homer's audience may well have known and worshipped in this way some of the characters mentioned in the *Iliad*. A likely instance is Sarpedon, whose body Apollo snatches from the battlefield at Zeus' request and gives to Death and Sleep to transport to his native Lykia, "where his brothers and kinsmen will solemnly bury him / with tomb and stele, for this is the special honor of the dead" (16.674–75). The word translated as "will solemnly bury," *tarchusousi*, appears to be a word used technically of hero-cult practice, originally meaning "to make a hero of someone" or "to treat someone as a god."[8] This makes it seem as if, in historical terms, the poet is saying to his audience, "Sarpedon was taken, at the command of Zeus, to be worshipped as a hero, like the heroes we worship." But in terms of the *Iliad*, what is important is that Sarpedon is dead. Having Zeus as his father no more grants him an exemption from the defining limit of the human condition than Achilles' having Thetis as his mother enables him to escape death. When in *Odyssey* 11 Odysseus encounters Achilles' ghost (*psuchē*) in Hades, Achilles' ghost says, "I would rather serve as a hired laborer in the field of another, / a man without his own portion who has a meager livelihood, / than be lord over all the dead corpses" (*Od*. 11.489–91). In other words, mortal life on earth is what counts. There is no immortality after death for Achilles or any other Homeric hero, except through being immortalized for his achievements in epic verse.[9]

Apart from the contradiction between the immortality of the heroes worshipped in hero cults and the thoroughgoing mortality of Homer's heroes, there is another important reason why mention of these traditional cults is suppressed in the *Iliad*. Since each of them was associated with a particular tomb at a particular site, hero cults were local cults. The power of the dead figure was considered effective only at the place of burial, and he was worshipped only by inhabitants of that region. It was pointed out long ago by E. Rohde that Homer's Olympian religion is Panhellenic. That is, the actual differences among the innumerable local cults of the Olympian gods are ignored in the *Iliad* (and *Odyssey*), as Homer transcends the limits of regional and local worship to create in poetry a religious uniformity that did not exist historically.[10] Recently, G. Nagy has stressed that this religious Panhellenism is only one aspect of a general Panhellenic trend in eighth-century Greece, manifested also in the establishment of the Olympic games and of the sanctuary and oracle of the Pythian Apollo at Delphi, in the organized colonization in the Black Sea region and Sicily and Italy by citizens of various city-states, sometimes acting cooperatively, in the spread of literacy, and in the Homeric epic itself, which "synthesizes the diverse local traditions of each major city-state into a unified panHellenic model that suits most city-states but corresponds exactly to none."[11] If Homer had introduced hero cults into the *Iliad*, he would have violated the poem's general Panhellenic orientation as well as its thematic emphasis on mortality and human sufferings and achievements.

2

As stated above, the stories and representations of the Olympian gods in the *Iliad* are consistent with what we find elsewhere in poetry derived from the same tradition. Nevertheless, the portrayal of the gods is not identical in each genre of this tradition. Just as there are radically different conceptions of heroes and different myths told about heroes in the various kinds of archaic Greek poetry, so the gods act differently in a heroic epic like the *Iliad*, concerned with human achievement in the face of death, than in Hesiod's *Theogony*, a poem about the evolution of the divine order of the universe from control by Earth and a variety of female, Chthonic powers to the patriarchal rule of Zeus and the Olympian gods.[12] The *Theogony* narrates such literally cosmic events as the defeat and imprisonment of Kronos and the Titans as well as other sufferings and combats among divinities competing for power. In the *Iliad*, such sufferings and battles of the gods are a thing of the past, which no longer occur, though they are occasionally recalled.[13]

Thus, there are references to the imprisonment of Kronos and the Titans at 5.898, 8.478–81, and 15.187–93; in this last passage we learn of the threefold division of the universe by lot among Zeus, Poseidon, and Hades. At 1.397–401, we hear of the desire of Hera, Athene, and Poseidon to "bind" Zeus and of his rescue by Thetis, who "summoned to great Olympos the hundred-handed one / whom the gods call Briareos and all men call Aigaion" (1.402–3); his display of power frightened the rebellious gods into desisting.[14] In 5.383–402, Dione tells Aphrodite how on different occasions Hera and Hades were wounded by Herakles, and how Ares almost perished when he was "bound" by Otos and Ephialtes, while at 6.130–40 Diomedes recalls how Dionysos was chased into the sea by Druas. Several times we hear that Zeus used to hurl gods from heaven—Hephaistos, for example, at 1.590–94 and 18.395–99; or other gods, 15.23–24—and how he once hung Hera between heaven and earth (15.18, 47). Yet no such divine violence takes place in the *Iliad*, apart from the battle between some of the gods on the Greek side and some of those helping the Trojans (21.385–513).

This battle is introduced by lines that closely resemble those that in the *Theogony* set the stage for the great battle between Zeus and Tuphoeus.[15] There,

> The whole earth seethed, and the heaven and the seas,
> and the great waves raged around and about the beaches
> beneath the rushing of the immortals, and an unquenchable
>   shaking arose.
> Hades, ruling the dead below, trembled,
> and the Titans under Tartaros around Kronos,
> from the unquenchable din and dread conflict.
>   (*Theogony* 847–52)

In the *Iliad*,

> The father of gods and men thundei ed terribly
> from above, and from below Poseidon
> shook the endless earth and the steep summits of the
>   mountains.
> All the foothills of Ida, with many springs, were shaken,
> and the peaks, and the city of the Trojans and the ships of the
>   Achaians.
> And from below the lord of the dead, Aidoneus, was afraid,
> and in his fear he leapt from his seat and shouted, lest up
>   above
> the shaker of the earth, Poseidon, might break open the earth,
> and to both immortals and mortals would be visible the
>   dwellings,
> wide and terrible, which even the gods hate.
>
> (20.56–65)

In the *Theogony* the conflict between Tuphoeus and Zeus climactically affirms the son of Kronos in his henceforth-unchallenged rule over the universe. But the divine battle in the *Iliad* is utterly without serious results and laughable in contrast to the deadly, tragic fighting among the humans in the poem. What is a significant event in a poem whose subject is the divine order of the cosmos is a "sublime frivolity" in a poem about mortal suffering and achievement; in the *Iliad* the actions and nature of the gods emphasize by contrast the seriousness of what human beings do and suffer.[16]

Yet the true sublimity of certain of Homer's descriptions of the gods is undeniable. In fact, "Longinus" quotes part of the description of the divine battle (20.61–65) for its imaginative genius, and comments admiringly: "The earth is torn from its foundations, Tartarus is laid bare, the whole universe overthrown and broken asunder, so that all things—Heaven and Hell, things mortal and things immortal—war together and are at risk together in that ancient battle" (*On the Sublime* 9.6–7, trans. D. A. Russell). But then "Longinus" goes on to speak of the passage as "irreligious" (*athea*), and remarks that "as far as possible Homer made the humans in the *Iliad* gods and the gods humans," thus in effect acknowledging the "frivolity" of the Olympians relative to the poem's mortals. As a "better" representation of the divine as "pure and truly great and unalloyed" with anthropomorphism, "Longinus" quotes a portion of the description of Poseidon's chariot ride over the sea to Troy (13.18–19, 27–29), which he compares with the account of creation in Genesis (*On the Sublime* 9.8–9). In this passage the quivering mountains and forests, the gamboling dolphins (*kētē'*), and the sea "parting with joy"—the only time in Homer that inanimate nature is endowed with human feelings—evoke with true grandeur the presence and progress of a god.[17] But once again, the main effect of so sublime an image of divine majesty and ease is to reflect more clearly the human toil and struggle that precede and follow it in Homer's narrative.[18]

Another good example of such emphasis by contrast occurs at the end of Book 5, when Ares, speared in the belly by Diomedes with Athene's help, returns to Olympos, where his wound is quickly healed by Paieon, the god of healing, at Zeus' command. Ares then takes his seat beside Zeus "rejoicing in his triumphant glory" (*kudeï gaiōn*, 5.906). Here we have a revealing Homeric joke. *Kudos*, which I have translated as "triumphant glory," seems originally to have designated an irresistible magic power, a property of gods who might occasionally bestow it on a favorite mortal and thus assure his victory.[19] In the *Iliad* it normally is used to denote triumphant power leading to the glory that comes when one man kills or routs another, though it is used at 1.405, in the same phrase *kudeï gaiōn*, for the power of Briareos sitting beside Zeus. The ancient critic Aristarchos considered line 5.906, in which the phrase is used of Ares, spurious and a later interpolation—presumably on the ground that Homer would not have used this expression when Ares had just been defeated. But the point is that since Ares is a god, his defeat really doesn't matter. An occasion which would be fatally serious in the case of a mortal is merely an occasion for wit in the case of the god of war, who simply retreats from mortal sufferings and reassumes his divine essence with no further consequences.[20]

The gods in the *Iliad* are unaging, immortal, and far superior to mortals in knowledge and power. Everything they possess is correspondingly better: for example, their clothing, armor, and horses. Ichor, not blood, flows in their veins. They eat ambrosia and drink nektar, which seem etymologically to mean "not mortal" and "overcoming death," respectively.[21] But the contrast between them and the humans in the poem would not be nearly so effective were it not for the fact that, notwithstanding these differences, the gods are essentially anthropomorphic. Physically, psychologically, and sociologically they are modeled on humans, and these similarities serve to make the crucial differences more emphatic and meaningful. The gods have the same appetites and desires as do mortals; their extended family is a patriarchy, an immortal aristocracy with a social organization like those of the Greeks and Trojans; their ethical values, including their obsession with "honor" (*timē*), are identical to those of humans. Since they are perfect, "blessed" (*makares*) in their freedom from the decline and darkness in which everything human must end, the gods by contrast make the human condition in the poem, however brilliant the achievements of any hero, seem ephemeral and pathetically limited. On the other hand, since they are "unaging and immortal," they risk nothing essential and the honor they are obsessed with winning and losing is not truly significant. In this respect, their existence is trivial compared with that of humans, who seek to make their lives meaningful by fighting for this reward until they are finally killed.[22] Despite, or because of, their perfection, the gods serve as a foil to clarify by contrast the seriousness, or one might say the tragedy, of the human condition.

As well as "having their homes on Olympos" (*Olumpia dōmat' echontes*) and being the "blessed gods who exist always" (*makares theoi aien eontes*), the gods in the *Iliad* are *rheia zōiontes*, "the ones living easily." The distinction between living easily and living with pain and toil is one of the most frequently mentioned and most important differences in the poem between the human condition and that of the gods. In Homer, *rheia*, "easily," and related words denoting "easy" or "easily" are used typically of gods and only rarely of mortals, unless these mortals are being assisted or inspired by gods or, like Achilles in Books 20 and 21, have temporarily ceased to act human and are functioning with the power of gods. Thus, Aphrodite rescues Paris, snatching him away from the victorious Menelaos "very easily, like a god" (*rheia mal' hōs te theos*) and transporting him to his bedroom (3.380–82). The major exception to this typ-

ical usage, which really proves the rule, occurs in the *Odyssey*,
where *rheia* and its cognates are repeatedly used of the Phaia-
kians and their way of life, that is, of those mortals who are
closest to the gods and most exempt from the pain and toil of
human existence.[23] Penelope's suitors seem to think that they
can live like gods:

> These men are concerned with the lyre and song,
> easily, since they devour the livelihood of another without
>   paying,

says Telemachos to Athene/Mentes (*Od.* 1.159–60). But the
suitors eventually learn their limitations the hard way. In the
Iliad no one is exempt from human pain and toil; these constitute reality for the "wretched mortals" (*oizuroisi brotoisi*), the
"pitiful mortals" (*deiloisi brotoisi*), of the poem. At 17.443–47,
Zeus rhetorically asks the horses of Achilles, "Ah, you
wretches, why did we give the two of you to lord Peleus, / a
mortal, while you are unaging and immortal? / Was it so you
might have sorrows along with miserable men? / For there is
surely nothing more painfully wretched than a man, / of all the
things that breathe and crawl over the earth."

Numerous details reveal almost casually the differences between gods and men, always in a way that defines by contrast
what it means to be human. For instance, when Poseidon's
horses skim his chariot lightly over the waves, and the bronze
axle beneath the chariot is not even wet (13.29–30), we are reminded of the description at 11.531–37, where Hektor's horses
carry his chariot through the Trojans and Greeks "trampling
corpses and shields; the axle beneath / was all spattered with
blood, and the rims around the chariot, / which were being
struck by drops thrown from the horses' hooves / and the
wheels"; or, again, we recall the similar passage at 20.498–502,
where Achilles' horses likewise trample corpses and shields as
he presses on to win glory and avenge Patroklos.

Perhaps the clearest and most illuminating example of how
such defining contrasts between men and gods are strengthened by the anthropomorphism of the Olympians occurs in
Book 1. After the Greek embassy, led by Odysseus, has
brought Chryseis back to her father Chryses, the young men
join in a sacrificial feast, drink wine, celebrate Apollo all day

with singing, and at sundown go to sleep beside their ships. In the morning they return to the Greek camp; the quarrel with Chryses and the plague sent by Apollo have ended. But the next thing we hear is that Achilles still "was furiously angry" (*mēnie*, 1.488), and we understand that this anger and conflict with Agamemnon will continue, with the deadly consequences already announced in the opening lines of the poem. Later in Book 1, when the gods are gathered in the house of Zeus on Olympos, he and Hera quarrel over his promise to Thetis that he will destroy many of the Greeks among their ships for the sake of Achilles (1.539–67). This dispute is resolved when Hephaistos intervenes by serving nektar to all the gods, who then feast all day, listen to Apollo accompany with his lyre the Muses' singing, and at sundown go home to sleep. In particular, we are told that Zeus went to bed with Hera beside him. The parallels between the way the immortals and the mortals quarrel and resolve their quarrels are obvious, but unlike the conflict between Achilles and Agamemnon, that between Zeus and Hera has no tragic result and is almost comic. When they see Hephaistos limping around the house to serve nektar, "an unquenchable laughter arose among the immortal gods" (1.599). If humans were to laugh at a lame man serving as cupbearer, it might seem obscene. But moral condemnation of the essentially amoral Olympians would be as pointless as blaming them for never growing old or dying.

The difference between humans and gods is even clearer on another occasion in archaic Greek poetry when the Muses sing at a gathering of the Olympians. In the Homeric *Hymn to Apollo*, they "sing of the immortal gifts of the gods and the sufferings of men, / as many as they have at the hands of the immortal gods / as they live witless and helpless and are not able / to find a cure for death and a defense against old age" (*H. Ap.* 190–93). For an audience schooled in the poetic tradition, such a scene on Olympos with a song of the Muses was undoubtedly formulaic, and this traditional formularity would have better enabled listeners to understand the differences between the tragic, strife-ridden condition of humans and the easy existence of the gods. Furthermore, it has recently been shown by G. Nagy that one of the major motifs of traditional epic poetry was strife breaking out at a feast with tragic consequences for

Greeks and Trojans.[24] Demodokos, the Phaiakian bard, sings of such a quarrel breaking out between Achilles and Odysseus at Delphi (*Od*. 8.72–82), and we recognize the theme in the story (referred to but not told in the *Iliad*) of the wedding of Peleus and Thetis and the conflict that was the original cause of the Trojan War. The way in which, in Book 1 of the *Iliad*, the dispute between Zeus and Hera is resolved harmoniously would have been especially pointed for an audience familiar with this traditional motif of the tragically interrupted mortal feast.

3

In the *Iliad* whatever is positive in human life and in the world can be said to come from the Olympian gods, who are at once the sources and symbols of beauty, strength, ability, success, honor, and glory—of all that makes life worth living. Different gods preside, as it were, over different activities and skills: when someone performs a specific activity or exercises a specific skill, he or she is said to be aided by, or to be the recipient of the gift of, the particular god in charge of that activity or skill. Thus a warrior who makes an excellent spearcast and succeeds in killing his opponent, or who has a long string of such successes, may be said to be helped by Ares or Athene. Helen and Paris are the recipients of the favor and gifts of Aphrodite. Agamemnon and other kings have honor from Zeus, the supreme king. But not all the gods' gifts are of equal importance: Paris tells Hektor (3.64–65) not to reproach him for the gifts of Aphrodite, since "the glorious gifts of the gods are not to be thrown away"; but we know that in the *Iliad*, an epic about heroic warfare, the gifts of Aphrodite are more trivial, of less weight, than those of Athene. Like the rest of Troy's domestic and civilized qualities, the gifts of Aphrodite cannot prevent its eventual, inevitable fall.

The gift-relation between humans and gods in the *Iliad* can be illustrated by the origin of Pandaros' bow.[25] In 4.105–11, just before Pandaros breaks the truce by shooting an arrow at Menelaos, we are told by Homer how the bow was made by a craftsman, a worker in horn, out of the horns of a wild goat Pandaros had killed. But in the catalogue of Trojan warriors (2.827) Homer says that Apollo himself gave Pandaros his bow. There really is no contradiction between the two passages. That Apollo gave Pandaros his bow does not refer to a specific event but to the fact that Pandaros was a particularly good archer and therefore must have been gifted by the god of archery. Similarly, we learn at 15.441 that Teukros, the foremost Greek archer, was given his bow and arrows by Apollo.

Homer may speak not only of the gift of a god but also of the inspiration of an idea or of strength by a god, or of direct physical intervention by a god, as when Athene guides Diomedes' spear into Pandaros' face (5.290–91) or into Ares' belly (5.856–57). In the *Iliad* a god is manifest in any kind of outstanding success, or indeed on any occasion on which a person seems to be or to do something more (or something less) than would normally be expected.[26] In this sense divinity for Homer might be said to consist in exceptional human achievement.

The relationship between success and a divinity, especially Athene, is marked throughout the *Iliad*. Indeed, M. Willcock has aptly defined Athene's "function," that "which in her case is parallel to sexual attraction for Aphrodite and killing for Ares," as "*winning, success*, and specifically Greek success. . . . [T]he favourites of Athene are Tydeus, Diomedes, Odysseus, Achilles—the naturally successful, the natural winners."[27] Because Homer tells us, in any given instance, that Athene or another god has made something happen, we tend to make the god the cause or agent. But in fact the achievement or excellence shown by a hero, or any unusual or striking occurrence, indicates retrospectively both to the poet and to his audience that a god has been present; actually the god is an *ex post facto* explanation, not a cause or agent of what happened.

For modern readers a rational or rationalized explanation of this kind of divine presence usually is possible. For instance, we may say in the case of Achilles heeding Athene's suggestion that he not kill Agamemnon (1.193–222) that Achilles had second thoughts, that he thought the better of it, in a manner we find psychologically plausible. Similarly, when Apollo makes Diomedes drop his whip during the chariot race in the funeral games (23.383–84) or when Athene makes Ajax, son of Oileus,

slip on some dung during the footrace (23.774–77), we can explain these as accidents that can happen in such races. But
when, in the chariot race, Athene returns the whip to
Diomedes (23.389–90), or when she returns to Achilles the
spear that he had hurled vainly at Hektor, with which he then
kills him (22.276–77), the inadequacy of such rational or plausible explanations is clear. In these instances no rational explanation is available, yet these supernatural interventions are ex-
plicable in terms of the poem's poetic structure, and in terms of
what has been said about Athene and heroic success. As Willcock puts it, Diomedes and Achilles are naturally winners; if no
gods had been present, they would have won without any
help. "Indeed, it is precisely because [Achilles] did not need
her help that he gets it; Athene helps him because he is going
to win."[28] To modern readers it may seem unfair that a god
takes part so decisively in human action. Yet for Homer and his
audience, the presence of the god was the traditional poetic
means of calling attention to the greatness of the victor and the
victory, and it likewise conferred a special dignity on both victor and victim by showing that the gods themselves were concerned to intervene in their struggle.[29] Otto has called attention
to "the magnanimity of conception which makes the goddess
. . . actually help [Hektor] achieve an honorable and glorious
death."[30]

    That the gods intervene in human actions or motivate hu-
man behavior does not mean that the humans are not morally
responsible agents. B. Snell has argued that "Homer lacks a
knowledge of the spontaneity of the human mind; he does not
realize that decisions of the will, or any impulses or emotions
have their origin in man himself."[31] Yet usually, if one looks
carefully, a given action or decision is obviously motivated both
by a god and by the human in question.[32] E. R. Dodds invoked
the Freudian concept of "overdetermination" to account for
the mixture of human and divine motivation for specific behavior, as when Diomedes says (9.702–3) that Achilles will rejoin
the fighting "whenever the time comes / that the heart in his
chest urges him to and a god drives him."[33]

    Homer, perhaps because he is telling a story about heroes,
tends to describe gods as physically present and active only at
times of specially heightened action or perception. When this

happens, he usually describes the physical effect on the person or persons influenced. For example, when, at 13.66–80, the two Ajaxes feel that their hands, knees, and feet are filled with energy (*menos*) as a result of Poseidon's exhortation and his touching them with his scepter, they are more eager to do battle; and when, at 17.451–58, Zeus breathes strength (again, *menos*) into Achilles' horses, they shake the dust from their manes and lightly bear their chariot through the field. Although readers are aware of the gods chiefly at such moments of heightened or abnormal experience, we should remember that the gods in the *Iliad*, because they are within nature and the world, are always present to humanity.

For some scholars, the presence and power of the gods and their contributions to human decisions and actions mean that they, in particular Zeus, inflict the events of the war and of the poem on the helpless mortals. These scholars cite the words, "and the plan of Zeus was accomplished" (1.5), which follow the announcement that the subject of the poem will be the destructive wrath of Achilles and its deadly consequences, in support of this interpretation. For them, the moral of the poem is: "As flies to wanton boys are we to th' gods. / They kill us for their sport."

In fact, "the plan of Zeus" refers neither to the entire war nor to all that happens in the *Iliad*, but rather to Zeus' decision to grant Achilles' request, as conveyed by Thetis, to honor him and support him in his quarrel with Agamemnon by destroying many Greeks at their ships (1.408–12, 505–10). At 8.473–76 and 15.61–71, we learn that in the long run Zeus' plan will involve not only the temporary triumph of Hektor and the Trojans but also the successive deaths of Sarpedon, Patroklos, and Hektor (and, we learn later, of Achilles), and the fall of Troy. But the plan itself is simply to honor Achilles by granting temporary victory to the Trojans.

We know from a fragment of another epic in the Epic Cycle, the *Kypria*, that according to the traditional mythology, Zeus brought about the Trojan War to relieve Earth of a heavy burden of overpopulation; this fragment concludes with the words, "the heroes were killed / in Troy, and the plan of Zeus was accomplished." We also hear, at *Od.* 8.81–82, in a song of Demodokos, that as the war began, "the beginning of woe was rolling / on both the Trojans and Greeks through the plans of great Zeus." The similarity of wording between these two passages and *Il.* 1.5 has led some scholars to conclude that "the plan of Zeus" in the *Iliad* is identical with that mentioned in the *Kypria* and referred to in the *Odyssey*, and that Zeus is the cause of human sufferings in the *Iliad*. But this interpretation does not appreciate how in the *Iliad* Homer consistently plays down those aspects of the tradition that emphasize the gods' responsibility for the war, and instead brings the responsibility of mortals to the fore. In the *Iliad*, "the plan of Zeus" is the plan of Achilles, or rather, as it turns out, the plan of Achilles gone tragically astray.[34]

4

From the point of view of the humans in the poem, the gods are everywhere, constantly intervening in human affairs. From the gods' own point of view, as it were, their usual, most characteristic position vis-à-vis mortals is that of spectators.[35] Repeatedly they are said to "look on" or "watch over" the doings of mortals, occasionally with but usually without moral approval or disapproval. J. Griffin recently has likened them to spectators of a drama, "a tragedy rather than a comedy, feeling pity and sorrow, though not of course terror."[36] To be sure, they are a special kind of audience precisely because of their interventions, which help to arrange the plot of the drama they are viewing. Thus, at 7.59–61 Apollo and Athene, in the form of vultures, sit on an oak tree "delighting in the men" (*andrasi terpomenoi*) as they might delight in an artistic performance, while the men are behaving just as the two gods have decided they should.

Griffin suggests that the gods watch humans struggling and suffering just as the aristocratic mortals on whom they are modeled enjoy watching, for example, such athletic competitions as the funeral games of Patroklos in Book 23.[37] In fact, at one especially tense moment Homer himself seems to make this comparison:

> In front a good man was fleeing, but a much better man was
>   pursuing him
> swiftly; it was not a sacrificial victim or an oxhide which
> the two were trying to win, which are prizes for swiftness of
>   foot among men,
> but they ran for the life of Hektor, tamer of horses.
> As when prize-winning, solid-footed horses run very lightly
> around the turns, and there is a great prize waiting,
> a woman or a tripod, when a man has died,
> so the two circled three times around the city of Priam
> on swift feet; and all the gods were looking on.
>
> (22.158–66)

In this scene Zeus pities Hektor (22.169–70), just as he pities
Sarpedon (16.433–34) and as he is ready to make peace between the Greeks and Trojans and spare the city of Priam (4.16–
18). But in each case the pity, though real, is passing; the most
Zeus does is pour to earth a light drizzle of blood in honor of
Sarpedon whom Patroklos is about to kill (16.459–61). The ultimate indifference of the divine spectators to human suffering
is made clear at 4.37–39, when Zeus tells Hera, who has in-
sisted that Troy be destroyed so her "sweat and toil" should not
have been for nothing (4.26–27), that in that case she had better
not object when in the future he wants to sack a city and a people dear to her. She replies, "Three cities are dearest by far to
me— / Argos and Sparta and Mycenae of the broad streets. /
Sack them whenever they become hateful to your heart; / I
won't protect them and I don't begrudge you" (4.51–54).[38] Of
course, as she goes on to say, she couldn't stop him even if she
wanted to, "for you are much stronger. / But my toil must not
be unfulfilled, / for I am a god too . . ." (4.56–58). Hera's "sweat
and toil" and all-too-human jealousy, like Zeus' insistence on
getting even, contrast notably with their divine power to destroy both human life and the civilization humans have worked
to achieve.

What is a mere spectacle to the gods, or the subject of their
petty squabbling, is of ultimate importance to humans. At the
beginning of Book 13,

> When Zeus had brought Hektor and the Trojans near to the
>   ships,

he let them have toil and misery there
unceasingly, but he himself turned his shining eyes in the
    opposite direction,
looking far off toward the land of the Thracians

(13.1–4)

For Zeus and the other gods, who view human events as spectators, it is easy to turn away when they lose interest. For Hecuba and Priam watching from the walls or for Achilles gazing from his shelter it is impossible. The gods' amusement is life and death to the mortals of the poem.[39]

Homer's Olympians are presented in a double perspective: they are frivolous and their existence is lacking in seriousness when compared with the tragic reality of human strivings for heroic achievement and meaning in life; yet in contrast to their cosmic power and perfection, human existence is limited and unimportant. Homer never lets his audience forget either side of this double view. This may have been part of what Herodotos had in mind when he said (2.53) that Homer and Hesiod were responsible for distributing the names, functions, and forms of the Olympian gods. At any rate Homer was responsible for the religious view, characteristic throughout the archaic and classical periods, that emphasized human ignorance and powerlessness in the face of a higher cosmic order even while it made human beings the subjects and objects of all significant action, suffering, and speculation.

APPENDIX: On Fate

The Homeric Greek words usually translated as "fate" or, when personified, as "Fate," are *moira*, its variant form *moros*, and its synonym *aisa*. These words literally mean "allotment" or "portion" or "share," as of land (16.68) or booty (18.327), though *moros* is used so often of someone's death or doom that lexicons offer these meanings also. Unlike the Latin word *fatum*, from which "fate" is derived, *moira*, *moros*, and *aisa* do not mean "a thing said" or, by extension, "a predetermined course of events"—a meaning of "fate" that has been strengthened for us by Christian notions of predestination, as well as by such artistic concepts as "the tragedy of fate." When we translate *moira, moros,* or *aisa* as "fate," we must avoid importing with the translation a concept of destiny that is in no way Homeric.

Of course, all humans in the *Iliad* are mortal; they know that they will die, and in this general sense they know their *moira . . . thanatoio,* their "portion of death," though only the gods know precisely when and how someone will die—specifically what his *moira* is. From the human point of view, only when something happens to someone does he realize (or Homer tell us) that it was his *moira.* And though the gods know what will happen, they do not directly cause it or bring it about: with one possible exception (Ares at 5.842), no god actually takes a human life. At the hour of *moira* a protecting god may depart, as Apollo does from Hektor at 22.213; or, as in the case of Patroklos, a human may be opposed by a god who is protecting his opponent. In all such instances, the human chooses to act in such a way that he comes to be killed, and the most that can be said is that *Moira,* a personification of "what, in retrospect, was bound to happen," cooperated with divine and human agents (cf. 16.849–50).[40]

While a god never causes *moira,* there are occasional passages where a god prevents it from happening prematurely or inopportunely. In these instances, Homer says that something almost happened "beyond portion" (*hupermoron, huper moiran, huper aisan*): for example, one man almost killed another, or the Greeks almost captured Troy. What almost happened never is contrary to what is known to have happened according to the traditional mythology (for example, Troy eventually did fall), but rather is an anticipation of it. When Homer says that something almost happened "beyond portion," he is saying that a hero's achievement was so exceptional, or the course of events so remarkable, that *even this* would have happened on this occasion, if the oral poetic tradition did not tell us—the poet and his audience—otherwise. On two occasions, in the case of Sarpedon (16.431–38) and of Hektor (22.167–76), Zeus contemplates saving a man from death and thus altering his portion; in other words, Zeus thinks of doing something "beyond portion." But when Hera and Athene tell him that the other gods "will not approve," he refrains from the contemplated action.

While Zeus clearly is able to change a *moira*, at the same time, paradoxically, he cannot do so for the same reason that other things do not happen "beyond portion": that is not the way the traditional story goes, and any change in the tradition is inconceivable for both poet and audience.[41]

Notes to Chapter 2

[1]W. Otto, *The Homeric Gods: The Spiritual Significance of Greek Religion*, trans. M. Hadas (1954; reprint, Boston, 1964), p. 135.

[2]Ibid., p. 15.

[3]Ibid., p. 17.

[4]Homer never refers to the *Moirai* in the plural except in 24.49, where they are said to have placed in mortals "an enduring heart." This line is anomalous not only because of the plural number but because of the gift of something good. Elsewhere, when Homer personifies *Moira*, "Fate," it gives to mortals only death. See below, p. 47.

[5]Significantly, in Hesiod Night is the mother of the *Moirai* and *Keres*, as well as of Death, Sleep, Blame, and Woe (*Theogony* 211–14, 217).

[6]Otto, *Gods*, p. 269. See the appendix on Fate at the end of this chapter, pp. 62–64.

[7]On hero cult, see E. Rohde, *Psyche*, trans. W. B. Hillis, 2 vols. (1925; reprint, New York, 1966), vol. 1, pp. 115–55; L. R. Farnell, *Greek Hero Cults and Ideas of Immortality* (Oxford, 1921). For the archaeological evidence, see A. M. Snodgrass, *The Dark Age of Greece: An Archaeological Survey of the Eleventh to the Eighth Centuries* (Edinburgh, 1971), pp. 398–99; J. N. Coldstream, "Hero-cults in the Age of Homer," *Journal of Hellenic Studies* 96 (1976), pp. 8–17.

[8]On the meaning of *tarchusousi*, see P. Chantraine, *Dictionnaire étymologique de la langue grecque. Histoire des mots*, 4 vols. (Paris, 1968–80), vol. 4.1, p. 1095, s.v. *tarchuo*.

[9]Cf. W. Kullmann, *Die Quellen der Ilias (Troischer Sagenkreis)*, Hermes Einzelschriften, no. 14 (Wiesbaden, 1960), p. 35 n. 1; *Das Wirken der Götter in der Ilias: Untersuchungen zur Frage der Entstehung des homerischen "Götterapparats"* (Berlin, 1956), p. 131. Human heroes, including Achilles, can and do achieve immortality in hero cult in other epics in the Epic Cycle. On Achilles' immortality after death in the *Aithiopis*, see Chapter 4, pp. 95, 123n15.

[10]Rohde, *Psyche*, vol. 1, pp. 25–27.

[11]G. Nagy, *The Best of the Achaeans: Concepts of the Hero in Archaic Greek Poetry* (Baltimore and London, 1979), p. 7.

[12]Ibid., pp. 151–210; J.-P. Vernant, "Le mythe hésiodique des races: Essai d'analyse structurale," in *Mythe et pensée chez les Grecs: Etudes de psychologie historique*, 2d ed. (Paris, 1969), pp. 19–47.

[13]See J. Griffin, *Homer on Life and Death* (Oxford, 1980), pp. 184–85. When the gods do suffer in battle in the *Iliad*, for example, Ares and Aphrodite in Book 5 and Ares, Aphrodite, and Artemis in Book 20, the effect is not cosmic but comic.

[14]On this attempt to "bind" Zeus, see Chapter 4, pp. 91–92.

[15]Griffin, *Life and Death*, p. 185.

[16] Ibid., p. 199, translating Karl Reinhardt's phrase "erhabener Unernst."

[17]On Poseidon's journey over the sea, see J. Th. Kakridis, *Prohomerika, Homerika, Hesiodeia* (Athens, 1980), pp. 77–88, especially pp. 86–88. (In Greek.)

[18]See below, pp. 53–54.

[19]On *kudos*, see E. Benveniste, *Indo-European Language and Society*, trans. E. Palmer, Miami Linguistics Series, no. 12 (Coral Gables, 1973), pp. 346–56.

[20]There is a similar, revealing contrast between gods and humans in *Odyssey* 8.266–366: Demodokos' song about Ares and Aphrodite. For the humans of the poem adultery, even would-be adultery, with its violence to the property of another, is a serious transgression, which, for example, costs the suitors their lives. But among the gods, adultery and its punishment are an occasion for humor, without serious consequences. Just seven lines after she has been released by Hephaistos, Aphrodite has been bathed and anointed, has put on lovely garments (cf. Ares in *Il.* 5.905), and is a "wonder to behold."

[21]On *ambrosia*, see Chantraine, *Dictionnaire*, vol. 1, pp. 197–98, s.v. *brotos*. On *nektar*, ibid., vol. 3, pp. 741–42, s.v. *nektar*, and F. W. Householder and G. Nagy, *Greek: A Survey of Recent Work* (The Hague and Paris, 1972), pp. 52–53.

[22]See Chapter 3, pp. 68, 70–72. As Mark Griffith has suggested (in a letter), the gods are "immune from real tests of character—which are normally conducted in the *Iliad* in the face of death." Cf. R. Bespaloff, *On the Iliad*, trans. M. McCarthy (1947; reprint, New York, 1962), pp. 73–74.

[23] Cf. Nausikaä's description of the Phaiakian King Alkinoös at *Od.* 6.309: "Sitting he drinks his wine like an immortal."

[24]Nagy, *Best of the Achaeans*, pp. 22–25, 64–65.

[25]Here I follow M. Willcock, "Some Aspects of the Gods in the *Iliad*," *Bulletin of the Institute of Classical Studies in London* 17 (1970), pp. 3–4 = J. Wright, ed., *Essays on the Iliad. Selected Modern Criticism* (Bloomington and London, 1978), pp. 62–63.

[26]Cf. E. R. Dodds, *The Greeks and the Irrational* (Berkeley and Los Angeles, 1951), p. 13: ". . . all departures from normal human behaviour whose causes are not immediately perceived, whether by the subjects' own consciousness or by the observation of others, are ascribed to a supernatural agency, just as is any departure from the normal behaviour of the weather or the normal behaviour of a bowstring." Dodds observes (p. 17) that this is "especially likely to happen when the acts in question are such as to cause acute shame to their authors."

[27]Willcock, "Aspects of the Gods," p. 6 = Wright, *Essays*, p. 67.

[28]Ibid., p. 7 = p. 68.

[29]See H. E. Barnes, *The Meddling Gods* (Lincoln, 1974), p. 100.

[30]Otto, *Gods*, p. 278.

[31]B. Snell, *The Discovery of the Mind: The Greek Origins of European Thought*, trans. T. Rosenmeyer (Cambridge, Mass., 1953), p. 31.

[32]See A. Lesky, *Göttliche und menschliche Motivation im homerischen Epos* (Heidelberg, 1961).

[33]Dodds, *Greeks and the Irrational*, pp. 7, 13.

[34]For a different interpretation of "the plan of Zeus" in 1.5 and a convenient summary of several other views, see J. M. Redfield, "The Proem of the *Iliad*: Homer's Art," *Classical Philology* 74 (1979), pp. 105–8.

[35]On what follows, see Griffin, *Life and Death*, pp. 179–204.

[36]Ibid., p. 201. Cf. H. Fränkel, *Die homerischen Gleichnisse*, 2d ed. (Göttingen, 1977), p. 32 n. 1, cited by Griffin, p. 180 n. 3.

[37]Griffin, *Life and Death*, p. 193. Cf. J. M. Redfield, *Nature and Culture in the Iliad: The Tragedy of Hector* (Chicago and London, 1975), pp. 158–59.

[38]The epithet "of the broad streets" (*euruaguia*) movingly summons up a vision of a civilized culture which Hera is willing to see destroyed. The epithet is used elsewhere of Troy. Cf. Chapter 6, p. 169.

[39]Cf. Griffin, *Life and Death*, p. 201.

Appendix Notes

[40]See Otto, *Gods*, p. 280.

[41]Cf. Nagy, *Best of the Achaeans*, pp. 40, 81–82 §25n2. Of course, at the level of the action of the poem there is another good reason, spelled out by Hera (16.445–49), why Zeus does not change Sarpedon's *moira*: if he does, all the other gods whose sons are fighting on the Greek and Trojan sides will wish to do likewise, and chaos will ensue.

3

War, Death, and Heroism

1

The *Iliad* has been called "from beginning to end a poem of death."[1] This description is obviously accurate in a literal sense: the poem begins with an invocation to the muse to sing the *mēnis*, the "wrath," of Achilles, "which hurled forth to Hades many strong souls / of heroes and made them [the heroes] prey for dogs / and all the birds" (1.3–5); it ends with a description of the burial of Hektor. More generally, most of the action of the epic consists of Greeks and Trojans killing one another. By the end, Hektor, the main figure on the Trojan side, has been killed and his city symbolically sacked; Achilles, the chief figure on the Greek side and the central character in the poem, has lost and buried his beloved comrade Patroklos and, by killing Hektor, has in effect brought about his own death, which has been repeatedly prophesied and prefigured. The funeral games of Patroklos in Book 23 and the mourning and burial of Hektor in Book 24 are, in a sense, not only for these two heroes but for everyone in the poem. They form a ritually appropriate, aesthetically and spiritually satisfying conclusion to the relentless killing and dying; they help us, as well as the

Greeks and Trojans, to endure the pain and loss entailed in being mortal.

Yet one could also argue that "from beginning to end" the *Iliad* is a poem of life, or, as E. Vermeule has suggested, a poem "of mortality and mortal accidents, and of the kinds of behavior only mortals need have to confront these."[2] In the world of the poem, war is the medium of human existence and achievement; bravery and excellence in battle win honor and glory and thus endow life with meaning. Heroes affirm their greatness by the brilliance and efficiency with which they kill. The flashing action of a warrior's triumph represents the fullest realization of human potential, despite the pain and loss for the victim, his family, and his community. And even for the victim, death that "yields glory to another" (12.328, 13.327) can be more than simply pain and loss. Some glory can be won, too, by dying bravely, in an act that sums up and puts a seal on a life lived in accordance with the generally acknowledged standards of heroic "excellence" (*aretē*). Thus when Hektor realizes that Athene has tricked him and that he is about to die at Achilles' hands, he says, "At least let me not perish without a struggle, ingloriously, / but after having done something great, for future generations to learn of" (22.304–5).[3]

Homer's descriptions of killing and dying are traditional and formulaic in action and style, but as always he selectively reworks the tradition in accordance with the characteristic themes of his poem and achieves a depiction of human existence that is distinctively Iliadic. The main reason why winning honor and glory in war can endow life with meaning is that in the world of the *Iliad* there is no significant afterlife. For Homer, as Vermeule says, "The realm of death is more a series of standard expressions and a few deliberately pointed contrasts [with life] than a serious focus of imagination."[4] The word *psuchē*, usually translated "soul," has none of the intellectual or spiritual significance that it came to have for later Greeks and for the West. Etymologically, *psuchē* seems to mean "wind-breath." In the *Iliad* it is simply an entity that, when it is in a human body, makes that body alive, and that, when a person is killed, departs to Hades; there it is a ghost, with no significant physical or mental existence.[5] The *psuchē* is not particularly important for Homer, who, in 1.3–5, contrasts to the "souls" (*psuchas*) hurled forth to Hades the "selves" (*autous*) left as prey for dogs and birds. This conception of the body as the "self" both accounts for Homer's much greater concern with what happens to bodies than with what happens to "souls" and explains his characters' sense that what counts is what one can do and win and suffer in the only life there is for a mortal.

This was not always the case in the poetic tradition. In Hesiod's *Works and Days*, for example, after death the mortals of the golden race live on as good "divinities" (*daimones*) above the earth, watching over mortal men, keeping evil away from them, and rewarding them with prosperity (121–26); those of the silver race survive death as "blessed mortals below the earth," that is, as heroes with hero cults (140–44).[6] In the *Odyssey* Menelaos, because he is Helen's husband and Zeus' son-in-law, will not die but will be sent to the Elysian plain to live "the life that is easiest for mortals" (4.561–69)—a life like a god's.[7] But in the *Iliad*, regardless of what the audience may have expected from their familiarity with the traditional conceptions of an afterlife, Homer suppresses all mention of any continued or posthumous existence for mortal warrior-heroes.

Homer's attitude toward heroism can be seen in the very word *hērōs*, which elsewhere denotes a figure worshipped in hero cults (see Chapter 2, pp. 47–49), but in the *Iliad* signifies a warrior who lives and dies in the pursuit of honor and glory. *Hērōs* seems to be etymologically related to the word *hōrē*, "season."[8] Although a "hero" might originally have been "seasonal" in the sense of going through the cycle of seasons and being, as it were, reborn when the cycle begins anew—that is, as an immortal "hero" to be worshipped in cult—in Homer *hōrē* means in particular the "season of spring," and a "hero" is "seasonal" in that he comes into his prime, like flowers in the spring, only to be cut down once and for all. In 2.468 the Greek army is compared in numbers to the leaves and flowers that arise "in the season," and in a famous passage (6.146–49) Glaukos, speaking to Diomedes, compares the generations of leaves to those of men: the wind pours some down to the ground, and the living stock puts forth others when the season of spring returns. As befits an aristocrat boasting of his family tree in a passage that ends with an affirmation of ancestral guest-friendship between the two opposing fighters, Glaukos puts his emphasis as much on the stock that survives to put out new leaves as on the leaves that bloom and are poured to the ground like dead warriors.[9] Still, we can see that the vegetal imagery expresses the *Iliad*'s conception of a hero as a mortal who fights and dies with no afterlife as his reward other than the glory of celebration in epic song.[10]

In the *Iliad*, although death can be a source of anxiety for mortals, it "is not the enemy of creativity but its cause, since the contemplation of death is the single factor that makes us long for immortality."[11] As Sarpedon says to Glaukos (12.322–28), "If . . . we two were going to be unaging and immortal forever, / neither would I myself fight in the front ranks / nor would I send you into the battle where men win glory. / But as it is, since the spirits of death stand over us / numberless, which it is not possible for a mortal to flee or avoid, / let us go—either we will give glory to boast of to someone else, or someone will give it to us."

As was explained in Chapter 2 (p. 53), since the gods by definition are "unaging and immortal," they can neither win nor lose significant glory. Since they cannot die, they risk nothing; for this reason their existence, compared with that of mortals, is trivial. They emphasize by contrast the seriousness of the human condition, in which winning honor and glory alone makes a brief life meaningful and enables an individual to stand out in his own and in others' eyes.[12]

Winning honor and glory, however, makes life meaningful not only because humans are mortal but also because of the social value system that is normative throughout the poem. This value system is most clearly stated earlier in the same speech of Sarpedon to Glaukos:

> Glaukos, why, then, are we two especially honored
> with a seat of honor and with meats and with full wine goblets
> in Lykia, and all look at us as at gods
> and we are assigned a great estate by the banks of the river
>   Xanthos,
> a fine one of vineyard and wheat-bearing plowland?
> Therefore it now is right that among the front ranks of Lykians
> we stand and encounter the blazing battle,

so that someone of the Lykians who wear thick armor will say:
"By no means without glory do they rule Lykia—
our kings—and they eat fat sheep
and drink exquisite, honey-sweet wine; but their strength, too,
is good, for they fight among the front ranks of Lykians."
                                        (12.310–21)

This same code of values is illustrated by the dispute between
Agamemnon and Achilles in Book 1, which turns on Achilles'
sense that in violation of the societal norm he has been robbed
of the honor he has earned.

   This "honor" is not merely an abstraction. The basic meaning of *timē*, "honor," is "price" or "value" in a tangible sense.
The word can be used of a woman like Briseis, who was a *geras*
or special "gift of honor" from the army to Achilles, as well as
of the seat of honor, full wine goblets, meats, and fertile land
mentioned by Sarpedon as rewards for prowess in battle and
reasons for continued bravery and achievement. Those who
win such tangible honors also receive honor conceived ab-
stractly; from this comes their *kleos*, "glory and reputation,"
what is said about them near and far, even when they are dead.
To be sure, in the course of the *Iliad* Achilles comes to question
and contradict the validity of the normative social value system. This disillusionment enhances Achilles' tragedy and constitutes part of Homer's critical exploration of the nature and
conditions of heroism and of human life. Nevertheless, for
Achilles and for everyone else in the poem, there is no real alternative. Life is lived and death is died according to this code
of values: to be fully human—that is, to be a hero—means to
kill or be killed for honor and glory.

   The human situation in the *Iliad* might well be called tragic,
because the very activity—killing—that confers honor and
glory necessarily involves the death not only of other warriors
who live and die by the same values as their conquerors, but
eventually, in most cases, also of the conquerors themselves.
Thus, the same action is creative or fruitful and at the same time
both destructive and self-destructive. Odysseus states the situation well and plainly when he says to Agamemnon (14.84–
87), "Would that you were giving signals to some other, vile
army, / and were not lord over us, to whom Zeus / has given

from our childhood even to our old age to wind up the thread /
of difficult wars, so that finally we perish, each of us."[13]

The fact that "each of us" will perish through the very warfare that makes life meaningful indicates the cost as well as the
rewards of the heroism Homer celebrates. When a warrior
dies, limbs which have been warm and active become cold and
still. Darkness prevails where eyes had previously been bright.
Feelings of love for and solidarity with comrades, family, and
native land are suddenly ended. Though Homer's account of
the war may appeal to different emotions at different places in
the poem, he never becomes naively sentimental or thought-
lessly brutal about death. He balances equally the greatness of
the slayers and the pathos of the slain.

2

The Homeric attitude toward death is especially
clear in the descriptions of the fates of numerous minor warriors, the little heroes who exist merely to be killed, whose
deaths are the occasions for brief remarks or vignettes about
their lives and manner of dying.[14] As Jasper Griffin has demonstrated, these "lesser heroes are shown in all the pathos of
their death, the change from the brightness of life to a dark and
meaningless existence, the grief of their friends and families. . . ."[15] Certain motifs recur in their "obituaries": a man's
life was brief; he died far from home and family; his comrades
or parents or wife and children were bereaved; they were unable to help him and could not make good his loss. When the
husband or son is young or newly married, the description of
the death is especially moving; when emphasis is placed on the
victim's ignorance of what was in store for him, or on his
beauty and potential cut short, we are even more affected.
Clearly, many of these motifs were traditional, but they are in-
tegrated with important themes of the *Iliad* itself. For example,
as Griffin points out, "The bereaved father is a dominant figure
in the plot from Chryses to Priam, who appeals to Achilles in
the name of another tragic father, Peleus."[16] And all the young

warriors who fall far from their parents and wives, whose comrades can do nothing for them, who die even as their ignorance of destiny becomes certain knowledge, culminate in Hektor. The descriptions of the deaths of the minor heroes help to create by their content and tone the consistent, unsentimental view of death and of life, that we think of as Homeric. They help us to interpret the overall dramatic situation and main story of the poem in a particular way.[17] Homer never lets us forget that the minor warriors really are minor compared with the greater heroes who kill them, but the pathos he endows their deaths with makes us see what is lost in the glory of these greater heroes.

One passage that well illustrates Homer's attitude toward death is the description of the death of the Trojan warrior Simoeisios (4.473–89). This is one of the richest and most exquisite of many passages that recapitulate a central theme of the *Iliad*: the cost in human terms of heroic achievement. The death of the Trojan youth is analogous on a small scale to the death of Hektor and the destiny of Troy as they are portrayed and prefigured elsewhere in the poem. Simoeisios' death makes a particularly strong impression on us also because he is only the third character killed in the *Iliad*; the description helps to establish a pattern of meaning that prevents us from simply becoming habituated to or dulled by the many later reports and descriptions of killing and dying:

> Then Ajax son of Telamon killed the son of Anthemion,
> unmarried, blooming Simoeisios, whom once his mother
> coming down from Ida beside the banks of the Simoeis   (475)
> gave birth to, when she followed along with her parents to see
>   the flocks.
> Therefore they called him Simoeisios. Nor did he give a return
> to his dear parents for rearing him, but his life was brief,
> conquered beneath the spear of great-hearted Ajax.
> For as he was moving in the front ranks, Ajax hit him in the
>   chest beside   (480)
> the right nipple; straight through his shoulder the bronze
>   spear
> went, and he fell to the ground in the dust like a black poplar,
> which has grown in the lowland of a great marsh,

smooth, but its branches grow at the very top;
and which a man who makes chariots cuts down with the
  shining   (485)
iron, so he can bend it into a wheel for a beautiful chariot;
and it lies hardening beside the banks of a river.
Such then was Anthemion's son, Simoeisios, whom Ajax
sprung from Zeus killed.

The passage is framed by statements in lines 473 and 488–89 that Ajax killed Simoeisios. It is notable that Ajax is described as son of Telamon in 473 and merely as "sprung from Zeus," a standard epithet of kings in the *Iliad*, in 489, while Simoeisios in each case is called the son of Anthemion. In the case of Ajax the patronymic merely tells us which Ajax is in action; there is no reason to repeat it. In Simoeisios' case the repeated patronymic calls attention to itself. It suggests the word *anthos*, "flower," thus associating the youth with natural growth.

This botanical association is reinforced by the comparison of Simoeisios' fall beneath Ajax's bronze spear to that of a tree cut down by the "shining iron" of a chariotmaker. Just as the chariotmaker puts an end to a living poplar, which then lies hardening, so Ajax ends the life of the youth, whose body, as corpses do, will grow rigid in death. That the chariotmaker cuts down the tree for a productive purpose, to make an instrument of war, a chariot, is ironically appropriate to Simoeisios' own effort to be a hero in war: he is killed "moving in the front ranks."

Simoeisios, as befits the son of Anthemion, is called "blooming," an etymologically botanical word used elsewhere in the *Iliad* of young men, especially husbands. But he is also "unmarried." We get an idea of a youth both blooming and potentially a husband, of warmth and energy that might have been directed toward a peaceful, fruitful life but were instead turned to war, where death put an end to warmth, flowering, and potential. This sense of unfulfillment is strengthened by the statement that Simoeisios did not repay his dear parents for rearing him.

The vignette about Simoeisios' birth is as moving as the details of his death. Like many other vignettes and similes in the *Iliad*, it moves from the realm of battle and death to a contrasting world of peacetime and everyday life. His mother had been visiting flocks with her parents on Mount Ida, an activity no longer possible during the war, and gave birth to him by the banks of the Simoeis river: one feels the rhythm of a normal, peaceful pastoral life. There is a particular significance, too, to the river as birthplace. As a source of fertility for the Trojan plain and a landmark associated with the city, the Simoeis, like the Skamandros, serves as a landscape symbol for Troy itself. Simoeisios' death is felt, indirectly and on a small scale, as the death of Troy.[18]

The poplar's "hardening by the banks of a river"(487), though in itself not an especially significant detail, echoes "beside the banks of the Simoeis" (475), thus associating the fall of the tree more closely with the death of the youth. It almost makes us see the gradual stiffening of his body. Similarly, one can associate the description of the poplar, "smooth, but its branches grow at the very top," with the appearance of Simoeisios. We visualize the smooth body of an adolescent, entirely without hair except that on his head. This vividness makes the whole scene more poignant; so also does the moving detail that Ajax's spear struck beside the right nipple. The bronze spear, passing straight through the shoulder, coldly destroys what is tender, warm, rooted in life like the poplar. Yet the youth is destroyed by the highest Homeric excellence, heroic *aretē*, both his own ("moving in the front ranks") and that of Ajax, whose status and glory are based on just such killing of lesser warriors. And the chariot for the sake of which the poplar is cut down is "beautiful."

As I have said, the Simoeisios passage is but one of many such vignettes and similes about young men whose deaths Homer narrates. None of the others is so carefully wrought, but each to some extent makes us aware of what the war with its splendid killing costs in human terms. It is significant that almost all of the young victims are Trojans, for the greatest cost of the war is to Troy itself, whose eventual destruction is most clearly prefigured by the death of Hektor (22.410–11, 24.728–38).[19] Indeed, Hektor's visit with Andromache and Astyanax in Troy in Book 6 is set in the action of the poem as an expanded vignette of how a man had gone to war leaving his wife and child whom he was never to see again. Homer achieves a similar effect by the description of how Achilles pursued Hektor past the twin springs of Skamandros and the washing troughs "where the wives and beautiful daughters / of the Trojans used to wash their shining garments / before, in peacetime" (22.147–56). Homer suspends an image of the normal, domestic life of Troy "before the sons of the Achaians came" (22.156) in the midst of the climactic episode of the war and of the poem. The effect of this juxtaposition is to remind us of the cost of Achilles' supreme heroic act. Hektor dies fighting not only for glory but also for the life of tender domesticity, characteristically Trojan in the *Iliad*, of which he and Andromache are the poem's prime exemplars.

3

The description of the death of Simoeisios, like all of Homer's battle narrative, is conventional in style, form, and content; Homer's achievement is the meaning that emerges from this and other such descriptions. As noted in Chapter One, poems about heroes killing and dying for their own imperishable glory and the sake of their communities seem to be very old in the Indo-European poetic tradition. The formulaic style of the *Iliad*'s battle scenes, as of the rest of the poem, is derived from this tradition. It has been shown, too, that not only descriptions of individuals killing and dying but also the various sequences of Greek and Trojan deaths, and of kinds of wounds, are patterned. In other words, the battle scenes are thematically as well as linguistically formulaic,[20] and they share several other important formal features that would have made them readily intelligible and meaningful to an audience schooled in the conventions of the oral poetic tradition.

For our understanding of the nature and significance of war in the *Iliad*, perhaps the most important shared feature of the numerous scenes of killing and dying is that the combats are generally decided quickly, by one fatal blow.[21] Rarely does a warrior need as many as two moves to finish off an opponent. Correspondingly, those who are hit, with a couple of exceptions, are killed immediately; Homer describes very few nonfatal wounds other than those dealt to the Greek kings in Book

11, when he is motivating the entry of Patroklos and the Myrmidons into the battle. This emphasis on killing rather than
wounding shows that Homer is interested not so much in the
technique of battle or the detailed, anatomical description of
wounds—vivid as this is—as in questions of death itself. Descriptions of warfare are essentially descriptions of death.

On the other hand, the fighting among the gods, and between Diomedes and the gods in Book 5, always results in
wounding and never, of course, in a god's death. In contrast to
human conflict, which is literally a matter of life and death, divine warfare is a game without serious consequences, a game
that, as W. Marg says, can always be replayed. For mortals,
death is the end, death is everything.[22]

Just as interesting as the almost universal fatality of wounds
inflicted by Homer's heroes are the verbal threats, boasts, and
taunts made by warriors to their opponents before and after
individual combats. The threats and battle mockery are intended primarily to deny or reduce the opponent's bravery and
warcraft; as Vermeule says, "The aim [of a warrior's taunts] is
to turn the opposing soldier into a female, or into the weaker
animal role."[23] She has pointed out, too, that often the vocabulary of these taunts exploits semantic ambiguities in such
words as *meignumi*, "mingle," which is used of mingling in battle or in sex, and *damazō* or *damnēmi*, "subjugate" or "domi-
nate," verbs used of taming an animal or raping a woman or
killing a man. A warrior who is killed has become in effect a
subdued animal or a subjugated woman. It is no accident that
the phrase *krēdemnon luesthai*, "to loosen a veil," can mean
either to sack a city or to breach a woman's chastity.[24]

In different battles and different books of the *Iliad* there is a
striking variety in the wounds inflicted and in the tone and details of the verbal threats, boasts, and mockery. Some scholars,
not realizing that every battle scene is traditional and formulaic, have suggested that these differences might serve as re-
fined criteria for the "analysis" of the *Iliad* into various historical layers on stylistic grounds.[25] Rather than drawing such
historical conclusions, we should recognize that differences in
the kinds and details of killing, dying, threatening, and boasting reflect Homer's varying poetic emphases, since in different
places in the poem he stresses different consequences of war

for mortals. For example, Book 13 is remarkable for the grue-
someness of the wounds described and for frequent, rather
baroque boasts, especially by victorious warriors over their
victims.[26] These grotesque wounds and boasts should be
connected with the fact that in Book 13, though there is a great
deal of killing, neither side makes any progress in the battle.
The controlling image of the book is the "knot of powerful strife
and of war equal for all" which Zeus and Poseidon "drew tight
for both sides, / unbreakable and unable to be loosened, but
which loosened the knees of many men" (13.358–60).[27] There
is a strong sense that mortal effort is futile because of this conflict of wills between the older and younger divine brothers;
that strife on a cosmic level parallels the quarrel between Agamemnon and Achilles. The words "unbreakable and unable to
be loosened" are particularly effective because they occurred
earlier in the same book (13.37) in the idyllic description of Poseidon's chariot ride over the sea on his way to Troy, but there
is nothing idyllic about the knot of war. Books 13 and 14 are a
study of what makes war seem primarily futile and painful for
mortals, especially when, as in these books, the gods intervene
directly. The characteristically Homeric play on words, "unable to be loosened, but which loosened the knees of many
men," is of a piece with the humor of the deceitful seduction of
Zeus by Hera in Book 14. The gruesome wounds, grisly taunts,
and lack of progress in Book 13 are the other, mortal side of this
humor. Together, the two sides add up to a meditation on warfare that remains for a reader's or listener's consideration and
enjoyment alongside the imagined sight of war. There is no
contradiction between the fact that Homer and his audience
could aesthetically enjoy as mere performance the skillful narrative of warfare in the traditional style and the fact that scenes
of battle in the *Iliad* can be appreciated intellectually and be
thought-provoking in a variety of ways.

One mark of the traditional nature of Homeric battle descriptions is the way they make use of "formal patterns long
used for animal combats and hunting scenes" in visual art.[28]
Such "animal art" typically "expressed valor and pathos in
duels between a predator and a grass-eater, usually a lion attacking a bull or a deer. . . . On the battlefield of Troy the duel
between enemy heroes is handled in precisely the same formal

patterns as the animal fight."[29] Just as in the visual art "the lion was . . . the image of success in both war and hunting," so in the *Iliad* the greatest of heroes at the peak of their prowess are compared to lions.[30] Such comparisons, like those to wild boars and other animals, show Homer's self-consciousness of his artistic tradition. He not only arranges his individual combats like the animal combats in art, but he says over and over to his audience in lengthy similes how his human warriors act or feel like wild animals. These similes make explicit the implied predatory animality of the poem's heroes; they testify that the psychological connection between hunting and warfare, so well known in many ancient and modern cultures (including our own), is present in the minds of Homer's audience as well as those of his characters.

There is, to be sure, a certain decorum in Homer's comparisons of his heroes to wild animals and in the heroes' own animalistic behavior. Although on a couple of occasions we hear that one or another mortal would like to hack an enemy to pieces and eat him raw, such "cannibal impulses and . . . animal language stay in the realm of rhetoric, like almost all 'ugly actions' in the *Iliad*."[31] This is a major difference between Homeric epic and other traditional Greek oral poetry, which told such stories as that of Tydeus' punishment by Athene for eating the brain of a dead enemy during the campaign of the seven against Thebes.[32] The greatest lapse into savagery in the *Iliad* is Achilles' sacrifice at the pyre of Patroklos (23.175–76) of twelve Trojan youths captured near the river Skamandros for that purpose (21.26–32). Such deliberate savagery, however, really is not animalistic but distinctively human in its planned brutality and its perversion of an activity (sacrifice) that is supposed to bring humans closer not to animals but to the gods. Clearly Homer is portraying Achilles at this stage of the poem as beyond a boundary that humans in the *Iliad* normally do not cross. As we shall see in more detail, he is at once superhuman and subhuman, almost like a god in his power and a force of nature in his destructive savagery. Yet in thus "having made savage his great-hearted spirit" (9.629) and temporarily losing his civilized sociability, Achilles in fact acts like a deranged human, not like an animal; it would eat its victims raw, not sacrifice them alive.

Another important traditional feature of Homer's description of war in the *Iliad* is the *aristeia*. *Aristeia* is a word used in later Greek for "excellence" or "prowess," including, in particular, the excellence or prowess of a Homeric warrior when he is on a victorious rampage, irresistibly sweeping all before him, killing whomever of the enemy he can catch or whoever stands against him. *Aristeia* is an abstract noun, closely related to the verb *aristeuō*, which in the *Iliad* means "to be (or try to be) the best and bravest in battle." This verb is used by Glaukos when he tells Diomedes (6.207–9; cf. 11.783) that his father sent him to Troy and told him "always to be best and bravest and to surpass all others, / and not to disgrace the line of my fathers, who were / much the best." It also is the word used by Odysseus when he reminds himself (11.408–10) that while cowards may flee, whoever "is best and bravest in battle" must stand strongly and either himself be hit or hit another. In Greek of all periods, the adjective *aristos*, "best," is the superlative of *agathos*, "good," but in the *Iliad*, whose world is a world of war, "good" and "best" mean "good [or: best] in battle."

In the *Iliad* the *aristeia* is the main compositional unit of battle narrative. One can distinguish five sections of a normal *aristeia*.[33] First there is a description of the hero arming himself, including an especially detailed description of his triumphantly gleaming armor. Next the hero turns the tide of a deadlocked battle by killing an opponent who stands against him. Thirdly, the hero breaks into the grouped ranks of the enemy and wreaks havoc among them. Thereafter the hero is himself wounded (which causes a temporary setback for his side), but he prays to a god, is healed or strengthened, and reenters the battle to kill an important enemy. Finally, there is a fierce battle over the corpse of this enemy, until it is taken (often with divine aid) from the clutches of the hero. Although not every *aristeia* in the poem has all these sections in identical sequence and form, the normal *aristeia* would have been present in the minds of both poet and audience, since it was a major element of the oral poetic tradition; the audience would have been able to appreciate both the fulfillment of the norm and artful, meaningful variations on it. Thus, a description of a hero arming would have raised in their minds the expectation that he would stand out in the ensuing battle, and nuances of the description would foreshadow the precise degree of his success.

The different sections of the *aristeia* were characterized by particular kinds of similes. Each kind was associated with a certain type of event or action. An audience schooled in the tradition would have been prepared by the similes for the associated event or action and, conversely, would have expected a given kind of simile in a given narrative context. The fact that five-sixths of the similes in the *Iliad* occur in scenes of battle indicates the close connection of similes to the *aristeia*, the typical form of Homer's battle narrative.[34] The similes were one means by which Homer, and presumably every poet in the tradition, could both control the expectations of his audience regarding descriptions of warfare and, by breaking the narrative flow, adjust their attention to his own poetic performance.[35]

Achilles is the main hero of the *Iliad*, and his *aristeia*, concluding with the killing of Hektor and the eventual return of his body at the gods' behest, is the culmination of the poem. But there are three other Greek heroes, Diomedes in Book 5, Agamemnon in Book 11, and Patroklos in Book 16, whose *aristeiai* prepare the way for Achilles': in contrast to them Achilles is absolutely outstanding. Some scholars have spoken of these heroes as surrogates or substitutes for Achilles, as if the original form of the poem had been a story of Achilles and the other *aristeiai* were directly modeled upon his. Such a supposition fails to recognize the traditional formulaic nature of the *aristeia*. While Achilles is the real hero of the poem, we can appreciate his uniqueness only through juxtaposition and contrast with other heroes and *aristeiai*. For instance, while each of the others is wounded by a human opponent and/or rescued by a helper-god to whom he prays, Achilles is threatened by the river god Skamandros himself, reassured by Athene and Poseidon, and rescued by Hephaistos at Hera's request. His status as a hero beyond all others is enhanced both by his divine opponent and by his multiple divine helpers. Likewise, while the victims of the other *aristeia*-heroes are taken from them by divine aid on the battlefield (Aineias in Book 5, Sarpedon in Book 16), Achilles drags Hektor's body to the Greek camp and only restores it to Priam at Zeus' request. As

T. Krischer says, by this variation on the usual final element of the *aristeia*, the gods show Achilles not the limits of his power as a hero (as is the case with Diomedes, Agamemnon, and Patroklos) but the limits of the human condition itself.[36]

4

That the *Iliad* tells the story of a war for a city is central to Homer's conception of war and to our understanding of the poem. Although war in Homer is, as I have said, a socially validated way of life, it is at the same time supremely antisocial. The tragic situation that became clear in the case of Simoeisios—that the only way for an individual to achieve greatness and meaning in life is by the destruction of other individuals engaged in the same pursuit—is clear also on the level of society. The aim of the war is to destroy a socially evolved human community just like the community that each Greek left behind him when he set sail for Troy. The price of individual self-assertion and self-fulfillment is social annihilation. From the point of view that sees human beings as by definition social, the Greeks, cut off from their homes and families, are in effect less human than the Trojans.[37] From a point of view that sees war as the only way for a human being—or rather, a human male—to exist meaningfully, the Greeks are more successfully, and therefore more fully, human than the Trojans.

Despite the poem's unsentimental, realistic, and complex portrayal of war, several critics have interpreted the *Iliad* as simply an antiwar epic. In various ways these critics have held "that Homer's values were ultimately spiritual," and that the violence depicted in the poem must be viewed in a larger context within which, and only within which, it "can be understood in the poet's terms."[38] Undoubtedly the most eloquent and influential of these interpreters is Simone Weil in her essay *The Iliad or the Poem of Force*. This was written in occupied France and displaces onto the *Iliad* Weil's emotional and moral repugnance to the atrocities Nazi Germany inflicted on its victims.[39]

Weil argues that "the true hero, the true subject, the center of the *Iliad* is force," that "the human spirit is shown as modified by its relations with force, as swept away, blinded, . . . de-

formed by the weight of the force it submits to." Force she defines as "that *x* that turns anybody who is subjected to it into a
thing"; for example, it makes a corpse out of a man.[40] Weil fully
appreciates the sheer physicality of the poem's descriptions of
killing, dying, and supplicating for life. She does sensitive and
eloquent justice to the pathos and poignancy of war and death
in the *Iliad*, illuminating Homer's portrayal of the individual
and social cost of heroism. But her interpretation is one-sided
and fails to recognize the nobility and glory of the slayers along
with the humanity and pathos of the slain. Weil make this
omission because, like others who read the *Iliad* as an antiwar
poem, she tacitly substitutes for its social and cultural values
her own spiritual categories.

Weil views the *Iliad* through Christian lenses. She sees force
in the poem as exercising tyranny "over the soul," which "en-
slaved to war cries out for deliverance"; however, as has been
pointed out, such a concept of the "soul" does not exist in the
Homeric universe.[41] For Weil, the bitterness of the *Iliad*
"springs from the subjection of the human spirit to force, that
is, in the last analysis, to matter."[42] She compares the *Iliad* with
the Gospels: in both works, she says, we see reflected the "spiritual force" that "allowed the Greeks to avoid self-deception";
the same "sense of human misery" that "gives the Gospels
[their] accent of simplicity . . . endows Greek tragedy and the
Iliad with all their value."[43] "All their value" is an overstate-
ment, and the assimilation of the *Iliad* to Christianity is not only
anachronistic in its statements about the "soul" but arbitrary in
its assumptions about "the" human spirit. These flaws in
Weil's argument are grounded not in the poem but in her view
of life. Her interpretation is beautifully expressed and makes
sense in the light of her own spirituality and of Nazi violence;
it is not, however, an accurate reading of the poem.

We inevitably distort and misread the *Iliad* when we foist the
values of another time and culture upon its objective, inter-
nally consistent presentation of and attitude toward war and
death. Of course, we all bring our preconceptions, prejudices,
values, and beliefs to whatever we read. Still, there is a difference between evaluating a work of art in personal terms and
finding our personal terms in the work. Warfare in the *Iliad* has
a complexity which eludes one-sided interpretations, spiritual

or otherwise. As Rachel Bespaloff has written, Homer has a "virile love of war and a virile horror of it"; he presents war as it is, with no illusions, without condemning it.[44] This is only to be expected. In the poem, war and death *are* life itself—the medium in which life is lived and through which it amounts to something. The *Iliad* is filled with what J. G. Gray has called "the enduring appeals of battle": "the delight in seeing, the delight in comradeship, the delight in destruction."[45] Indeed, "delight" (*charmē*) is Homer's word for the joy of battle which warriors "remember" (*memnēmai*) and call on their comrades to "remember" in the uttermost stress of the fighting. To be sure, this delight is tempered by Homer's full recognition of the self-defeating nature of war, of the contradictions that make human life in the poem, and the poem itself, tragic as well as joyful. As Bespaloff says, "[I]n the *Iliad* force appears as both the supreme reality and the supreme illusion of life. Force, for Homer, is divine insofar as it represents a superabundance of life that flashes out in the contempt of death . . . ; it is detestable insofar as it contains . . . a blind drive that is always pushing it on to the very end of its course, on to its own abolition and the obliteration of the very values it engendered."[46]

The *Iliad* is both a poem of death and a poem of life: in other words, it is a poem of mortality. With unwavering and unsentimental realism it presents the necessities and opportunities of human existence, tragic limitations that are at the same time inspiriting and uplifting to live with and to contemplate. Its depiction of war and death is thoroughly traditional, but the tradition is transformed by Homer's characteristic artistry into a comprehensive exploration and expression of the beauty, the rewards, and the price of human heroism.[47]

Notes to Chapter 3

[1]K. Reinhardt, "Tradition und Geist im homerischen Epos," in *Tradition und Geist: Gesammelte Essays zur Dichtung* (Göttingen, 1960), pp. 5–15, where the words quoted appear on p. 13; J. Griffin, *Homer on Life and Death* (Oxford, 1980), p. 142. Cf. W. Marg, "Kampf und Tod in der Ilias," *Die Antike* 18 (1942), pp. 167–79, revised and expanded in *Würzburger Jahrbücher für die Altertumswissenschaft*, n.s., 2 (1976), pp. 7–19. In subsequent notes I cite the revised version of this fine essay.

[2]E. Vermeule, *Aspects of Death in Early Greek Art and Poetry* (Berkeley and Los Angeles, 1979), p. 97. Vermeule's chapter on "The Happy Hero," pp. 83–117 (with notes, pp. 232–38), is an excellent, if rather lighthearted, treatment of death in Homer.

[3]Cf. 7.89–91, and J.-P. Vernant, "*PANTA KALA* d'Homère à Simonide," *Annali della Scuola Normale Superiore di Pisa*, ser. 3, 9 (1979), pp. 1365–74, especially p. 1366.

[4]Vermeule, *Aspects of Death*, p. 97. Cf., too, ibid., p. 37: "Death is a negative, a cessation, an inversion of life. . . ."

[5]Ibid., p. 212 n. 12, points out that, "Loss of *psyche* can signify fainting . . . as well as death." Cf. 5.696, 22.467, *Od.* 24.348.

[6]On hero cult, see Chapter 2, pp. 47–49.

[7]On the significance of "easiest," see Chapter 2, pp. 53–54. The Elysian plain is one of a number of locations in early Greek literature to which certain mortals are transported and which are symbolic of a posthumous immortality. See E. Rohde, *Psyche*, trans. W. B. Hillis, 2 vols. (1925; reprint, New York, 1966), vol. 1, pp. 55–67.

[8]W. Pötscher, "Hera und Heros," *Rheinisches Museum für Philologie* 104 (1961), pp. 306–9.

[9]At 21.463–66, Apollo refuses to fight with Poseidon "for the sake of mortals, / wretches who, like leaves, at one time / are full of fire, eating the fruit of the fertile earth, / and at another time waste away lifeless." Significantly, the god, in contrast to the mortal Glaukos, mentions only the leaves which symbolize the human generations that succeed one another, not the stock of the tree that survives to put forth new leaves. From the divine perspective everything mortal is utterly and only transient. Cf. Mark Griffith, "Man and the Leaves: A Study of Mimnermus fr. 2," *California Studies in Classical Antiquity* 8 (1975), pp. 76–77.

[10]Vernant, "*PANTA KALA*," pp. 1367–70, compares the cultural function of epic with that of funeral rites: both are institutions "que les Grecs ont élaborées pour donner une réponse au problème de la mort, pour acculturer la mort, pour l'intégrer à la pensée et à la vie sociale" (p. 1367). As Vernant points out, Homeric epic goes further than funerary ritual in transforming an individual who has died in battle into a figure whose presence remains forever inscribed in the memory of his society, thus assuring his continued beauty, youth, and glory (p. 1370). See too Vernant's "La belle mort et le cadavre outragé," *Journal de psychologie normale et pathologique* 77 (1980), pp. 209–41.

[11]Vermeule, *Aspects of Death*, p. 94. Cf. Marg, "Kampf und Tod," p. 19: "Für den Menschen der Ilias und auch den Hörer bedeutet das Ernstnehmen des Todes nicht Resignation, sondern reinere Liebe zum begrenzten Dasein, zur Tat und auch zum Ruhm, der allein über

die Grenze des Todes hinausreicht." For a somewhat different formulation, see H. Fränkel, *Early Greek Poetry and Philosophy*, trans. M. Hadas and J. Willis (Oxford, 1973), pp. 84–85: "It is in conflict above all that a man confirms his own existence. For the suffering that he must bear in life and for the ineffable horror of annihilation in death, Homeric man knows only one compensation—glory." Cf. Vernant, "La belle mort," pp. 210, 218–19.

[12]Cf. Vernant, "*PANTA KALA*," p. 1367.

[13]A. W. Gouldner, *Enter Plato: Classical Greece and the Origins of Social Theory* (New York, 1965), pp. 13–15 = *The Hellenic World* (New York, 1965), pp. 13–15, aptly describes the competitive social situation in the *Iliad* as one in which the achievements of one man are another man's failure; a hero can only be supreme in honor and glory at everyone else's expense. Gouldner points out that the heroic society of the *Iliad* has an inbuilt instability and an inbuilt need to wage war (both for gain and for status).

[14]See G. Strasburger, "Die kleinen Kämpfer der Ilias" (diss. Frankfurt-am-Main, 1954).

[15]J. Griffin, *Life and Death*, p. 143.

[16]Ibid., p.123.

[17]Ibid., p. 140.

[18]Cf. the battle between Achilles and the river Skamandros in Book 21, where at first Skamandros calls to Simoeis to rise in defense of Troy (308–15), and where his ultimate surrender to Hephaistos explicitly symbolizes the fall of Troy (373–76). See C. H. Whitman, *Homer and the Heroic Tradition* (Cambridge, Mass., 1958), p. 140.

The death of Simoeisios, by its poetic elaboration, is made to bear a far greater significance than do those of the superficially similar Satnios (14.442–48), who also was named for the river by whose banks he was born, and of Skamandrios (5.49), Ilioneus (14.489–99), and Tros (20.463–72), whose names similarly suggest Troy or Trojan landscape. To some extent, every Trojan death prefigures the fall of Troy.

[19]As Strasburger, "Die kleinen Kämpfer," p. 125, says: "Die Troer stellen ja die weit grössere Zahl der Gefallenen, weil sie von vornherein die Schwächeren, die ihrem Untergang zueilenden Verlierer sind. . . ." It is no coincidence that, with one exception (5.559–60), all the warriors who fall like trees are on the Trojan side: 13.178–81, 13.389–93 = 16.482–86, 14.414–18, 17.53–60; cf. 13.436–41.

[20]See B. Fenik, *Typical Battle Scenes in the Iliad: Studies in the Narrative Technique of Homeric Battle Description*, Hermes Einzelschriften, no. 21 (Wiesbaden, 1968).

[21]In this paragraph I follow Marg, "Kampf und Tod," pp. 13–14.

[22]Ibid. notes, too, that the expressed lack of interest in taking pris-

oners alive, in contrast to what we several times learn was normal earlier in the war, enhances our perception of war as essentially "das
Tödliche."

[23]Vermeule, *Aspects of Death*, p. 101.

[24]M. N. Nagler, *Spontaneity and Tradition: A Study in the Oral Art of
Homer* (Berkeley and Los Angeles, 1974), pp. 44–60. On the association of war and sex common to many cultures, see J. G. Gray, *The Warriors: Reflections on Men in Battle* (New York, 1967), pp. 59–95, especially
p. 68. Cf. W. T. MacCary, *Childlike Achilles: Ontogeny and Phylogeny in
the Iliad* (New York, 1982), pp. 137–48, 152–62.

[25]W.-H. Friedrich, *Verwundung und Tod in der Ilias*, Abh. der Akad.
Wiss. Göttingen (Phil.-Hist. Kl.), ser. 3, 38 (Göttingen, 1956), especially pp. 78–83.

[26]See W. Leaf, ed., *The Iliad*, 2d ed., 2 vols. (1900 and 1902; reprint,
Amsterdam, 1960), vol. 2, p. 2.

[27]Cf. A. L. T. Bergren, *The Etymology and Usage of PEIRAR in Early
Greek Poetry*, American Classical Studies, no. 2 (New York, 1975), pp.
45–57.

[28]Vermeule, *Aspects of Death*, p. 84.

[29]Ibid., pp. 84–85.

[30]Ibid., p. 87, notes that, "In Greek myths the preeminent lion-sol-
dier was always Herakles." Herakles, at once the great lion-killer and
the hero "with the heart of a lion" (5.639; *Od.* 11.267), is the one mortal
to whom Achilles is several times compared; Achilles is the only other
character in the *Iliad* to receive the epithet "with the heart of a lion"
(7.228). In the *Iliad* Herakles represents the highest possible human
heroic achievement, including a previous sack of Troy (5.642, 14.251),
and he is also the paradigm of a mortal suffering and dying despite his
outstanding greatness. Cf. W. Kullmann, *Das Wirken der Götter in der
Ilias: Untersuchungen zur Frage der Entstehung des homerischen "Götterapparats"* (Berlin, 1956), pp. 34, 131.

[31]Vermeule, *Aspects of Death*, p. 94. On "ugly actions," see C. Segal,
The Theme of the Mutilation of the Corpse in the Iliad, Mnemosyne Supplements, no. 17 (Leiden, 1971), p. 15 with n. 1.

[32]The story of Tydeus and Athene probably was told in the *Thebaid*:
see J. D. Beazley, "The Rosi Krater," *Journal of Hellenic Studies* 67 (1947),
pp. 1–9, especially pp. 3–5, for sources and references. Tydeus' cannibalism is linked with a story of his almost evading death. Such an
evasion, unthinkable in the *Iliad*, is one example of "the fantastic, the
miraculous, and the romantic" in which other traditional Greek epics
apparently abounded. See J. Griffin, "The Epic Cycle and the Uniqueness of Homer," *Journal of Hellenic Studies* 97 (1977), pp. 39–53.

[33]On the *aristeia*, I follow closely the excellent discussion in T.

Krischer, *Formale Konventionen der homerischen Epik*, Zetemata, no. 56 (Munich, 1971), pp. 13–89. For the sections of a typical *aristeia*, see pp. 23–24.

[34]Ibid., p. 17. Book 8 describes a battle that contains no real *aristeia* before it breaks off; correspondingly, it contains only two similes in its battle description. See Krischer, pp. 17, 85–89.

[35]Cf. Fränkel, *Early Greek Poetry*, p. 40: "[In the similes Homer] adds something of his own and places himself in a man-to-man relationship with the hearer."

[36]Krischer, *Formale Konventionen*, pp. 27–28.

[37]Cf. Homer's comment at 2.453–54, after Odysseus has reversed the army's flight to the ships and he, Nestor, and Agamemnon have primed them for battle: "At once war became sweeter for them than to return / in the hollow ships to their dear fatherland." Of course, the Greeks' campaign against Troy is in the name of *Zeus Xeinios*, "Zeus the protector of the rights of guests and hosts," who, Menelaos argues, was angered by Paris' abduction of Helen from his home (13.623–25). Since *Zeus Xeinios* governs a social relationship, the Greeks' expedition might be considered a social enterprise.

[38]Nagler, *Spontaneity*, p. 161 with n. 42.

[39]S. Weil, *The Iliad or The Poem of Force*, trans. M. McCarthy, Pendle Hill Pamphlets, no. 91 (Wallingford, Pa., 1957).

[40]Ibid., p. 3.

[41]Ibid., pp. 10, 22.

[42]Ibid., p. 33.

[43]Ibid., pp. 34, 35.

[44]R. Bespaloff, *On the Iliad*, trans. M. McCarthy (1947; reprint, New York, 1962), p. 83.

[45]Gray, *The Warriors*, pp. 28–29.

[46]Bespaloff, *On the Iliad*, pp. 44–45.

[47]For a brief appreciation of how "the *Iliad* owes its tragic greatness to Homer's ability to appreciate and sympathize with [the contradictory] aspects of heroic war," see O. Taplin, "The Shield of Achilles Within the *Iliad*," *Greece and Rome* 27 (1980), pp. 14–17, where the words quoted appear on p. 16. Interestingly, Taplin (p. 17) argues that, "The scope of Homer's sympathy has perhaps never been more deeply expressed than in Simone Weil's essay, *The Iliad, or the Poem of Force*."

4

Achilles: One

In the following two chapters I examine closely the character and role of Achilles as they are developed throughout the *Iliad*. Achilles is the central figure of the poem, and such a close, systematic reading is necessary to appreciate in detail the poetic structure of Homer's epic and his distinctive transformation of the traditional themes of heroic poetry into a critical and tragic meditation on the human condition. My reading owes much to those studies of the poem's formulaic style and traditional mythology summarized in Chapter One; it assumes and builds on the interpretations of the gods and of the depiction of war, death, and heroism developed in Chapters Two and Three. I have divided my discussion of Achilles into two chapters because Achilles, after he learns of Patroklos' death at the beginning of Book 18, becomes the constant focus of attention and is portrayed by Homer in the final seven books as qualitatively different from what he had been earlier in the poem.

1

The tragic contradictions of warfare and heroism in the *Iliad* are nowhere more apparent and more moving than in the case of Achilles. As a hero, Achilles is the purest, the highest, the "best of the Achaians" (1.244, 412; 16.274). On the one hand, he fights and kills more brilliantly and more effectively than any other warrior; on the other hand, beyond the general knowledge shared by all the swiftly doomed heroes that their way of life is conditioned and determined by their mortality, Achilles knows that he is "most swiftly doomed" (1.505), that he is going to die at Troy and not return home. His own foreknowledge and a reader's awareness of his destiny become more and more specific and detailed in the course of the poem, especially from the beginning of Book 18 until the death of Hektor.[1] More than any other hero, Achilles is self-conscious and articulate about his choice of a short life with imperishable glory over a long life with no glory at all (9.412–16). As a result, we feel most poignantly the cost of his unparalleled greatness. We see him as the destroyer of Hektor, and therefore of Troy, but he resembles the Trojans whom he defeats in that his own death is as bound up with that of Hektor as is the fall of the city. The tragic contradiction discussed in Chapter Three—that a hero achieves greatness and meaning in life only through the destruction of other would-be heroes and through his own destruction—is most clearly and movingly exemplified in the case of Achilles.

The special quality of Achilles can be seen largely through parallels and contrasts to other heroes in the poem. These parallels and contrasts are not simply random or cumulative; rather, the structure of the *Iliad* makes us see Achilles as a particular kind of hero, for whom the others, especially the two with whom he is most in conflict, Agamemnon and Hektor, serve as backdrops or foils. But the character of Achilles is not constant. In order to understand his role in the *Iliad*, it is necessary to go through the poem from beginning to end, noting both the stages of Achilles' responses to the situation he finds himself in and the poet's sequence of causes and effects that forms the setting for Achilles' attempts to explain himself. The poem presents an evolving Achilles, out of whose initial resentment and later vacillation develops his unique absoluteness.

Achilles has much in common with other heroes. As S. Benardete has noted, he contains within himself or exemplifies "all the heroic virtues that are given singly to others."[2] He is not of a wholly different nature, but can be measured by the same measure as the "common" or typical warriors, though he is preeminent in beauty, swiftness, strength, and all-around fighting ability, as well as in his horses and armor. Most important, like the other warriors, Achilles, however outstanding, is a mortal. Homer suppresses any elements in the mythological tradition, such as the stories of Achilles' invulnerability and eventual immortality,[3] that might deflect from his being the prime instance of human greatness subject to the limits of imperfect human knowledge and of death.

Nevertheless, however much Achilles may resemble the other heroes of the poem, he is at the same time radically different from them, especially in his relationship to the divine. This relationship goes far beyond his blood tie to the gods through his mother, the sea goddess Thetis. It is clear from the first word of the poem, *mēnin*, a form of the word *mēnis*, "wrath," which Achilles feels first against Agamemnon and later, after the death of Patroklos, against Hektor and the Trojans. Elsewhere in the *Iliad* and in archaic Greek poetry generally, *mēnis* is used specifically of wrath felt by a god, usually toward humans, who fear and avoid it. *Mēnis* suggests something sacral, a vengeful anger with deadly consequences. Achilles is the only mortal in the poem of whom this word is used. The force and intensity of his anger are more than human, and his daemonic power sets him apart from all other mortals.[4]

Although there are other children of divinities in the Greek and Trojan armies, the *Iliad* contains no other long and intimate conversations between a divine parent and a son like those between Thetis and Achilles. No other hero either appeals to Zeus or comes prophetically to know his own destiny through his divine parent.[5] Furthermore, Thetis has a special relationship to Zeus: at 1.396–406 Achilles reminds her how she had often boasted that she alone among the gods had saved Zeus when Hera, Poseidon, and Athene in rebellion had wanted to bind him.[6] She had summoned the hundred-handed one, whom the gods call Briareos but men call Aigaion, to Olympos, where his show of power discouraged the gods from binding Zeus. Briareos is called by Homer "better in strength than his father" (1.404). This suggests, and would undoubtedly have suggested even more vividly to an audience schooled in the poetic tradition, a well-known story Homer seems to recall obliquely only to suppress: there was a prophecy that Thetis would give birth to a son mightier than his father, who would overthrow him. This prophecy discouraged both Zeus and Poseidon from mating with her and led to her being married perforce to a mortal, Peleus.[7] Achilles mentions this forced marriage at 18.85, as Thetis herself does in stronger terms at 18.430–34. The effect of Homer's calling attention to the story without actually telling it is to bring out the special way in which Achilles, even though he is descended from Zeus, is *not* his son, and to emphasize the tragically mortal nature of a child of Thetis who might have been the ruler of the universe had his mother borne him to Zeus, son of Kronos.[8] "Thetis enables us to view Achilles' life from a cosmic perspective which enhances its stature, as it sets in relief its brevity."[9]

"In fact," as E. T. Owen has observed, "Thetis's artistic role in the poem [is] to bring with her when she comes the thought of Achilles' approaching death."[10] This keynote of the poem is struck three times in the first book (1.352–56, 414–48, 505); it is echoed repeatedly in Book 18, when Achilles decides on his death once and for all,[11] and again in Book 24, when Thetis is lamenting her son's death (24.85) as Iris arrives to summon her to Olympos. Sometimes Thetis simply refers to Achilles as "swiftly doomed" (1.417, 505); at other times she prophesies in more detail (18.59–60, 95–96; cf. 9.410–16, 17.408–9). Always, whether she mourns for Achilles or simply mentions his death, she accentuates by her own immortality the pathetic brevity of his life. What would be moving enough were she a human mother lamenting her son's inevitable death is still more affecting owing to the infallibility of her divine knowledge. Similarly, her power as a goddess to whom Zeus owes the continuation of his rule and to whom he will grant what she asks contrasts strongly with her powerlessness to help Achilles when it really counts (18.62). She can inform him of the future, obtain armor for him from Hephaistos, and intercede for him with Zeus, but she cannot prevent or console him for the death of Patroklos or make him happy in his greatness. If anything, the fact that she dwells remote in the depths of the sea and comes to Achilles only in his grief—and only to vanish once more into her element—serves to enhance his, and our, sense of his all-too-human isolation and suffering. It even makes him wish that she had never married Peleus (18.86–87) so that he never would have been born.

Even apart from Thetis, Achilles has a special relationship to the Olympian gods, in particular to Zeus and Athene, the divinities most associated with victory. Achilles wears armor and uses a spear given by the gods to his father Peleus, a spear which no one else can wield (16.141–42). When Hektor captures this armor after the death of Patroklos, Hephaistos makes a new set for Achilles, which only the son of Thetis can look at without trembling and with delight (19.14–18). One obvious effect of this divine armor is to magnify Achilles' greatness beyond all heroes'. At the same time, the representation and description of the cosmos, including the human world of war and peace, on the shield made by Hephaistos, sets Achilles' sufferings and achievements in an immortal, artistic perspective that makes them seem small, temporally limited, merely human by comparison. Precisely the same effect is achieved in the case of Achilles' immortal horses, which were a gift from Poseidon to Peleus. They are incomparable, far better than all other heroes' mortal horses (2.770, 23.276–78). But Zeus asks:

> Ah, you wretches, why did we give the two of you to lord
>   Peleus,
> a mortal, while you are unaging and immortal?
> Was it so you might have sorrows along with miserable men?
> For there is surely nothing more painfully wretched than a
>   man,
> of all the things that breathe and crawl over the earth.
> (17.443–47)

Just as Thetis' power is juxtaposed with her inability to help Achilles, so the divine gifts which he owes to his parents' marriage magnify him as half-divine only to make his actual mortality that much clearer and more poignant. It is no accident that both Hephaistos in promising the new armor to Thetis (18.463–67) and the horse Xanthos in his miraculous speech to Achilles (19.408–17) refer to his imminent and unavoidable death.

From the beginning to the end of the poem, the gods take a special interest in Achilles. He knows this and accepts it as natural and appropriate. He tells his mother,

> . . . since you bore me to be short lived,
> the Olympian Zeus who thunders on high ought to have
>   conferred
> honor upon me.
>
> (1.352–54)

When Phoinix advises him to accept Agamemnon's gifts lest, when he finally returns to the war, he receive less honor (9.600–605), Achilles replies, "I don't need this honor, / I think I have been and am being honored by the portion of Zeus" (9.607–8). Agamemnon makes a similar claim (1.175), but he is wrong and Achilles is right. In Book 24, when the gods decide to ask Achilles to give up Hektor's body for burial, both Hera and Zeus are concerned to insure his honor (24.57, 66).

Hera also sends Athene at 1.195 and Iris at 18.165 to advise Achilles: in the first instance not to kill Agamemnon, in the second to appear at the trench before the Greek encampment to terrify the Trojans and rescue Patroklos' body.[12] In Book 1 Achilles is utterly enraged, in Book 18 he is desperately sorrowful, but on each occasion he treats the goddess with respect and follows her suggestion. To Athene, who has stopped his action by pulling his hair—an informal gesture indicating their friendly relationship—he speaks plainly and as an equal (1.202–5), though he immediately acknowledges the obedience owed by mortals to the gods (1.216–18). With Iris he is a bit more impatient—"How can I go into the moil of battle? They have my armor." (18.188)—but he at once springs up to follow her instructions (18.203). Thereupon Athene crowns his head with a golden cloud from which fire blazes to dazzle and terrify the Trojans (18.203–6, 225–27).

Occasionally the gods assist Achilles on the field of battle, speaking to him directly, rescuing him, and aiding his victory. Poseidon and Athene stand by him when he is threatened by the river Skamandros, assuring him that the gods are on his side and that he will pen the Trojans in the city and slay Hektor (21.284–97). Then Hephaistos, at Hera's instructions, kindles the fire that defeats the river (21.328–82). In Book 22, Athene, who had sustained Achilles' strength while he was fleeing from the river (21.304),first guarantees him that the two of them will destroy Hektor and bring a great boast of victory to the ships (22.216–18); then she tricks Hektor into standing and fighting and aids Achilles by returning to him the spear he had hurled in vain, with which he then kills his enemy (22.224–47, 276–77). Some readers, perhaps inspired by Hektor's realization that Athene had deceived him (22.299), have felt that the gods' constant care for Achilles, which goes far beyond what they give to any other mortal, diminishes his greatness and cheapens his triumph over Hektor. But Homer's mention of Athene's aid and the way the gods repeatedly are concerned for Achilles and honor him magnify rather than diminish the hero.[13]

Like his divine mother and divine armor and horses, Achilles' special closeness to the gods heightens our appreciation of his mortal limits. The very deities who aid him will do so, as Hera says, "today, but later he will suffer whatever his portion / spun for him when he was born, when his mother gave birth to him" (20.127–28). Hera thus calls attention to Achilles' mortality even as she refers to his divine parentage. We learn in Hektor's dying words (22.359–60) that Achilles will perish at the Skaian gates at the hands of Paris and Apollo. This death, appropriate for the half-human, half-divine hero, was described in the *Aithiopis*.[14] There Achilles' death was followed by his immortality when his mother transported him to the White Island.[15] But in the *Iliad*, Homer's emphasis is on Achilles' mortality. The details that remind the audience of his death and would remind them of this traditional immortality serve to emphasize still more strongly, like all relations between Achilles and the gods, his unqualified mortality.

There is a motif in Greek mythology whereby, like Thetis in the *Aithiopis*, certain other goddesses who mate with mortals obtain immortality for their lovers or their sons.[16] The prime example is Eos who does this in different myths for Tithonos and Memnon. Nothing could be further from what we find in the *Iliad*, where immortal connections in no way guarantee immortality. Homer transforms the traditional stories into his own poetic terms, as when he has a god or goddess rescue a favorite on the battlefield by shrouding him in cloud or mist and snatching him away. In the long run, however, for Homer to preserve Achilles or any warrior from death would be to deny him heroic life, that is, immortality through celebration in heroic poetry.[17]

2

It was noted in Chapter Three that Homer sometimes uses vegetal imagery to express his conception of mortal heroism. We saw in the description of the death of the Trojan youth Simoeisios (Chapter 3, pp. 73–76) that Homer calls Simoeisios "blooming" and names his father Anthemion, "Flowery." Furthermore, Simoeisios and all but one of the other warriors in the poem who fall like trees are on the Trojan side (see Chapter 3, note 18), and the fall of the city is imaged and prefigured in these vegetal deaths of its defenders.

The only Greek hero described in this characteristically Trojan vegetal imagery is Achilles. In Book 1, in his quarrel with Agamemnon, he swears a great oath

> by this scepter, which will never grow leaves
> and branches, since first it left its stock in the mountains,
> and it will not bloom again, for the bronze has stripped off
>   around it
> both leaves and bark, and now the sons of the Achaians
> carry it in their hands when they deliver judgments . . . .
>   (1.234–38)

This scepter is emblematic of Achilles' essential nature both as a force that destroys blooming life rooted in nature and as a life so destroyed. He swears by the scepter that the Greeks will miss him when they fall before manslaughtering Hektor, and that they will regret dishonoring him. But then he can only slam it down in anger and frustration, the fruitless, self-defeating anger and frustration that constitute the *mēnis* he will feel throughout the poem until his meeting with Priam in Book 24. When Agamemnon wields this same scepter (2.201–9), it is described in terms of its manufacture by Hephaistos and transmission through the hands of Zeus, Hermes, and three earlier mortal kings to Agamemnon. For the latter, it is an emblem of *his* essential quality, royalty. These two scepter descriptions effectively contrast the two preeminent figures on the Greek side, "the son of Atreus, lord of men, and brilliant Achilles" (1.7).

At 18.54–60, Thetis laments for her son:

> Ah me, wretched me, unhappy in having borne the best hero
>   as a son,
> since I gave birth to a son faultless and powerful,
> outstanding among heroes, and he shot up like a young tree;
> I nurtured him, like a plant in the slope of the orchard,
> and I sent him forth in the curved ships to Ilion
> to fight with the Trojans, but I shall not receive him again
> returning home into the house of Peleus.

The phrases "like a young tree" and "like a plant" corrrespond to the similes in Homer's descriptions of the deaths of Trojan youths like Simoeisios. Thetis' words are analogous to the vignettes in which, at the moments of warriors' deaths, Homer recalls the parents, wives, and homelands they will never see again. In this way Achilles is associated imagistically with his enemies, so many of whom he himself will destroy. Just as his closeness to the gods endows his humanity with a special pathos and poignancy, so his resemblance to the Trojans ironically qualifies the fact that he, more than any other Greek, destroys them and their city. Just as we are made aware several times that the death of Hektor at his hands involves both the fall of Troy and Achilles' own death, so we see in Achilles' resemblance to the Trojans the fundamentally self-destructive quality of his brilliant heroism.

Achilles resembles the Trojans and differs from his fellow Greeks in another, even more basic respect. He is consistently portrayed as tender, compassionate, and loving toward others—qualities which throughout the poem are characteristically Trojan. The Greeks are separated from their homes and families; we see them as warriors engaged in a massive act of destruction and vengeance. This portrayal reflects the needs and norms of life on an all-male military expedition. The Trojans, on the other hand, are fighting in their homeland before their families, who watch from the city walls and whom they visit from the battlefield. We see them in their domestic relations: husband with wife and baby, aged parents with children, siblings and in-laws with one another.

The Homeric Greek adjective used to describe a person participating literally or metaphorically in a "loving" or "friendly" relation with other people of the same group is *philos* (plural: *philoi*).[18] Originally this relation seems to have been social: relatives by blood or marriage, members of the same household, community, or army, and friends were obliged to support and protect one another and to provide hospitality to one another and to any stranger or guest with whom one of them was connected by *philotēs*, "friendship," "love," "being a *philos*."[19] Historically, the meaning of *philos* shifted from the "social" to the "personal," and in the *Iliad* "an emotional color," a "sentimental attitude" going "beyond the bounds of the institution" is attached to the word; it denotes someone who is "dear," a "friend," "beloved."[20]

The *Iliad* is as much about the *philotēs* of Achilles as it is about his *mēnis*. The love he feels for Patroklos, his conversations with his mother, and his tender relationships with his surrogate fathers Phoinix and Priam are as exceptionally human and as unparalleled among the Greeks as is his divine wrath. Achilles repeatedly refers to his own father, Peleus, and speaks or is described in images of parents and children. But for much of the poem his *mēnis* nullifies or paralyzes his *philotēs*: after he quarrels with Agamemnon, though he is almost bursting with love and deeply needful of solidarity with his comrades, he can neither express his own feelings nor reciprocate theirs. As Ajax says (9.629), "He has made savage the great-hearted spirit in his breast." Only when Patroklos is killed and the wrath is, as it were, transferred from Agamemnon to Hektor and the Trojans, can Achilles once more become social by rejoining the army in the fighting. But paradoxically, both his love and grief for Patroklos and his own imminent death, which is repeatedly prophesied and prefigured, isolate him even further from his comrades, and the savagery with which he routs and slays the Trojans cuts him off from all normal humanity. His *philotēs* disappears, or rather, it is redefined: he actually calls the Trojan Lykaon, who had begged and prayed for life in the most compelling human terms, *philos* (21.106) as he tells him that the only human solidarity between them is the fact that they are mortal, and that all he can do to express this solidarity is to kill him. At this point, for Achilles, love and hate are one and the same; his utter inhumanity and dislocation from himself are obvious in his foul mistreatment of Hektor's corpse and his sacrifice of twelve Trojan youths at Patroklos' tomb. Only in Book 24, when Achilles is touched by Priam's desperate supplication and the two virtually adopt one another as father and son (24.509–11), does Achilles put an end to his wrath. Priam is in an even worse condition than Achilles, with an even greater need for consolation and elemental human solidarity. These Achilles, his *philotēs* once again dominant, offers him. But while this adoption mediates Achilles' return to the world of humanity, of normal social values and individual decency, it does so only in a context of death, not only the death of Hektor and of Patroklos but of Achilles himself and of Troy. It emphasizes all the more Achilles' isolation and the tragic futility of both his *mēnis* and his *philotēs*.

3

We see the *philotēs* of Achilles for the first time in Book 1, when, at Hera's prompting, he calls the army to an assembly to suggest consulting "a seer or priest or even a dream interpreter" (1.62–63) to learn why Apollo is inflicting the plague on them and what they can do to induce him to end it. But as a result of his quarrel with Agamemnon, Achilles' social sentiments give way before his outraged sense of his own worth, and he requests his mother to ask that Zeus

> hem in the Achaians along the ships and the sea
> while they are being killed, so that all might profit from their
>   king,
> and even the son of Atreus, wide-ruling Agamemnon, might
>   recognize
> his blind folly, that he didn't at all honor the best of the
>   Achaians.
>
> (1.409–12)

Thetis transmits this request, beseeching Zeus to

> . . . honor him;
> for so much time confer victorious strength on the Trojans,
>   until the Achaians
> recompense my son and make him greater with honor.
>
> (1.508–10)

Although Achilles is asking that his own community, the Greek army, be defeated for the sake of his honor, his selfishness is not simply antisocial. Achilles' dispute with Agamemnon turns on his sense that he has been robbed of the honor he has earned:

> The son of Atreus, wide-ruling Agamemnon,
> dishonored me; for he took away my special gift of honor and
>   is keeping it, having robbed me himself.
>
> (1.355–56)

In robbing him, Agamemnon has violated the normal social "code" to which everyone in the poem would subscribe, according to which bravery and excellence in battle win wealth, honor, and glory, and thus endow life with meaning (see Chapter 3, pp. 68, 70–72). In Book 1 Achilles' refusal to fight and even his request that Zeus aid the Trojans are socially validated, if extreme, responses to Agamemnon's selfish breach of decorum. Achilles points out (1.152–60) that he is not fighting with the Trojans because they have done him any injury, but "to try to win honor" from them for Agamemnon and Menelaos. Since Agamemnon doesn't care about this and threatens to dishonor him—a threat he carries out by robbing him of Briseis—he will go home.

Many readers have felt that despite Agamemnon's selfishness, and although Achilles' withdrawal is socially validated, nevertheless Achilles goes too far in asking that the Trojans be victorious and his own comrades be killed at the ships. Such a judgment does not sufficiently take into account that Achilles, more than any other Greek or Trojan warrior, feels the need to be honored fully and fittingly for his achievements because, as he tells his mother, "you bore me to be short-lived" (1.352). Thetis confirms this:

> Would that you were sitting by the ships untroubled, without
>   weeping,
> since your portion of life is brief, not at all long;

> but as it is you are both swiftly-doomed and wretched beyond
>   all men. . . .

(1.415–18)

When she speaks to Zeus later in the book, she refers to Achilles, as already has been noted, as "most swiftly-doomed beyond other men" (1.505). We learn more fully (9.410–16) that Achilles has chosen a brief, heroic life at Troy with imperishable glory in preference to a long life at home with no future reputation; therefore he has from the beginning of the *Iliad* to its end a more acute and highly developed sense of his own mortality and his own worth than any other warrior. This makes him more touchy, more sensitive to Agamemnon's revoking of his honor, more easily insulted by this affront than another Greek might be. Achilles is "the limiting case" of what it is to be a hero and of the validity of the normal code of values by which heroes live and die.[21]

Between 1.490–92, where we learn

> Neither would he ever go into the assembly where men win
>   glory,
> nor into the war, but he kept wasting away his heart
> staying there, though he was longing for war and the battle
>   cry,

and Book 9, where an embassy is sent to him by the Greek kings, Achilles does not figure in the main action of the poem. But Homer keeps him present in a listener's or reader's mind by a series of references to what his absence means to both Greeks and Trojans.[22] Book 2 begins with Zeus pondering "how he might honor / Achilles, and destroy many men at the ships of the Achaians" (2.3–4). At 2.377–80, Agamemnon self-pityingly admits that he began the quarrel with Achilles "over a girl," and says that if they ever could agree with one another, the Trojans would be doomed immediately. Later in the same book, in the catalogue of ships and men, Homer mentions that the Myrmidons were not arming because they had no leader:

> For swift-footed, brilliant Achilles lay among the ships
> angry on account of the fair-haired girl Briseis,
> whom he had taken from Lyrnessos with much toil,
> when he sacked Lyrnessos and the walls of Thebe.

(2.688–91)

In these lines we get a clear sense of what Achilles did to deserve the kind of honor Agamemnon took from him; the reference to the sack of the two cities and to Achilles' toil recalls his words to Agamemnon (1.162) that he "toiled very much" for the gift of honor the Greeks had given him, and that he never receives a gift of honor equal to Agamemnon's when the Greeks sack a city, even though his hands do most of the fighting (1.163–66). Later in the catalogue (2.763–69), we learn in a different way how Achilles is missed: "Telamonian Ajax was far the best of the men / as long as Achilles was wrathful, for [Achilles] was much the mightiest" (2.768–69). And while Achilles' immortal horses were absent, the mares of Eumelos were the best in the army.

When the fighting begins, both gods and humans on each side refer to Achilles. The gods speak of his absence while exhorting the armies to fight. At 4.509–13, Apollo calls on the Trojans

> . . . not to yield in the joy of battle
> to the Argives, since their skin isn't stone or iron
> to withstand flesh-tearing bronze when they are hit.
> Nor indeed, neither is Achilles, the son of fair-haired Thetis,
> fighting, but he is nursing his heart-grieving anger at the
> ships.

At 5.787–91, Hera cries out to the Greeks to

> . . . have shame;
> while brilliant Achilles used to come regularly into the war,
> the Trojans would never even come out in front of
> the Dardanian gates, since they feared his heavy spear.
> But now they are fighting far from the city at the hollow ships.

The humans refer to Achilles' past deeds to clarify present circumstances. Thus Helenos at 6.98–100 calls Diomedes "the mightiest of the Achaians," and says, "We never feared even Achilles in this way." In Book 7, Agamemnon restrains Menelaos from accepting Hektor's challenge to a duel by saying, "Even Achilles shuddered to meet this man / in battle where men win glory—Achilles who is a much better man than you"

(7.113–24). And when Ajax advances to duel with Hektor, he tells him:

> Now, Hektor, you will know clearly man to man
> what sort of champions the Greeks have,
> even behind Achilles, the breaker of men with the heart of a
> lion.
> Though he among the curved, seagoing ships
> lies, angry at Agamemnon, shepherd of the people,
> we are such men as might oppose you, and there are lots of us.
> (7.226–32)

Undoubtedly the most moving and most revealing reference to Achilles in these books is Andromache's recollection (6.414–19) of how

> brilliant Achilles killed my father
> and sacked the well-inhabited city of the Kilikians,
> high-gated Thebe; he slew Eëtion,
> but he didn't strip him of his armor, for he had reverence in his
> heart in this respect,
> but he burned him along with his decorated weapons,
> and heaped up a tomb.

She goes on to describe how he killed all seven of her brothers in a single day, and captured her mother, whom he then released for a great ransom. Andromache recounts these events to Hektor when she urges him not to go back into the fighting: he is, she says, everything to her—father, mother, brother, and "blooming husband"—now that Achilles has destroyed her home and family. The Achilles she describes is terrible and deadly in his fighting, but humane and generous in his treatment of the dead and of captives. This picture of the pre-*mēnis* Achilles deepens our appreciation of his characteristic heroism prior to his emotional dislocation, and serves as a moving foil to his savage treatment of Hektor's corpse.[23] It is no accident that the only other time in the poem that Achilles is said to feel anything like the "reverence" with which he treated the dead Eëtion is in Book 24, after old Priam comes to ransom his dead son, when "he looked at the godlike Priam and admired him" (24.483); "he wondered at Priam, the son of Dardanos, / gazing at his noble appearance and hearing his speech" (24.631–32).

By his humane treatment of the Trojan king and surrender of his son's body for burial, Achilles is reestablished as the noble enemy whom Andromache remembers as respectful to, though the slayer of, her father.

4

When the Greeks assemble in Agamemnon's shelter on "the night that will either destroy or save the army" (9.78), it is clear that Zeus has shown Achilles the honor for which he had prayed: the Greeks are penned behind the makeshift ramparts they built at the end of Book 7 and the Trojans are camping out in the field, certain that on the next day they will set fire to the ships and destroy their enemies.[24] The confidence of the Trojans and the despair and panic of the Greeks are effectively shown in the contrasting similes at 8.555–61 and 9.4–8, where the myriad Trojan watch fires are compared to the stars on a clear night that gladden the heart of a shepherd, while the troubled hearts in the breasts of the Achaians are likened to the North and West winds churning up the sea, raising a terrifying wave and hurling seaweed onto the shore. At this point Nestor tells Agamemnon that, since he had "yielded to his great-hearted spirit" and "dishonored the mightiest man, whom the gods honor," they now must try to persuade him to return to the fighting "with gentle gifts and pleasing words" (9.109–13). Agamemnon admits that he has been blind and foolish—"worth many / men is the man whom Zeus loves in his heart, / as he now has honored this man and conquered the army of the Achaians" (9.116–18)—and offers to make amends to Achilles by returning Briseis and giving him "an incalculably abundant ransom" (*apereisi' apoina*). At Nestor's suggestion, Odysseus, Telamonian Ajax, and Achilles' old foster father Phoinix are named as ambassadors to convey Agamemnon's offer and to try to persuade Achilles to rejoin the army. It seems that the situation of Book 1 has been reversed and the conflict resolved. Agamemnon, who had refused Chryses' offer of "an incalculably abundant ransom" (1.13) now is offering one to Achilles, who in turn is receiving the "three times as many fine gifts" that Athene had predicted he would receive (1.212–14) if he refrained from killing Agamemnon on the spot. Given Achilles' demand in Book 1 for suitable honor and the normal value system of the poem, which defines such honor in terms of women, land, and the other tangible possessions that Agamemnon offers in such abundance, one would expect Achilles to accept Agamemnon's offer and return to battle, vindicated in his own and others' eyes.

But at this juncture the special quality of Achilles' wrath and his uniqueness in the *Iliad* and the entire poetic tradition become clear in his remarkable reply (9.308–429) to Odysseus' report of Agamemnon's offer. This reply oscillates between deliberate, almost palpable rationality and outbursts of confused, passionate illogicality. Achilles begins quietly enough with controlled, straightforward statements and clearly marked logical articulations (9.308–17). Then come three epigrammatic lines:

> There is an equal share for the one who stays back and if
>   someone fights strongly;
> in a single honor are both the coward and the brave man;
> the man who does nothing and the man who has done much
>   die alike.
>
> (9.318–20)

Lines 318 and 320 lack the connective conjunctions which normally coordinate clauses in Homeric verse. This striking syntactical harshness calls attention to these lines by setting them off from the smooth flow of the speech up to this point. When examined more closely, they signify a radical break from the heroic value system prevalent elsewhere in the poem.

When Achilles says,

> There is an equal share for the one who stays back and if
>   someone fights strongly;
> in a single honor are both the coward and the brave man,

he is contradicting the notion of honor he himself in Book 1 held strongly enough to quarrel over and to which everyone else in the poem subscribes. Achilles has just realized (9.316–17) that there is after all no "gratitude and recompense" (*charis*) for his fighting, as there should be according to the "code"; he responds by actually misusing the word "honor" (*timē*) in a way that implies a non-acceptance of the normal value system and suggests a groping toward some other that does not exist anywhere in the world of the poem and is no real alternative. As A. Parry has pointed out, Achilles' misuse of language enhances his tragedy: even linguistically he cannot "leave the society which has become alien to him," or rather, from which he has alienated himself.[25] When Achilles continues,

> The man who does nothing and the man who has done much
> die alike,

he no longer is misusing language, but he implies that just as, in fact, honor really has nothing to do with desert, so glory after death will be the same regardless of one's achievements.

Achilles echoes the disillusionment of 9.316–20 near the end of his speech, at 9.401–9:

> For not equal in value to my life are as many things as they say
> Ilion possessed, the well-inhabited citadel,
> previously, in peacetime, before the sons of the Achaians
> came,
> nor as much as the stone threshold of the archer holds within
> it,
> of Phoibos Apollo, in rocky Pytho.
> For oxen and fat sheep are to be plundered,
> and tripods and the tawny heads of horses can be acquired;
> but a man's life cannot be made to come back by plundering
> nor can it be captured again, when once it passes the barrier of
> the teeth.

Normally the wealth of Troy or of Apollo's temple at Delphi (Pytho) would be worth risking his life for: the oxen, sheep, tripods, and horses would mean honor, and fighting for them would produce glory. But the situation isn't normal. Achilles is led away from a hero's usual preoccupation with what he can do or win to a most atypical, but characteristically Achillean consideration of what he *can't* do: both live to old age and win imperishable glory (9.410–16). In effect he is asking, "What is glory?" Achilles is the highest expression of quality in the world of the poem, but for him at this point there is no longer any quality left in the world, only the quantities that Agamemnon offers and the newly understood value system provides. He might as well go home.

After so vividly expressing his alienation from the values of his society (9.318–20), Achilles expresses in a less startling way his perception that things are not as they should be. In a simile (9.323–27) he compares himself to a bird bringing back mouthfuls of food to her unfledged young, though she has a hard time herself. Thus, Achilles says, he brought back the spoils from numerous campaigns around Troy to Agamemnon, who distributed little and kept much for himself. Achilles' mention of fledglings is characteristic: at 16.7–11 he compares Patroklos to a little girl who runs to her mother crying to be picked up; at 18.318–22 he groans for the dead Patroklos like a grieving, angry lion groaning for cubs a hunter has stolen away; at 23.222–25 he weeps for Patroklos at his funeral pyre like a father grieving over the death of his newly married son. In all four passages there is a curious reversal of roles, for Achilles puts himself, and is put by Homer, in the position of the parent, although it is Patroklos and Agamemnon who, by virtue of age and position, should be caring for him.[26] The similes spoken by Achilles in Books 9 and 16 reflect his special sensitivity to parent-child relationships—a sensitivity perhaps rooted in his distance from his mother in the sea depths and from his father at home in remote Phthia.[27]

In fact, one important element in Homer's characterization of Achilles is his alienation from the various men who stand to him, at least symbolically, as father to son: Peleus, Phoinix, Agamemnon, even Patroklos. This alienation reflects and makes poignant his inability to do anything for them, and theirs to do anything for him, that will make life better and happier. Even in the case of Priam, as has already been remarked, the mutual adoption comes too late.[28] Like Achilles' groping misuse of language, the frustration of his *philotēs* and his isolation from parents and comrades, culminating in the death of Patroklos, evince his tragic loneliness in a world he qualitatively transcends but cannot leave. He cannot leave it, in part, because it is this very world that has established the terms in which he is transcendent, in which he is "the best of the Achaians."

As Achilles describes to Odysseus how he brought spoils back to Agamemnon, who kept much for himself and gave little to others, the memory of how Agamemnon robbed him of his honor sets him off on a series of passionate rhetorical questions (9.337–41): "Why should the Argives be fighting / with the Trojans? Why did Agamemnon gather and lead an army / here? Isn't it because of fair-haired Helen? / Are the sons of Atreus the only mortal men who love / their wives?" It might seem that Achilles' strongest feeling here is one of jealousy. He says, "Let him enjoy / sleeping with her" (9.336–37), and speaks of Briseis as one whom he "loves from the heart, even though she is only a captive of my spear" (9.343). The word "love," however, is misleading: *tēn/ek thumou phileon* means "I cared for her [or: I made her my own] from the heart," with no suggestion of erotic feeling. In the same sentence, the same verb, *phileei*, is joined with *kēdetai*, "is concerned for," to describe the feelings any good, sensible man has for his woman (9.342). Perhaps Homer depicts Achilles as led by his rage to say something a bit different from what he should mean; this impression is confirmed by his calling Briseis an *alochon*, normally signifying a "wedded wife," in 9.336 and implicitly again in 9.340. Achilles recalls himself from this extreme rage only in 9.344–45, when he says, quite rationally, that since Agamemnon has robbed him of his gift of honor and deceived him, he shouldn't try to persuade him to return to the fighting.

Achilles' emotional outburst is strongly marked by the unanswerable rhetorical questions he raises, for example, "Why should the Argives be fighting / with the Trojans?" (9.337–38). To be sure, this question seems to be answered in the very next line (9.339): "Isn't it because of fair-haired Helen?"[29] But such a literal answer really is no answer at all to what clearly is a more general question; Helen is only an occasion. If we recall Achilles' similar questioning of the justification for war at 1.152–54, where he points out that the real reason why he and the other Greeks "follow along with" Agamemnon is "to try to win honor" for him and Menelaos, we see that Achilles is here questioning the way the sceptered Agamemnon is perverting in his case what held good for Menelaos. Achilles' apparently illogical questions, despite their rapid movement and unelaborated connections, have a clear logic and consistency of argumentation. He is challenging the arbitrariness and inequity with which values and authority are applied. Once again we see an expression of Achilles' tragedy: although he can ask why the Greeks should be fighting with the Trojans, he has nothing to put in place of the only answer there is in the world of the poem: honor and glory—an answer he has become unable to accept.

After Achilles' outburst of passion, he becomes calm again. Somewhat sarcastically he tells Odysseus that since the army has gotten on well without him, building a wall and a trench—which, we realize, they did not need when he was fighting—let them figure out how to keep Hektor and the fire away from their ships.[30] Since he himself no longer is interested in fighting Hektor and winning honor and glory, he will go home with the possessions he still has left now that Agamemnon has taken his special gift of honor. Once again, when Achilles recurs to this wrong, he is swept away in an emotional tirade against Agamemnon. The smooth hexameters describing how he will go home (9.356–67) give way to lines broken by strongly punctuated exclamations (9.375–77):

> For he utterly deceived me and transgressed against me; but he
>   couldn't yet again
> cheat me with words; he's done enough; let him, at his leisure,
> go to hell!

Achilles goes on to say that he hates Agamemnon's gifts and considers him worthless. He is carried away into hyperbole when he says that Agamemnon couldn't persuade him if he gave him gifts as numerous as "the dust and the sand"; he wouldn't marry his daughter (as Agamemnon had proposed, 9.144–48, 284, 286–90) if she could compete with Aphrodite in beauty and Athene in works.[31] Achilles even demands that Agamemnon "pay back all my heart-rending injury" (9.387); this is an illogical demand, for although someone can pay another back *for* heart-rending injury, actually to undo a heart-rending injury that has been done is impossible. "The only form of compensation Achilles can dream of accepting is a form that Agamemnon is logically incapable of offering," just as, in his earlier emotional outburst, the only questions he could ask were ones that were impossible to answer.[32] Achilles presents radically the problem of how to measure worth: Agamemnon cannot buy off someone who is totally alienated, cannot offer him sufficient "honor" for his life. Agamemnon can only "pay back all my heart-rending injury" if he goes through what Achilles has gone through. Achilles wants Agamemnon to suffer as he himself has suffered. He forces to the surface the real moral question of the poem: what, in a heroic world, is the true measure of value?

The rest of Achilles' speech is relatively calm and reasoned, at least on the surface. He describes how he will go home, marry a girl his father will find for him, and enjoy his possessions (9.393–400). This leads him to the lines already quoted about the wealth and honor he can win in war not being worth risking his life for. Therefore, of the "two different death-destinies" his mother told him of, he prefers long life at home without noble fame to death at Troy with undying glory. Let the leaders of the Achaians find a better plan, since he won't give up his anger.

As A. Parry has said, "Achilles has no language with which to express his disillusionment. Yet he expresses it, and in a remarkable way. He does it by misusing the language he disposes of."[33] If, as seems likely, Parry is correct in assuming that "the language he disposes of" is the inherited oral vocabulary and style, then Homer shows us a hero alienated not only from the world of his poem but from the world celebrated by hundreds of years of poetic tradition and cultural values. In Achilles' great speech to Odysseus, Homer has painted a powerful portrait of absolute brilliance and excellence having to come to terms with a world that is not commensurate with it. The rest of the *Iliad* develops the tragic consequences of this awful disparity.

5

Achilles' speech to Odysseus ends almost casually with the suggestion that Phoinix spend the night in his tent so that they can go home together in the morning (9.427–29). This makes it appropriate that, after a long silence, Phoinix is the next speaker to appeal to Achilles to give up his anger, accept Agamemnon's gifts, and rejoin the fighting. Phoinix, as we learn at 9.485–95, is teacher and foster father to Achilles as the son he could never have. He had taken care of Achilles as a child, setting him on his knees and cutting up his meat and holding his wine for him. When Peleus sent the inexperienced youth to join Agamemnon's army, he sent along Phoinix to teach him "to be a doer of deeds and a speaker of words" (9.443). In conformity with the usual style of supplicating a god or a more powerful man for a favor, Phoinix reminds Achilles of all he has done for him in the past to induce him to grant in return what he now wishes: that he change his mind and come back to the army.

Apart from what Achilles owes Phoinix as a foster father, there are powerful circumstantial reasons why he might find his own situation reflected in that of Phoinix and therefore be moved by his plea. Phoinix was unable to have children because he had been cursed with sterility by his father, Amyntor, after the latter learned that Phoinix had made love to his concubine. Phoinix did this at his mother's request, so that the concubine "would hate the old man" (9.452). He even planned to kill his father (9.458), but

> some one of the immortals stopped my anger, who made me
> think of the rumor in the community and the many reproaches
> of people,
> so that I might not be called a parricide among the Achaians.
> (9.459–61)

Phoinix's kinsmen tried to keep a watch on him in his house, supplicating him repeatedly, but he escaped and fled to Phthia where Peleus generously took him in and "loved me as a father loves his own son, / an only child . . ." (9.481–82)—in other words, loved him as if he were Achilles.

The terrible conflict between Phoinix and Amyntor over a woman echoes that between Achilles and Agamemnon over Briseis. Just as Phoinix might have killed his father if a god had not "stopped [his] anger," so Achilles might have killed Agamemnon at 1.188–94 had he not been stopped by Athene.[34] Just as conflict with his father resulted in Phoinix's sterility, so conflict with the older Agamemnon, one of the men in the *Iliad* who stand as a "father" to Achilles (see above, p. 107, with note 26), makes Achilles unable to function as he should for much of the poem. Finally, just as Phoinix was alienated from his family and went into exile, so Achilles is cut off from the community of the Greeks and withdraws to the isolation of his shelter.

The situation of Phoinix resonates profoundly with that of Achilles, and Homer exploits the analogies to make his audience more aware of the cost to Achilles of his terrible wrath. Phoinix himself has other appeals in mind. He takes advantage of his status as surrogate father to preach to Achilles the story of the Prayers (9.502–14), the moral of which is that one should honor the divine principle of forgiveness when one is supplicated in the name of Zeus and receives an appropriate recompense (9.515–19). Phoinix adds that although there was no reason to find fault with his previous anger, now Agamemnon has sent him Achilles' "closest friends among the Argives" (*philtatoi Argeiōn*), whose visit and whose speech it would be wrong to render vain (9.520–23). In this way Phoinix appeals to Achilles' strong sense of *philotēs* and his need for solidarity expressed in his words of greeting to the ambassadors when they first came to his shelter:

> Welcome! You have come as friends, and I need you very
>   much,
> who of all the Achaians are dearest (*philtatoi*) to me even when
>   I am angry.[35]

> (9.197–98)

The theme of *philotēs* is central, too, to the long story Phoinix tells Achilles and the others (9.529–99) about Meleagros, a hero of an earlier generation who had a wrath very like Achilles', from whose example Achilles is meant to learn. There are several close parallels in action and diction between Meleagros and Achilles: each withdraws from battle and "nurses his heart-grieving anger" (9.565 ≈ 4.513); the heart of each "swells with anger" (9.553–54 ≈ 9.646); the wrath of Achilles arises from an attempt to appease the wrath of Apollo, that of Meleagros from an attempt to appease that of Artemis (9.533–39).[36] Most important, as J. Th. Kakridis has demonstrated, Homer has modified the traditional story of the wrath of Meleagros to make his "comrades" (*hetairoi*) who were "closest" (*philtatoi*) to him more prominent than they had been in the usual version of the tale, thus making Phoinix's mythological *exemplum* closer thematically to the situation in the *Iliad*.[37] Phoinix, Ajax, and Odysseus are themselves "comrades" of Achilles (9.630) who, as Ajax says, want to be "closest" to him (9.642) and to influence him in the name of *philotēs* to give up his wrath and return to the army. Furthermore, just as in Phoinix's story it is Kleopatra, the wife of Meleagros, who truly is closest to him, who changes his mind and persuades him to save the city (9.590–96), so in the *Iliad* it is Patroklos, undoubtedly Achilles' closest comrade (17.411, 655), who persuades Achilles to allow him to lead the Myrmidons back into battle and whose death induces Achilles to end his wrath and fight again himself.[38]

Phoinix ends his speech with a final appeal to Achilles as *philos* (9.601). He tells Achilles that although Meleagros finally did save his people, he did not receive the gifts that had previously been promised to him, and urges him that he ought to take Agamemnon's gifts now and let the Achaians pay him honor equal to a god, lest, if he should enter the fighting later without gifts, he, like Meleagros, might receive less honor.

Achilles replies to Phoinix that he does not need this honor—that he is being honored by the allotment of Zeus, which will keep him by his ships as long as he lives (9.607–10). Then he takes up the question of *philotēs*. He admits that he has been moved by Phoinix's speech—"Don't keep on confusing my spirit by lamenting and grieving" (9.611)—but he claims that Phoinix, as his own friend, ought not to show favor to the son of Atreus:

> Nor is it right
> that you love this man, lest you be hated by me who love you;
> it is a fine thing for you to cause pain to whoever causes me
> pain.
>
> (9.613–15)

Achilles then invites Phoinix to stay the night, and in the morning they will decide whether to go home or stay. Achilles really is "confused in spirit." The tender, loving side of him wishes to reciprocate his foster father's expressions of love, but under the influence of his wrath, the only love of which he can conceive is for Phoinix to hate the same enemy he himself hates. Whereas at the end of his long speech to Odysseus he had desired the old man to remain with him in order that they might sail home together the next day, Achilles has been swayed by Phoinix's speech to the point where he is not certain whether he will stay or go. He knows only that he cannot accept Agamemnon's gifts, and he successfully opposes Phoinix's exhortations.

As Achilles is signaling Patroklos to prepare a bed for Phoinix so that the others will think of leaving, Ajax intervenes, addressing Odysseus. In effect, he accuses Achilles of not loving and not reciprocating the love of his dearest comrades: Achilles

> has made savage the great-hearted spirit in his breast;
> he is hard-hearted, and is not swayed by the love (*philotēs*) of
>   his comrades,
> the love with which we honored him by the ships beyond all
>   others,
> the pitiless man.
>
> (9.629–32)

Similarly, at the end of his speech Ajax says to Achilles directly:

> Make the spirit in you gracious,
> and have respect for your own house. We are under your roof
>   with you
> out of the multitude of the Danaans, and we are eager more
>   than all others
> to be closest and dearest to you of all the Achaians.
>
> (9.639–42)

Ajax blurs the strength of his appeal as a friend and comrade by going on to develop the notion of Achilles' "savage" spirit: this, he says, is "bad and inflexible" because of one girl, whereas Agamemnon is offering him seven. Even in a much more serious matter, Ajax says, the murder of a brother or son, a man restrains his heart and spirit and accepts payment from the murderer, who remains in the community. Ajax raises once again the question of value, of what it means to repay a heart-rending injury. His exhortation to Achilles to act like any other man is a different way of making the same point Phoinix made in the story of the Prayers: "Yet, Achilles, you too allow that to the daughters of Zeus be granted / honor, which makes flexible the mind even of other good men" (9.513–14).

The mind of Achilles will remain inflexible (cf. 24.40–41) until the visit of Priam in Book 24. At 9.644–48 he responds to Ajax that even though he seemed to speak all that he said

> . . . in accordance with my own feelings,
>   nevertheless my heart swells with anger, when I remember
> those things—how the son of Atreus treated me degradingly
>   among the Argives,
> as if I were some dishonored outcast.

Achilles acknowledges Ajax's appeal in the name of *philotēs*; he is affected by it sufficiently to tell him and Odysseus to go and report that he will not consider making war until Hektor reaches his own ships and shelters, killing Argives and burning ships. "But around my shelter and black ship / I think Hektor will be checked even though he is eager for battle" (9.654–55). Achilles would like to accept and reciprocate Ajax's love, as he would have liked to accept and reciprocate Phoinix's, but an irrational impulse of anger, which he cannot articulate clearly but which involves a rejection of their values, prevents him from doing so. This is his *mēnis*, which makes that man who of all the Greeks is most full of love and has the most to gain from reentering the battle able only to express his hatred for Agamemnon and to punish himself and his comrades by his withdrawal and isolation.

Achilles comes to see this clearly only after the death of Patroklos, the one comrade who really is "closest" to him.[39] As he tells his mother (18.102–6),

> I was not a light of salvation to Patroklos nor to my comrades,
> those others, who were conquered in large numbers by
>   brilliant Hektor,
> but I sit beside the ships a fruitless burden on the fertile land,
> although I am such as no other of the bronze-greaved Achaians
> in war.

The death of Patroklos "restores the *philotēs* . . . between Achilles and the Achaians."[40] But the Achilles who rejoins his comrades is even more twisted by hatred than the Achilles of Book 9, and this hatred is directed not toward one man but toward all the Trojans (cf. 21.103–5, 133–35). Until the beginning of Book 18, when he learns of Patroklos' death, Achilles remains the isolated, inhibited, and dislocated figure we see in Book 9, caught between his feelings of love for his comrades and his inflexible, irrational anger at Agamemnon's insult to his honor, tragically unable to do the one thing that he can do best in the world, that alone can make his brief life meaningful.

6

This is certainly the case when we get a glimpse of Achilles in Book 11, standing "by the stern of his capacious ship, / gazing out at the sheer toil and the tearful onrush" (11.600–601), a picture that recalls Odysseus at *Od.* 5.158 "looking out over the barren sea, shedding tears." In these passages each hero is viewing and longing for the element and activity that gives meaning to his life and wins him imperishable glory in the poetic tradition: Odysseus for his return home over the sea, Achilles for war and killing. But whereas we are told that Odysseus no longer enjoyed Calypso's company, that his "sweet life was dripping away / as he wept for his return home" (*Od.* 5.152–53), Achilles addresses Patroklos as "you who delight my spirit" (11.608), and remarks with satisfaction,

> Now I think that the Achaians will position themselves at my knees
> in supplication, for an unbearable need has come upon them.
> (11.609–10)

These two lines have seemed to some Analytical scholars to contradict or ignore the embassy in Book 9, when the Achaians did come to supplicate Achilles. But such logic has nothing to do with Homer's poetic reality. The point is that even though they came to his knees in Book 9, even though he got what he wanted, still all Achilles can do in his unceasing wrath is dwell on the prospect that they will need him even more, which in fact is the case. Although, as I have said, he anticipates the Achaians' need with satisfaction, at the same time he gets no satisfaction from it either in the short run, since all he can do is gaze longingly at the toil and the rush of battle, or in the long run, since it leads to the death of Patroklos. This long-run consequence is duly noted by Homer, who remarks that

> Patroklos came out [from the shelter] the equal of Ares, and it
> was the starting point of evil for him.
>
> (11.604)

It is characteristic that this "starting point of evil" for his
dearest comrade arises from Achilles' *philotēs*. He has seen
Nestor's chariot rush past carrying Nestor and the wounded
Machaon. Achilles is not sure if it was in fact Machaon, because
the horses sped by so fast that he was unable to see his face; he
sends Patroklos to ask Nestor who the wounded man is. Patroklos obeys his "beloved comrade" (11.616) and sets out on
the errand that leads to his death. Just as in Book 1 Achilles'
concern for the Greeks being destroyed by the plague led him
to initiate the assembly that in turn led to his quarrel with Agamemnon, so here his concern for a wounded comrade leads
him to dispatch Patroklos to Nestor, who gives him the idea of
fighting in Achilles' armor that in turn leads to his death.[41]

Similarly, what brings Achilles to send Patroklos and the
Myrmidons into battle in Book 16 is an appeal to his *philotēs*,
which Patroklos makes in the most radical terms possible. As
Patroklos, weeping for the misfortune of the Greeks, returns
from his visit to Nestor, Achilles makes fun of him, comparing
him to a little girl who runs beside her mother wanting to be
picked up, pulling at her dress and gazing at her tearfully until
finally she is taken up (16.7–11). He then asks him if he has
heard bad news from Phthia, which might account for the
tears,

> or are you weeping for the Argives, how they are being
> destroyed
> at the hollow ships on account of their arrogant
> transgressions?
>
> (16.17–18)

This question releases a flood of emotion in Patroklos, and,
after describing how desperate the Greek situation is, he blows
up at Achilles, accusing him of being simply inhuman in his
anger:

> May this kind of anger never seize on me, this anger you are
> cherishing,
> you man of cursed excellence. What benefit will another man,
> born in the future, get from you,

> if you do not ward off for the Argives shameful destruction?
> Pitiless; the horseman Peleus wasn't your father,
> nor Thetis your mother. Rather the gray sea bore you
> and the tall rocks, since your feelings are so estranged from us.
>
> (16.30–35)

Patroklos is right to associate Achilles' nature with sea and rock: there is something hard and irreducible, truly elemental, about his wrath, just as there will be something elemental about his furious rampage on the battlefield after his comrade's death—only in that instance the element is not earth or water but fire. Nevertheless, despite his hardness, Achilles is touched by Patroklos' appeal, even more than he had been by that of Ajax in Book 9. He reiterates his "dire sorrow" at the way in which Agamemnon robbed him, his equal, of his gift of honor and treated him like a "dishonored outcast" (16.59 = 9.648), but he gives way to his beloved comrade as he would not and could not give way to others:

> But we will let these be things of the past; there was no way,
>   after all,
> for me to be angry in my heart unceasingly; and yet I said
> that I would not stop my wrath, until the time when
> the war and the sound of battle reached my ships.
> But you put my glorious armor on your shoulders,
> and lead the war-loving Myrmidons to battle,
> if indeed the dark cloud of Trojans stands around
> the ships in overwhelming strength, and on the breaking of the
>   sea
> they have been bent back, holding still a small portion of land,
> the Argives; and the whole city of the Trojan stands over them
> courageously, for they do not see the face of my helmet
> flashing close at hand; fleeing quickly would they stuff full
> the river gulleys with corpses, if the ruler Agamemnon
> were kindly disposed toward me; as it is, they are fighting
>   around the army's encampment.
>
> (16.60–73)

This passage reflects Achilles' tortured feelings as he finally gives way. His refusal to "stop [his] wrath" and reenter the fighting before his own ships are threatened is in effect an attempt to preserve his sense of himself, to address the question of under what conditions he can function as Achilles. His inner

struggle is marked by the unusual syntactical articulation of
16.60–63, with no end-stops in 61 and 62 and strong sense
breaks two-thirds of the way through 60, 61, and 62, as well as
the emphatic "and yet I said."[42] The structure of the next ex-
tremely long sentence, with eight lines (66–73) attempting to
justify in his own mind his yielding in 64–65 to Patroklos' request, is similarly eloquent: enjambment at the ends of six lines
reflects the barely controlled rush of Achilles' thoughts, and
the unusually complicated word order in 66–69, which is only
partly conveyed by my translation, indicates the difficulty he
has in articulating verbally the *philotēs* for the Greek army that
actually motivates his decision.

As he sends Patroklos out to "ward off destruction from the
ships" (16.80), Achilles seems to take into rational consideration both his own prerogatives and Patroklos' safety. On the
one hand, he urges him to come back when he has driven away
the Trojan army,

> so you might win great honor and the glory of victory for me
> from all the Danaans, and they might return
> the fair-cheeked girl and provide in addition glorious gifts.
> Don't you be eager to fight apart from me
> with the war-loving Trojans: you will make me more
>   dishonored.
>
> (16.84–90)

On the other hand, he warns him that if he presses on to Troy,
one of the gods may oppose him,

> for Apollo who works from afar loves them very much.
> Rather, turn back, when for the ships a light of salvation
> you make, and leave them to struggle in the plain.
>
>   (16.94–96)

At this point, however, as so often in his speeches, Achilles
moves suddenly from rationality to emotion:

> Father Zeus and Athene and Apollo, would that
> neither any of the Trojans might avoid death, as many as there
>   are,
> nor any of the Argives, but we two might emerge from the
>   destruction,
> so that alone we might breach the sacred citadel of Troy.
>
> (16.97–100)

This passionate outburst, especially emphatic because it comes as the climax of a speech fifty-two lines long, undercuts not only the rational considerations of honor and safety but also the feelings of *philotēs* for the army which had been aroused in Achilles by Patroklos. The only *philotēs* that counts for him is that between himself and his comrade, and both the intensity and the tragedy of their relationship are shown in Achilles' ni-hilistic wish that it be fulfilled in the total destruction of every-one else in their world, whether friend or enemy. Such a fulfill-ment would be simultaneously fruitless and satisfying, a perfect expression of the inseparable feelings of love and hatred at Achilles' core, of that impulse toward death and de-struction as the fullest, most "creative" expression of life and self that will be actualized in his *aristeia*.[43]

The scene in which he sends Patroklos into battle illustrates clearly the special closeness and the limitations of Achilles' re-lationship to Zeus. At 16.233–48, Achilles prays to Zeus, in the fullest, ritually correct manner, that he "send forth the boast of victory" along with Patroklos, and "then let him return un-scathed to the swift ships / with all his armor and with the com-panions who fight nearby him" (16.247–48). Zeus, Homer tells us, "heard him" and granted one part of his prayer but denied the other: he allowed Patroklos to push back the battle from the ships, but he refused to allow him to return safely. As in the first book, when he appeals to Zeus through Thetis, Achilles apparently receives what he asks for, but he is unable to govern what happens next; when he tries to alter the plan of Zeus that he himself has set in motion, he is helpless. Even with his spe-cial divine source of information, his knowledge and control of events is partial and fallible—in other words, mortal. Only at 18.8–11, after Patroklos is dead, does he recall that his mother had told him that while he still was alive, "the best of the Myr-midons / would leave the light of the sun at the hands of the Trojans." Not only does Patroklos not return alive, but the ar-mor and many of the comrades mentioned at 16.248 are also lost. The audience or reader of the poem knows, perhaps from the traditional story and certainly from 8.473–75 and 15.64–77, that the wishes of Achilles have already been superseded in the plan of Zeus. This knowledge sets Achilles' prayer in an ironic perspective that renders it tragic.[44]

Notes to Chapter 4

[1]Cf. J. Griffin, *Homer on Life and Death* (Oxford, 1980), p. 163 n. 39, on the major points in "the crescendo of increasing detail and exactness": "Achilles will have 'a short life,' 1.352, 416, 505; choice of two destinies, 9.411; 'after Hector,' 18.95; 'a god and a man will slay you,' 19.417; 'by Apollo, near the wall,' 21.275; 'Paris and Apollo at the Scaean Gates,' 22.359."

[2]S. Benardete, "Achilles and the *Iliad*," *Hermes* 91 (1963), p. 1.

[3]On Achilles' immortality, see below, p. 95, with n. 15. It is not certain that the familiar story of Thetis trying to make Achilles invulnerable by dipping him as a baby into the river Styx (or, in other versions, by treating him with fire or boiling water) was known by Homer. The earliest mention of dipping him into the Styx is by the first-century A.D. Roman poet Statius *(Achilleid* 1.134); the first reference to the treatment with fire is found in the third-century B.C. Greek poet Apollonius of Rhodes *(Argonautika* 4.869–70; cf. the treatment of Demophoön by Demeter in the Homeric *Hymn to Demeter* 239–42). Nevertheless, it seems likely that a traditional myth about Thetis' efforts to make Achilles invulnerable is alluded to on a proto-Corinthian vase, ca. 680–670 B.C., which shows Achilles dead, pierced by an arrow sticking out of his heel—the only part of his body, according to the story, which was vulnerable, because Thetis had held him by it as she dipped him in the Styx. See K. Schefold, *Myth and Legend in Early Greek Art* (London, 1966), p. 46, fig. 14. See too the similar depiction on a vase from the first half of the sixth century in E. Pfuhl, *Masterpieces of Greek Drawing and Painting*, trans. J. D. Beazley (London, 1955), p. 19, fig. 13. It is well known that archaic vase-paintings often preserve traditional myths not referred to in the *Iliad* or *Odyssey*, and it is reasonable to conclude that the story of Achilles' near-invulnerability was such a traditional myth, which Homer suppressed because it conflicted with his thematic emphasis on Achilles' mortality, as well as with his general avoidance of descriptions of magic. For references to other versions of the invulnerability myth in late antiquity, see J. G. Frazer, ed. and trans., *Apollodorus, The Library*, 2 vols. (London and New York, 1921), vol. 2, pp. 69 n. 4, 214–15 n. 1.

[4]On *mēnis*, see C. Watkins, "A propos de *MENIS*," *Bulletin de la Société de linguistique de Paris* 72 (1977), pp. 187–209. By "daemonic" I mean (literally) in the manner of or under the influence of a *daimōn*, a divinity.

[5]In 5.311–17, Aphrodite rescues her son Aineias from death at the hands of Diomedes, but she does not speak to him; at 20.335–39, Po-

seidon prophesies to Aineias his destined safety in battle after Achilles' death.

[6]For a god, to be "bound" is analogous to death; it is the ultimate punishment in the divine realm. At 5.385–91, Dione recalls to Aphrodite how Otos and Ephialtes had "bound" Ares in a bronze pot for thirteen months, and how he was being worn out and conquered by the harsh "binding" and would have perished, had not Hermes rescued him. Cf. Hesiod, *Theogony* 501–2, where Zeus sets free from "bonds" the sons of Heaven whom his father Kronos had bound, and 521–22, where he "binds" Prometheus in cruel, unbreakable bonds.

[7]See Pindar, *Isthmian* 8.26a–37 Snell. This prophecy, of course, is Prometheus' secret weapon against Zeus in *Prometheus Bound*.

[8]Achilles himself stresses his descent from Zeus in his vaunt over the dead Asteropaios (21.184–99), and Homer keeps it in our minds by repeatedly referring to Achilles by his father's patronymic, *Aiakidēs*, "son of Aiakos." Hearing this, an audience familiar with the poetic tradition would have recalled that Aiakos was not only the father of Peleus and grandfather of Achilles but also the son of Zeus.

[9]Laura Slatkin, "Thetis, Achilles, and the *Iliad*" (Ph.D. diss., Harvard, 1979), p. 21. In this dissertation Slatkin has shown the significance not only of the description of Briareos as "better in strength than his father" and of Thetis as the rescuer of Zeus, but also of other references in the *Iliad* to Thetis as a rescuer of gods: Dionysos (6.135–37), Hephaistos (18.394–405). Slatkin demonstrates that behind the *Iliad* lies a body of traditional mythology about Thetis in which she is a cosmogonic power capable of ordering the universe and preserving its stability. In the *Iliad*, Thetis' traditional power and her wrath at her mortal marriage—a wrath parallel to that of Demeter in the Homeric *Hymn to Demeter*—have been deemphasized and transformed in accordance with the themes and values of a poem about mortal heroism. But diction associated with her in the *Iliad* recalls her traditional power: for example, apart from Zeus, Apollo, and Achilles, only Thetis is said "to ward off destruction" (*loigon amunai*) successfully, and thus, by implication, to have the power to cause it (on a cosmic scale). The traditional motif of her wrath is absorbed in that of her son's, once again in accordance with the poem's thematic emphases. As Slatkin shows, it is no accident that the son of Thetis, and no other mortal, is the hero of the *Iliad*, and that this apparently minor goddess is given the role of asking Zeus to set in motion the events of the poem. In a (metaphysical) sense, Slatkin argues, the forced marriage of Thetis and the tragic mortality of Achilles are the price paid for preserving the hegemony of Zeus and the cosmic order.

[10]E. T. Owen, *The Story of the Iliad* (1946; reprint, Ann Arbor, 1966), p. 11.

[11]See W. Schadewaldt, *Von Homers Welt und Werk*, 4th ed. (Stuttgart, 1965), pp. 234–67.

[12]There are many parallels in action and speech between Books 1 and 18, especially in connection with the visits of Thetis. See Owen, *Story of the Iliad*, pp. 178–79, and K. Reinhardt, *Die Ilias und ihr Dichter* (Göttingen, 1961), pp. 368–70. Book 18 begins the last major section of the poem as Book 1 begins the first.

[13]See Chapter 2, p. 58.

[14]See Chapter 1, pp. 25–26.

[15]For the story of Achilles' immortality on the White Island, see Proclus, *Chrestomatheia* 2, in H. G. Evelyn-White, ed. and trans., *Hesiod, The Homeric Hymns and Homerica* (1936; reprint, Cambridge, Mass. and London, 1959), pp. 508–9, and E. Rohde, *Psyche*, trans. W. B. Hillis, 2 vols. (1925; reprint, New York, 1966), vol. 1, pp. 64–66.

[16]See Slatkin, "Thetis," pp. 13–16, who refers to D. D. Boedeker, *Aphrodite's Entry into Greek Epic* (Leiden, 1974).

[17]Slatkin, "Thetis," p. 26; cf. J.-P. Vernant, "*PANTA KALA* d'Homère à Simonide," *Annali della Scuola Normale Superiore di Pisa*, ser. 3, 9 (1979), pp. 1365–74, especially pp. 1367–70.

[18]On *philos*, see E. Benveniste, *Indo-European Language and Society*, trans. E. Palmer, Miami Linguistics Series, no. 12 (Coral Gables, 1973), pp. 273–88.

[19]Benveniste, *I-E Language*, p. 278, notes, "This is why the verb *philein* expresses the prescribed conduct of the person who welcomes a stranger to his hearth and whom he treats according to ancestral custom." Cf. 3.205–7, 6.12–15, and *Od.* 8.208–11, cited by Benveniste. In later Greek *philein* came to have the special meaning of "kiss," originally as a gesture of (hospitable) greeting between *philoi*, then as a mark of affection.

[20]Ibid., pp. 281–83, remarks that often the use of *philos*, "going beyond the sphere of human relations, is extended to objects of various kinds to which the common and constant meaning of 'dear' could hardly apply." Such objects include "things which are most closely linked with the person: soul, heart, life, breath; parts of the body: limbs, knees, chest, and eyelids . . . with terms designating places which are presumably 'dear,' notably the 'homeland'. . . , or the 'return' (*nostos*). Finally, we have a short list of terms which do not seem to involve any emotional colouring: gifts, house, clothes, bed. . . ." In these cases *philos* has been considered by most scholars since antiquity to be a simple possessive adjective, but in fact detailed examination shows in almost every instance that the word is used in a *context* ex-

shows in almost every instance that the word is used in a *context* explicitly or implicitly suggesting "institutions of hospitality," "usages of the home," or "emotional behavior" (p. 288).

[21]Slatkin, "Thetis," p. 21, notes that "Achilles . . . has special diction which distinguishes him as the limiting case of the experience of mortality." She discusses this diction at pp. 18–21.

[22]In what follows, I do not cite every instance on which Achilles is mentioned, only those that seem particularly significant.

[23]Cf. Ophelia's portrait of Hamlet as he was prior to his disestablishment from himself, "O, what a noble mind is here o'erthrown. . . ," *Hamlet* 3.1.150–61.

[24]7.436–41. In a well-known passage (1.11) Thucydides implies that the Greeks must have built the wall when they first landed on the Trojan shore at the beginning of the war, and in modern times the construction of this wall has seemed to Analytical critics to be a late interpolation into the *Iliad*. But poetically it is appropriate that the Greeks should build the wall at the end of Book 7, when, after the first day of battle without Achilles (i.e., the first day narrated to us by Homer; we learn at 1.493–94 that the fighting had gone on for eleven days between Achilles' conversation with Thetis and Thetis' appeal to Zeus), they realize that in his absence they need such a bulwark. It also enables Homer to have Achilles refer sarcastically to the futility of this construction at 9.349–50.

[25]A. Parry, "The Language of Achilles," *Transactions of the American Philological Association* 87 (1956), pp. 1–7 = G. S. Kirk, ed., *The Language and Background of Homer* (Cambridge, 1964), pp. 48–54. The words quoted appear on p. 7 = p. 54. Despite criticism by D. B. Claus, "*Aidōs* in the Language of Achilles," *Transactions of the American Philological Association* 105 (1975), pp. 13–28, and P. Friedrich and J. M. Redfield, "Speech as a Personality Symbol: The Case of Achilles," *Language* 54 (1978), pp. 263–88, Parry's thesis of Achilles' misuse of language seems to me fundamentally correct. Cf. W. T. MacCary, *Childlike Achilles: Ontogeny and Phylogeny in the Iliad* (New York, 1982), pp. 56–58.

[26]For Patroklos, see 11.786–89; for Agamemnon's relative age, 9.161. Agamemnon almost (but not quite) acknowledges a parental relationship to Achilles at 19.132–36: as Zeus grieved when he saw his son Herakles forced to carry out the shameful commands of Eurystheus, so he [Agamemnon] grieved when—Hektor was destroying the Argives. Here Agamemnon implicitly adopts a parental role vis-à-vis the whole army, but we cannot help thinking primarily of Achilles as the comparand to Herakles, both because we have seen him suffering profoundly since the beginning of Book 18, and because he has

explicitly associated himself with Herakles in his acceptance of death and mortality (18.117–21).

[27]Griffin, *Life and Death*, p. 75 n. 48, observes the unusually high frequency of similes in Achilles' speeches: four of the fourteen extended similes occurring in speeches in the *Iliad* are spoken by him. Griffin notes too the high incidence of unique words in Achilles' speeches, as well as his "staccato utterances"—brief clauses often taking up less than a line of verse, as in 9.375–77 discussed below (p. 109). Just as characteristic as these "staccato utterances" are Achilles' long, expansive sentences running for three or four lines with no end-stop or other strong sense-break, e.g., 16.60–73, 18.122–24.

[28]In a sense, Achilles here succeeds in realizing the role-reversal of his similes by caring for Priam.

[29]Cf. M. D. Reeve, "The Language of Achilles," *Classical Quarterly*, n.s., 23 (1973), p. 194.

[30]See above, n. 23. Achilles emphasizes his point by calling Hektor *androphonoio*, "manslaughtering," in 9.351 rather than the metrically equivalent *hippodamoio*, "tamer of horses." Cf. his similar choice of epithet in a similar context at 1.242. In fact no Greek ever refers to Hektor as *hippodamoio*; that is not how they perceive him. Cf. Chapter One, p. 8.

[31]Homer cleverly makes Achilles (9.391–92) answer Agamemnon's statement to Odysseus at 9.160–61, a statement Odysseus did not transmit and which Achilles, therefore, cannot have heard. This device effectively emphasizes that aspect of the quarrel between the two men which has to do with Agamemnon's royal prerogatives: cf. *basileuteros*, "more royal," in 9.160 and 9.392.

[32]Reeve, "Language of Achilles," p. 195.

[33]A. Parry, "Language of Achilles," p. 6 = Kirk, *Language and Background*, p. 53.

[34]*cholon pauseien* (1.192) ≈ *pausen cholon* (9.459).

[35]The verbs "Welcome," "you have come," and "are" in these lines are in the *dual* number, a grammatical form used in Greek to describe or express the actions or attributes of two, and only two, subjects. Most of the verbs used of the three ambassadors in 9.182–98 are in the dual, and this fact has given rise to a notorious scholarly controversy. While Analytical scholars have found in these lines evidence for multiple authorship of the *Iliad* (e.g., D. Page, *History and the Homeric Iliad* [Berkeley and Los Angeles, 1959], pp. 297–300, 324–26), others recognize merely a narrative inconsistency arising from Homer's reworking of a traditional story in which only two ambassadors were sent to Achilles. Most of the latter group have assumed that the traditional story involved Ajax and Odysseus and that Homer added Phoinix for

the sake of thematic resonances and increased poetic significance. Recently, however, in view of the distribution of the duals and the "pattern of self-assertion on the part of Odysseus," G. Nagy has suggested that "an 'Embassy of Ajax and Phoenix to Achilles' had been a stock theme of Greek epic tradition," and that Odysseus was inserted into the story in *Iliad* 9 in conformity with another traditional motif of "conflict between Odysseus and Achilles." See G. Nagy, *The Best of the Achaeans: Concepts of the Hero in Archaic Greek Poetry* (Baltimore and London, 1979), pp. 49–55.

[36]Nagy, *Best of the Achaeans*, pp. 104–5.

[37]See J. Th. Kakridis, *Homeric Researches* (Lund, 1949), pp. 21–25. In the typical pattern, discovered by Kakridis, comrades are less close and beloved by a hero than parents, siblings, or a spouse, but at 9.585–86 Meleagros' "comrades, who were closest and dearest to him of all," are mentioned as beseeching him (unsuccessfully) after his father, sister, and mother have done so but before his wife, thus implying that he loves them more than his father, sister, and mother though less than his wife. Undoubtedly the situation in the *Iliad* has led Phoinix to give the comrades of Meleagros their unusually high position in the "ascending scale of affection." It is worth noting, too, that the order of the speakers in Book 9 also is in line with this revised scale: first Odysseus, then the foster father Phoinix, and finally the comrade who speaks in the name of *philotēs*, Ajax. Cf. D. Lohmann, *Die Komposition der Reden in der Ilias*, Untersuchungen zur antiken Literatur und Geschichte, no. 6 (Berlin, 1970), p. 259.

[38]On Kleopatra and Patroklos, see E. Howald, *Der Dichter der Ilias* (Erlenbach-Zurich, 1946), p. 132; W. Schadewaldt, *Iliasstudien*, 3d ed. (Darmstadt, 1966), pp. 139–40; Kakridis, *Homeric Researches*, pp. 29–31; Nagy, *Best of the Achaeans*, p. 105.

[39]See Nagy, *Best of the Achaeans*, p. 105.

[40]Ibid., p. 106.

[41]There is a further indication of the tender or *philos* side of Achilles near the end of Book 11. As Patroklos is returning from Nestor's shelter to Achilles, he meets the wounded Eurypylos, who asks him to cut an arrow out of his thigh, wash away the blood with warm water, and "spread kind drugs on the wound, / good ones, about which they say you were taught by Achilles, / whom Cheiron taught, the most just of the Centaurs" (11.830–32). In these lines we have a fleeting glimpse of Achilles as healer and teacher, which is as striking and instructive as the glimpse of him as bard, "delighting his spirit" by playing the lyre and singing "the glorious deeds of heroes" (9.186–89). It has been remarked by scholars ever since antiquity that the traditional myth of the education of Achilles by Cheiron is inconsistent with the story told

by Phoinix in 9.485–95, and with Homer's usual avoidance of the theriomorphic in his adaptations of traditional mythology. This inconsistency is poetically motivated by Homer's desire to emphasize the *philos* aspect of Achilles at this point in the *Iliad*, even though such an emphasis requires a mention of Cheiron, with whose instruction this aspect was traditionally associated in the mythology known to both the poet and his audience.

[42]A. Parry, "Language of Achilles," p. 7 = Kirk, *Language and Background*, p. 54 n. 14, says: "On the [emphasis on 'I said'], I am tempted to say, hangs the whole tragic decision."

[43]The special quality of 16.97–100 was seen by ancient commentators of the Hellenistic period, who, however, utterly misinterpreted it. They judged the passage to be a late interpolation into the poem by someone anachronistically depicting the relationship between Achilles and Patroklos as sexual. See W. Leaf, ed., *The Iliad*, 2d ed., 2 vols. (1900 and 1902; reprint, Amsterdam, 1960), vol. 2, p. 163. In fact, the earliest extant portrayal of this relationship as sexual is in a fragment of Aeschylus' *Myrmidons*, which was composed more than two centuries later than the *Iliad*. See B. Snell, *Scenes from Greek Drama* (Berkeley and Los Angeles, 1964), pp. 1–21.

[44]It may have been from these scenes, or others like them in the poetic tradition, that Sophocles developed his characteristic techniques of making a character speak words that mean more to the audience than to himself and of having someone remember an oracle only after it already has come true. Cf. R. B. Rutherford, "Tragic Form and Feeling in the *Iliad*," *Journal of Hellenic Studies* 102 (1982), pp. 145–60, especially pp. 145–49. B. M. W. Knox, *The Heroic Temper: Studies in Sophoclean Tragedy* (Berkeley and Los Angeles, 1964), p. 51, observes that Sophocles seems to have modeled his typical "hero's situation, mood, and action" on those of Achilles, and speaks of "Sophocles' obsession with the Achillean temperament and situation" (p. 59).

5

Achilles: Two

When Achilles receives the news of Patroklos'
death (18.18–21), the *Iliad* moves onto a heightened plane of
action and passion. From this point on, Achilles is no longer
intermittently present as in the first seventeen books but is the
constant focus of attention. His behavior is more extreme and
desperate than it was earlier in the poem. He remains a figure
of *mēnis* and *philotēs*, "wrath" and "love," but his love and sorrow for his dead comrade lead him to transfer his anger and
hatred from Agamemnon to Hektor and the Trojans. As he
avenges Patroklos by ruthlessly massacring the Trojans, killing
Hektor, and mistreating his corpse, he becomes transformed,
disestablished from his distinctive, generous humanity and
heroism. Homer conveys the nature and extent of Achilles'
transformation in three distinct but complementary ways.
Firstly, he emphasizes his alienation from his earlier humane
self by symbolically representing him as dead, and therefore
less than fully human. Secondly, he depicts him as behaving
like an extreme version of a conventional warrior-hero of a kind
that was familiar from the poetic tradition but that the *Iliad*, for
the most part, is not concerned with. Thirdly, he represents
him as increasingly daemonic, not merely human, in his actions and the values these actions imply.[1] As a result of these

three ways of representing the change in Achilles, he comes to be seen as both less than than and more than human, both less than and more than his previous self; he can no longer be measured either by the same standards as other heroes or by his own previous standards. Only his eventual restoration of Hektor's body to Priam, whom he treats with regained humanity and compassion, marks his own restoration to his characteristic, Achillean self; but this reversal comes too late to affect the doom of Troy or of Achilles himself.

1

Death is the dominant theme of the final seven books, even more than of the preceding seventeen. Characteristically, Homer gives equal attention to the ruthless *aristeia* of Achilles, culminating in his slaying of Hektor, and to the burials and lamentations for Patroklos and Hektor. Throughout it is repeatedly made clear that the deaths of these two figures involve the death of Achilles himself, a death that symbolizes the extreme dislocation of Achilles from his normal sentiments and standards of behavior. Homer suggests and foreshadows the death of Achilles by adapting certain mythological motifs, diction, and perhaps specific passages of poetry associated in the poetic tradition with the death of Achilles to the death, lamentation, and burial of Patroklos.[2] Furthermore, he makes Achilles die symbolically, when both Patroklos and Hektor are killed in the armor so intimately bound up with his identity. By the end of the poem, as J. Th. Kakridis has said, "Achilles . . . belongs to the underworld, although the Iliad does not [actually] describe his death."[3]

When Achilles hears that Patroklos is dead and that Hektor has captured his armor,

> . . . a dark cloud of grief covered him;
> with both hands he grasped the grimy dust
> and poured it over his head, and disfigured his lovely face;

> and the dark ashes settled on his tunic which was as fragrant as
>   nektar.
> He himself, great in his greatness, stretched out in the dust
> lay, and he disfigured his hair, tearing it with his hands.
>
> (18.22–27)

These lines, which describe Achilles' sorrow, contain several words and formulas conventionally used in connection with death, thus suggestively depicting Achilles as if he were dead. "Darkness" often "covers" a man's eyes when he is killed; a "dark cloud covers" the dying Polydoros at 20.417–18 (though a different word for "dark" is used in 18.22 than in 20.418). On five occasions a man "grasps" the earth with his hand as he falls "in the dust."[4] The verb "he lay" (*keimai*, imperfect tense-form *keito* in 18.27) is commonly used of warriors "lying dead," including Patroklos a few lines earlier at 18.20 and again at 23.210 (present tense-form *keitai*), as well as of Achilles himself at 18.121.[5] Finally, the phrase "great in his greatness" (*megas megalōsti*) is used elsewhere only with a form of *keimai* and only of dead warriors, including Achilles himself in the description of his funeral at *Od*. 24.40.[6]

In the description that follows, "the slave women whom Achilles and Patroklos had taken as booty" (18.28) cry out in grief and rush

> around fiery-minded Achilles, and with their hands they all
> were beating their breasts and the knees of each one were
>   loosened,
>
> (18.30–31)

as if they were mourning for him rather than Patroklos. This effect is enhanced by the parallel passage a few lines further on, when Achilles' terrible cry of grief reaches Thetis "in the depths of the sea" (18.36):

> Then she cried out in distress, and the goddesses gathered
>   around her,
> all of them, as many Nereids as there were in the depth of the
>   sea.
>   .   .   .   .
> The bright cave was filled with them; together they all
> were beating their breasts, and Thetis led off the lament:
> "Listen, my Nereid sisters, so you may all

know well, hearing them, how many sorrows are in my spirit.
Ah me, wretched me, unhappy in having borne the best hero
  as a son,
since I gave birth to a son faultless and powerful,
outstanding among heroes, and he shot up like a young tree;
I nurtured him, like a plant in the slope of the orchard,
and I sent him forth in the curved ships to Ilion
to fight with the Trojans, but I shall not receive him again
returning home into the house of Peleus.

(18.37–38, 49–60)

When Thetis' cry (18.37) echoes that of Achilles, and the Nereids beat their breasts (18.50–51) just like the slave women (18.30–31), the world of lamentation for Patroklos is extended so that nature itself seems to be mourning for him.[7] But the mourning really is not for Patroklos. Lines 54–60, with the unique word *dusaristotokeia*, "unhappy in having borne the best hero as a son," and the emphasis on the fact that Achilles will never return home to the house of Peleus, clearly are a lament for the death of Achilles, though we are reminded of the actual situation in the poem at 18.61–64:

But while he lives and sees the light of the sun,
he sorrows, and I am not able to do anything for him, though I
  go to him.
But I will go, so I may see my dear child, and hear
what grief has come to him while staying away from the war.

The sense that Thetis is mourning for her son's death is reinforced by her use of the word *göoio* (18.51), which properly means "lament for the dead" (cf. 24.723, 747, 761), to introduce her comments about him. An even more striking indication occurs at 18.70–72:

As he groaned heavily the lady his mother stood beside him,
and, crying shrilly, took her son's head in her hands,
and, weeping, spoke winged words to him.

Elsewhere in the *Iliad* (23.136, 24.712, 714), and in the iconography of contemporary Geometric vase painting, it is the gesture of the chief mourner—usually the closest female relative—in the funeral ritual for a dead man to hold his head in her hands.[8] In the context of the preceding seventy lines, Thetis' gesture in 18.71 indicates clearly that Achilles is being depicted by Homer as if he were dead.

The systematic representation of Achilles as dead is by no means surprising. It has been clear since Book 1 that Achilles is "short-lived" (1.352) and "swiftly-doomed beyond other mortals" (1.505); we know from 9.410–16 of his "two different death-destinies," either a brief life ending in death at Troy with imperishable glory or a return home with a long life and no glory. Now we see Achilles actually make a decision and choose to "be absolute for death." When Thetis reminds Achilles that Zeus has accomplished all that he prayed for in Book 1, Achilles replies:

> My mother, yes, the Olympian has fully accomplished these
>   things,
> but what pleasure do I have from them, when my dear
>   comrade has perished,
> Patroklos, whom I honored beyond all comrades,
> as much as my own head. I have lost him, and as for his armor,
>   Hektor,
> who killed him, stripped it away, gigantic, a wonder to behold,
> beautiful, which the gods gave to Peleus as glorious gifts
> on the day when they threw you into the bed of a mortal man.
> . . . .
>   nor does my spirit bid me
> to go on living and be among men, unless Hektor
> is the first to be struck by my spear and lose his life,
> and pays back the spoils of Patroklos, son of Menoitios.
>   (18.79–85, 90–93)

Achilles equates the death of Patroklos with the end of his own life; in his mind their two identities merge. By calling attention to the armor, a wedding gift of the gods to Peleus, Achilles really is calling attention to his own mortality, which resulted from Thetis' being compelled to marry a mortal rather than a god.[9] As often in the *Iliad*, Achilles desires what is impossible to achieve. He envisions that Hektor's death would "pay back the spoils" of Patroklos; this is in line with the conventional value system, illustrated so often in the poem, whereby loyalty to a comrade and heroic honor are satisfied by the death of the slayer of that comrade, or at least by the death of another enemy warrior. But for Achilles, Hektor's death can no more "pay back" the irrevocable doom of his comrade than Agamemnon at 9.387 could "pay back" with his profferred gifts the outrage he had done to him. This is made clear at the beginning of Book 24, when Achilles vainly continues to try to exact revenge from Hektor by dragging his corpse around Patroklos' tomb. In Book 18, however, he still can imagine that Hektor's death will be adequate compensation.

When Thetis informs him,

> Then, my child, you will be swiftly doomed, the way you are
>   talking,
> for immediately after Hektor your doom is ready,
> (18.95–96)

Achilles bursts forth:

> Then I would die immediately, since for my comrade I was not
>   there
> to stand in defense as he was killed; very far from his native
>   land
> he perished, and he lacked me to defend him from destruction.
> As it is, since I am not going back to my beloved native land,
> and I was not any light of salvation to Patroklos, nor to my
>   comrades,
> those others who were conquered in large numbers by brilliant
>   Hektor,
> but I sit by the ships, a fruitless burden on the fertile land,
> although I am such as no other of the bronze-greaved Achaians
> in war, though in assembly there are others who are better—
> I wish that strife would perish from among gods and men,
> and wrath, which incites even a sensible man to become angry,
> and which rises in men's breasts like smoke
> and is far sweeter than dripping honey;
> thus on this occasion the lord of men, Agamemnon, angered
>   me.
> But we will let these be things of the past, even though we are
>   grieving,
> mastering the spirit in our breast by necessity;
> now I will go, so I may catch the slayer of a dear head,
> Hektor, and then I will accept death, whenever
> Zeus wishes to accomplish it, and the rest of the immortal
>   gods.
> (18.98–116)

In these lines, with their unique and vivid imagery, their ir-regular, almost out-of-control syntax, and their passionate self-reproach and impossible wishes, we recognize the Achilles of Books 9, 11, and 16. But he is now transformed, out of charac-ter, as it were, no longer able to balance his fury with his love for Patroklos; rather, he is driven by this love to vengeance even at the cost of self-annihilation. When he blames himself for being of no use to Patroklos and his other comrades, we see again the social side of Achilles that has been inhibited since Book 1. But so much else in him also has been unblocked that this social side seems insignificant. Whereas Thetis had spoken of him as growing "like a young tree / . . . a plant in the slope of the orchard. . . ," Achilles can only view himself as a "fruit-less burden on the fertile land," unproductive both for himself and for others. Achilles states clearly and accepts matter-of-factly his supreme excellence in war and comparative inferior-ity in assembly, where, we remember, his quarrel with Aga-memnon began. His earlier realization—that even though Zeus gave him what he had wanted, this was in no way gratify-ing (18.79–84)—is raised to a recognition that even the greatest hero is subject to the limitations of mortality:

> For no, not the strength of Herakles avoided death,
> who was closest to the lord Zeus, son of Kronos,
> but his portion mastered him, and the hard anger of Hera.
> (18.117–19)

Herakles is the traditional warrior-hero par excellence: he rep-resents the highest possible heroic achievement, including a previous sack of Troy (5.642, 14.251). He is the only mortal to whom Achilles compares himself and to whom Achilles is com-pared by others.[10] This comparison prepares the way for Achil-les' fierce battlefield exploits in Books 20–22, which in effect constitute a second sack of Troy; it expresses eloquently Achil-les' recognition of his own special greatness. It also sets a seal on his decision to die, since Herakles in the *Iliad*, for all his su-preme heroism, is in the end nonetheless a mortal who died. In accordance with the themes of his poem, Homer ignores, and makes Achilles ignore, the alternate tradition that Hera-kles achieved deification for his heroism (*Od.* 11.602–4).

At the same time Herakles is a hero of an earlier generation, a hero of a particular kind that is several times contrasted to the kind of warrior fighting in the Trojan War. Old Nestor refers frequently, as at l.266–72, to this earlier generation, with which he associated in his youth:

> Those were reared as the mightiest of mortal men:
> they were the mightiest and they fought with the mightiest,
> the mountain beasts, and they destroyed them terribly,
>
> · · · · · · · · · · · · · · · · · · ·
>
> And with these men no one
> of those who now are mortals upon the earth could fight.

This reference to men who "fought with . . . the mountain beasts," probably an allusion to the battle of the Lapiths and Centaurs, summons up a picture of a half-savage world of warriors far more powerful and far cruder than those of the *Iliad*'s heroic age. That Herakles belongs to this earlier world is clear not only from references to certain of his adventures and battles with mortals of a bygone age (11.690–91, 14.250–51, 15.24–30) but also from allusions to his combat with the sea monster (*kētos*, 20.145–48) and to his having wounded Hera and Hades with arrows (5.392–97) in combats that, like all serious combats involving divinities, are a thing of the past in the *Iliad*.[11]

Another indication of Herakles' older kind of heroism is the formulaic phrase "the Heraklean violence" (*biē Heraklēeiē*), consisting of a feminine noun and a proper adjective, which Homer uses five times in the poem as an equivalent to the simple name Herakles.[12] It usually is thought that this periphrasis, and others combining the words *biē*, "violence," *is*, "strength," and a few other nouns with the possessive form of a name, exist only for the sake of fitting metrically recalcitrant forms of certain names into the dactylic hexameter, which otherwise could not accommodate them.[13] But it is noteworthy that in Hesiod's *Works and Days*, a product of the same poetic tradition as the *Iliad*, one important feature of the violent bronze race of men, who directly precede the "better and more just" race of heroes who fought at Troy, is their *megalē biē*, "great violence" (148). In this light, it is striking that all the periphrases in the *Iliad* and *Odyssey* combining *biē* with a proper adjective are equivalents to the names of heroes of a previous generation—Herakles, Eteokles, Iphikles—although periphrases combining *biē* or another noun with the possessive form of a name are used for heroes of the present age as well as for those of the past.[14] Therefore, the formulaic periphrasis *biē Heraklēeiē* helps to characterize Herakles as an older kind of hero from an earlier age. The use of this periphrasis has led G. Nagy to argue that, "In the case of Herakles . . . the [traditional] theme of *biē* is actually embodied in the hero's identity."[15] If this is so, it is appropriate that at the point in the *Iliad* when Achilles is becoming more violent and, as it were, regressing into more of a Herakles-type hero, he explicitly compares himself with Herakles, using a *biē* periphrasis (18.117). Homer clearly is aware of a variety of possible modes of heroic behavior in the poetic tradition. By making Achilles compare himself with Herakles and assume a Heraklean identity, he exploits both this variety and his audience's familiarity with the traditional associations of the periphrastic formula—the theme of violence and Herakles' older kind of heroism—thus suggesting that Achilles' radical dislocation from his distinctive values and behavior consists, in part, of a change in the direction of a cruder warrior-heroism specifically associated with overwhelming power and with the sack of Troy.

This extreme change in Achilles is clear in his words to his mother at 18.120–26, immediately following his self-comparison with Herakles:

> So I, too, if a similar portion has been made for me,
> shall lie dead when I die. But now I would win noble glory,
> and force some one of the women of Troy or the deep-girdled
>   Dardanian women
> to groan in bursts of grief, as she wipes away her tears
> with both hands from her delicate cheeks,
> and thus they might know that I have ceased from the war for
>   too long.
> Don't hold me back from battle, mother, even if you love me;
>   you will not persuade me.

Achilles' vivid picture of a warrior's widow groaning as she wipes away her tears illustrates his own and the poem's perspective on his changing heroism, even while it foreshadows his destruction of the city. This picture is expressed in unusually vivid, characteristically Achillean language and style. The long, expansive sentence, with no end-stops in 123 and

124, is typical of his impassioned speeches.[16] The striking phrase, "to groan in bursts of grief" (*hadinon stonachēsai*, 18.124) is formulaic, but is paralleled in the *Iliad* only by the virtually identical formulaic phrases *hadina stenachizōn* (23.225) and *hadina stenachonta* (24.123), both of which are used of Achilles himself at moments of deepest sorrow, when he feels as devastated as the widow in his description. At 23.224–25,

> Achilles wept for his comrade as he was burning his bones,
> dragging himself on the ground beside the funeral-pyre,
>   groaning in bursts of grief.

At 24.122–23, Thetis

> arrived at her son's shelter; him there
> she found groaning in bursts of grief.

By an artistically appropriate and effective device, Homer makes Achilles use the same formula to express the future effect of his *mēnis* on others as the poet uses to express its effect on Achilles himself. In this way his heroic achievements are shown to be both destructive and self-destructive.

Despite its specifically Achillean qualities, Achilles' description of the lamenting widow is thematically conventional. Achilles sees himself as doing what city-sackers usually do.[17] He reverts to a traditional type of heroism far more brutal and one-dimensional than his own, which was expressed, for example, by his humanity to Eëtion during the sack of Thebe, as Andromache recalls at 6.414–19. The exceptional tenderness of his vision of the widow is the result of his characteristic *philotēs*, his human sympathy, which makes him especially sensitive to the terrible results of his *mēnis* for his enemies. But the effacing of that *philotēs* by the *mēnis* only serves to make him seem even more grim and inhuman.

Achilles' inhumanity is reflected in the increasingly daemonic character of his actions. After Thetis departs to obtain new armor for him from Hephaistos (18.146–47), it appears that Hektor will succeed in carrying off Patroklos' body (18.165). At this point Iris comes with instructions from Hera that Achilles show himself to the Trojans at the ditch surrounding the Greek camp. As he rises to do so,

> Athene threw her tasseled aegis around his strong shoulders,

and, brilliant among goddesses, circled his head with a cloud
of gold, and from it kindled glittering fire,

(18.204–6)

whose blaze towers to heaven. Standing at the ditch, he shouts
as loudly "as screams out a trumpet / of life-destroying enemies
besieging a city" (18.219–20); this shout is echoed by Athene,
and when the Trojans hear "the bronze voice of the son of
Aiakos,"

> the spirit was stirred in all of them; the beautiful-maned horses
>   turned their chariots around, for in their hearts they foresaw
>   pains.
> The charioteers were dumbstruck, when they saw the
>   unwearying fire
> over the head of the great-hearted son of Peleus terrifyingly
>   blazing, which the goddess grey-eyed Athene had kindled.
> Three times brilliant Achilles shouted loudly over the ditch,
> and three times the Trojans and their renowned allies were
>   thrown into panicked disorder.
> Then and there twelve of their best men perished
> among their own chariots and spears.
>
> (18.223–31)

The aegis, the supernatural fire, and the divinely enhanced
shout are miraculous, sublime emblems of Achilles' transcendent power and personality that make it possible for the Greeks
to carry the body of Patroklos back to their camp. From this
point to the end of the poem, Achilles is sustained by the gods
in such a way that he seems more a divine force than a human
one. This is the opposite, complementary side of the repeated
representations of him as dead. Described as dead, he is less
than a mortal; described as daemonic, he is far greater. In both
ways he has ceased to be human and can no longer be measured by the same standards as other heroes, whether Greek
or Trojan.

As the body of Patroklos is brought back to Achilles, Homer
tells us, Hera "sent the sun / toward the streams of Ocean,
though it was unwilling to go"(18.239–40). This setting of the
sun "signifies the end of Hektor's triumph."[18] At 11.192–94
(= 11.207–9), Zeus had promised him

> . . . triumphant power
> to keep on killing until he reaches the well-benched ships
> and the sun sinks and sacred darkness comes over.

Now his day is done, and Achilles, who will slay him, is ascendant. Accordingly, at this juncture we hear Hektor refusing Poulydamas' advice to retreat into the city and making his vain assertion that he will stand against Achilles—a refusal and assertion which Homer explicitly designates as mad (18.310–11). Without Zeus' help, Hektor is only human, and no human can stand against the increasingly daemonic son of Peleus. Homer indicates how transformed, by ordinary standards of the poem and especially by his own standards, Achilles now is by making him savagely threaten to "cut the throats of twelve glorious children of the Trojans" at Patroklos' pyre after bringing back the arms and head of Hektor (18.334–37).

Achilles' divinely enhanced power and fury are further marked in Book 19 by his refusal to join the rest of the Greeks in eating before they march out to do battle. On the one hand, he no longer is a man who eats, and to this degree is no longer a mortal.[19] On the other hand, he has no place in the community of the army, for whom a meal is a shared social ritual. When Odysseus, almost as a choric voice, asserts the need for the army to eat so that they will be physically able to fight for a whole day (19.155–72) and exhorts Agamemnon to produce Briseis and all the gifts he had promised in Book 9 so that the requirements of propriety and social form will be fully and formally satisfied (19.172–83), Achilles could not care less. He already had said that it would have been better if Briseis had died on the day he captured her (19.56–60) and that he was not concerned about the gifts (19.146–47). Now he tells Agamemnon:

> For my part, I
> now urge the sons of the Achaians to make war
> without eating, fasting, and at sunset
> to prepare a great meal, after we have paid back the outrage.
> Before then, there is no way that either food or drink will go
>   down
> *my* throat, at least, since my comrade has perished,
> who in my shelter torn by the sharp bronze
> lies dead, turned toward the forecourt, and around him the
>   comrades

> are mourning. Food and drink are no concern to my mind,
> but slaughter is, and blood, and the painful groaning of men.
> 　　　　　　　　　　　　　　　　　　　　(19.205–14)

Odysseus insists, in the name of ordinary human needs and of what is socially practical, on having his way: too many men, he says, die in war to mourn by fasting; we have to bury them "weeping for a day, [then] making the heart pitiless" (19.229) and get on with eating and drinking so we can fight the enemy. But Achilles can think only of his own particular sorrow and his need for revenge; while the others dine, he remains apart. At Zeus' suggestion, Athene instills nektar and ambrosia into his breast so that he does not grow hungry (19.345–54)—a clear indication of how far he has gone beyond ordinary humanity in the direction of the daemonic.[20]

Another such indication is the armor which Hephaistos forges for Achilles at Thetis' request. When she delivers it to Achilles,

> . . . the decorated armor clashed loudly.
> Trembling took hold of all the Myrmidons, nor did anyone else
> 　　dare
> to look directly at it, but they shrank back in fear. But Achilles
> looked, and as he looked, anger entered into him even more,
> 　　and his eyes
> shone forth from under his eyelids like a blaze,
> and he rejoiced to hold in his hands the god's glorious gifts.
> 　　　　　　　　　　　　　　　　　　　　(19.13–18)

When he puts on this new armor, his teeth grind and his eyes again flash like the blaze of fire (19.365–66). The light reflected from his shield reaches to heaven (19.379), like the fire Athene had kindled over his head (18.206, 214).

The shield is described in detail in a beautiful ecphrasis at 18.478–608.[21] It contains on it the entire cosmos—sun, moon, stars—but Homer's emphasis is on the human world within which, as it were, the events of the *Iliad* take place. The similes in the *Iliad* often move from the world of war to the everyday world of peaceful human life and then return from this contrasting realm to the plain of Troy, "relieving and heightening the tragic impression of the whole."[22] So, too, the description of the shield that is to be carried by Achilles in his *aristeia* in

Books 20 and 21 places this *aristeia* and the entire war in a larger setting and views them from an explicitly artistic perspective of generalized human life that makes them seem not only heroic but also tragic. Yet the similes, though functionally akin to one another, differ widely; each is chosen only for its particular place in the poem. In contrast, the images on the shield are related to one another and arranged into a coherent description of human reality—including the reality of war, which is absent from the similes precisely because they stand in contrast to it.[23] Hephaistos fills the shield with contrasting scenes of war and peace, city and country, sowing and harvesting, working and dancing.[24] He shows the joy and fruitfulness of life as well as its conflicts and sorrows. These scenes are appropriate to all the warriors in the *Iliad*, but especially so to Achilles: "At the highest moment of his glory and his sorrow, strong, young and beautiful, and so near death, the hero goes to fight his battle with a shield on which Hephaistos has emblazoned both the sweetness and uncertainty of life."[25]

The shield is especially appropriate to Achilles in other ways, too. In the first place its manufacture is closely bound up with his mortality: Thetis prefaces her appeal to Hephaistos with a lament for her having had to marry Peleus and "endure the bed of a mortal man / very much against my will" (18.433–34), a compulsion that is, as it were, the precondition of Achilles' mortality. In the same words as in her earlier complaint to the Nereids (18.56–60 = 437–41), she speaks of having given birth to a son "outstanding among heroes . . . / . . . whom I shall not receive again / returning homeward into the house of Peleus." When Hephaistos promises that he will provide "beautiful armor" for Achilles, which will be wondered at by whoever sees it, he says, "Would that in this way I could hide him far away / from sorrowful death, when his dire doom comes upon him" (18.464–65).

Furthermore, many of the details of the shield are thematically connected to events elsewhere in the *Iliad* and to Achilles as its hero.[26] For example, the women and old men of the besieged city watching from the wall suggest the Trojans' situation, and the battle to drag off dead bodies (18.539–40) calls to mind similar fighting in the poem, especially over the body of

Patroklos in Book 17. In particular, one of the scenes created by Hephaistos shows two men quarreling over the compensation (*poinē*, "payment," 18.498) for a dead man:

> One man, making a declaration to the community, was saying that he paid [the other] back in full, but he [the other] was refusing to take anything.[27]

(18.499–500)

This total inflexibility on the part of the second man recalls that of Achilles in Book 9, where the word used by Ajax (9.633, 636) for the payment accepted for the death of a brother or son also is *poinē*. It resonates, too, with Achilles' sense at 18.79–82 that nothing in the world can make up for the death of Patroklos as well as with his subsequent savagery in battle and refusal to return Hektor's body for ransom.

The description of the shield comes at a point in the *Iliad* after Achilles has decided on his own death and before he goes out to avenge Patroklos by killing Hektor in the poem's climactic battle. It forms an interval of calm in a world of heroic passion and fury, and its emphasis on the beauty of Hephaistos' artwork contrasts strongly with the increasingly savage fighting in Books 16–17 and 20–21. By temporarily setting aside Achilles and the events of the poem and describing the greater world beyond the plain of Troy, Homer clarifies the terrible disparity between the full range of human life and the transcendent yet pathetically limited heroism of the hero who carries the shield into battle. The shield is both the result of and a compensation for Achilles' suffering; its detached, objective, cosmic beauty arises from his personal tragedy. But, as W. Marg notes, it means nothing to Achilles himself, who is so absorbed in his own grief and anger that he registers no appreciation whatsoever of its beauty and meaning. Hephaistos says whoever of humans sees it will admire it (18.466–67). In the same way, the *Iliad* as a whole, while grounded in the sufferings of the Greeks and Trojans, evokes admiration from us, those humans who hear or read it. Both the poem and the shield are transformations of human experience into sublime art that, in the words of one formula, is a "wonder to behold."[28] As J. T. Sheppard said, the tragically significant "pattern" of the shield is, in brief compass, "the pattern of the *Iliad*."[29]

2

From a purely formal point of view, a description of armor and of a hero arming himself prepared an audience familiar with the conventions of traditional oral poetry for the hero's subsequent *aristeia*.[30] But, as K. Reinhardt asks, what would such an audience have made of the unparalleled description of Achilles' shield?[31] Achilles does not put on his armor until 19.364–98; his *aristeia* does not begin until 20.75. In his description of the shield Homer has exploited the poetic convention to make his audience understand not only that Achilles' *aristeia* would be greater than those of other heroes but also that it would be more meaningful.

Before the fighting begins in Book 20, Homer again emphasizes the certainty of Achilles' imminent death both in the hero's own mind and as an objective reality. At 19.315–37, while the Greeks are breakfasting before going out to fight, Achilles addresses the dead Patroklos. Recalling how they used to eat together prior to a battle, he reiterates that now he will fast

> in longing for you; since there is nothing worse I could suffer,
> not even if I should learn that my father had died,
> who must now in Phthia be shedding a tender tear
> for the lack of a son like me, while in a foreign land
> for the sake of Helen who causes men to shudder I make war
>   on the Trojans;
> or if I learned of the death of my son who is being raised in
>   Skyros,
> if, in fact, godlike Neoptolemos is still living.
> Previously my heart in my breast expected
> that I alone would perish away from horse-pasturing Argos
> here in Troy, but that you would return to Phthia,
> so that in a swift, dark ship you might bring
> that child of mine from Skyros and show him each of those
>   things—
> my property and slaves and my great, high-roofed house.
> Since by now I think that Peleus either must altogether
> be dead, or else that he is barely alive to sorrow
> in his hateful old age, and that he is constantly awaiting

the painful news about me, when he will learn that I am dead.
So he spoke weeping. . . .

(19.321–37)

In these lines Achilles is absorbed with thoughts of death: the death of Patroklos, of himself, of his father, even of his own son. His knowledge that nothing worse can happen to him sets him apart from everyone else in the *Iliad*.[32] This alienation is more extreme than it was earlier in the poem, when he could share his wrathful isolation with Patroklos and envision bad news from home for both of them (16.12–16). Homer's audience would rightly have expected the most terrible deeds of warfare from an Achilles who is so utterly cut off from the human community and who has nothing left to lose.

Achilles' death is prophesied yet again at the end of Book 19 in a striking, even uncanny, way; his response to this prophecy sums up his attitude as he is about to begin his *aristeia*. When he calls chidingly to his horses not to leave him dead on the battlefield as they left Patroklos, the "flashing-footed" Xanthos miraculously replies that it was not their fault that Patroklos was slain and his armor captured by the Trojans:

> We two could run together with the blast of the West Wind,
> which they say is the swiftest; but for you,
> it is your portion to be conquered mightily by both a man and a
> god.

(19.415–17)

Achilles responds:

> Xanthos, why are you prophesying my death? You needn't.
> I myself know that it is my portion to perish here,
> far away from my dear father and mother. But all the same
> I shall not leave off until the Trojans have their fill of my
> fighting.

(19.420–23)

The Trojan one most expects to have his fill of Achilles' fighting is Hektor, whom Achilles was most eager to meet in battle (20.75–78). But the two do not encounter one another until Book 22, except for a brief moment when Hektor comes forward to oppose him, moved by the sight of his brother Polydoros, whom Achilles has speared, "falling to the ground, holding his guts in his hands" (20.420). After the two taunt one another and Achilles springs forward for the kill, Apollo rescues Hektor by hiding him in a cloud; the frustrated Achilles goes on to kill other Trojans (20.429–54). Homer delays the killing of Hektor so that it comes as the climax of Achilles' rout of the Trojan army.[33] This allows him to portray the fury and prowess of Achilles as going far beyond anything done by Diomedes, Agamemnon, Patroklos, or Hektor himself in their earlier *aristeiai*.

Achilles' slaughter of the Trojans begins at 20.381, after an inconclusive duel with Aineias, whose rescue by Poseidon, like Hektor's by Apollo, shows that the greatest Trojan warriors are unable to survive combat with Achilles without the help of the gods. Aineias' fated survival and destined progeny of kings (20.302–8) stand in marked contrast to Achilles' imminent death. Achilles' *aristeia* is characterized both by the unparalleled variety of wounds with which he destroys his victims and by Homer's concentration on his unrelenting fury. From 20.378 to the death of Hektor in Book 22, no other mortal on either side kills an enemy. In Book 20 Achilles kills fifteen Trojans in succession, six with blows to the head or neck—a much higher proportion of such wounds than usual. He is utterly ruthless, with neither patience for suppliants nor inclination to spare life. He has virtually ceased to be human both physically and ethically; he has become a force of sheer destructive energy, annihilating whatever gets in his way:

> As a fire that humans can't cope with rages through the deep
> glens
> of a dry-wooded mountain, and the depths of the forest are set
> ablaze,
> and in every direction the driving wind rolls on the flame,
> so in every direction Achilles rushed with his spear like an
> immortal,
> harrying them as they were being killed, and the dark earth
> flowed with blood.
>
> (20.490–94)

Book 20 ends with another simile that expresses even more eloquently what Achilles has become:

As when a man yokes together broad-foreheaded male oxen
to crush white barley on a well-founded threshing-floor,
and quickly the barley is stripped under the feet of the loud-
     bellowing oxen,
so under great-hearted Achilles the single-hoofed horses
were trampling corpses and shields alike, and the axle beneath
was all spattered with blood, and the rims which went around
     the chariot,
which drops from the horses' hooves and from the chariot
     wheels
were striking. He was eager to win the boast of triumph,
the son of Peleus, and his unconquerable hands were
     spattered with gore.
                                        (20.495–503)

This vision of Achilles' overwhelming power, impressive in itself, is all the more effective when we realize that the destruction he is wreaking is expressed in terms of threshing, an activity associated positively with fertility and life, as the threshed
barley is used to produce sustaining food. The man who had
been, in his own words, a "fruitless burden on the fertile
land"(18.104) now is a thresher, but the results, though per-
sonally productive or fruitful, are at the same time destructive
and fruitless. This figurative negation of fertility and life recalls
Achilles' oath at 1.234–37

by this scepter, which will never grow leaves and branches,
since first it left its stock in the mountains,
and it will not bloom again, for the bronze stripped off
both leaves and bark. . . .

Both the scepter and the simile of the threshing oxen are emblems of Achilles' tragedy: he is fruitful, productive, and most
himself only when he is associated with the destruction of life
and the perversion of activities that should sustain life.

After the slaughter of the fifteen Trojans and the similes of
the forest fire and threshing oxen, half of the Trojans escape
over the plain to the city, while Achilles drives the other half
into the river Skamandros and plunges in after them to wreak
havoc with his sword. As Homer says,

He planned evil actions in his mind,
and he struck, turning in succession from one to another.

(21.19–20)

After Achilles captures twelve Trojans to sacrifice on Patroklos'
pyre, he meets a son of Priam, Lykaon, whom he had once captured and sold into slavery.[34] Lykaon had been ransomed by a
friend, then made his way back to Troy and his father's home.
There twelve days later "a god threw him into the hands of
Achilles" (21.47). Lykaon's appearance when he meets Achilles is such as to arouse great sympathy: he is

naked, without helmet and shield, and he didn't have a spear,
but he had thrown them all away on the ground, for the sweat
    was wearying him
as he escaped from the river, and exhaustion had overcome his
    knees.

(21.50–52)

But Achilles, though surprised, is not at all touched by his appearance and decides to let him "taste the point of my spear"
to see if he can return from Hades as he did from overseas. As
Achilles prepares to stab him, Lykaon eludes the spear, which
passes over his shoulder, and, crouching at Achilles' feet, em-
braces his knees in the posture of a suppliant. The ensuing conversation between the two speaks volumes:

"I take your knees, Achilles; have respect for me and pity me.
I am in the position of a suppliant, O loved of Zeus, who
    should be respected.
Beside you first I tasted the bread of Demeter,
on the day when you took me prisoner in the well-founded
    orchard,
and bringing me away from my father and friends you sent me
to holy Lemnos, and I was worth a hundred oxen to you.
Just now I was ransomed for three times as much, and this
    dawn
is the twelfth, since I came to Ilion.
· ·
And now there will be evil for me here, for I do not think
that I shall escape your hands, since a god brought me to them.
I will tell you something else, and you take it to your heart:
do not kill me, since I am not from the same womb as Hektor,

who slew your strong and gentle comrade."
Thus the glorious son of Priam spoke to him,
supplicating him in words, but he heard the pitiless voice:
"Fool, don't propose a ransom to me or go on speaking;
before Patroklos met his apportioned day,
then it was my heart's way to spare
the Trojans, and I took many alive and sent them away.
But now there is not one who shall escape death, whomever a
     god
may throw into my hands before Ilion, not one
of all the Trojans, and beyond all others, not one of the children
     of Priam.
But friend, die, you too. Why are you sorrowing so?
Patroklos died too, who was much better than you.
Do you not see what kind of man I am, how fine and great?
And I am the son of a noble father, and the mother who gave
     birth to me is a goddess.
Still death is upon me too and my overpowering portion;
there will be a dawn or an evening or a midday,
when someone shall take the life from me too in the fighting,
either by hurling a spear or with an arrow shot from a
     bowstring."

                                   (21.74–81, 91–114)

This speech, as E. T. Owen has said, presents "the various aspects of Achilles as a unity, by combining them in one complex of tortured feeling—his ruthlessness and brutality. . . , his strange compassion that broadens into a vision of the ruthlessness of life itself and of the splendid, pitiable futility of the human adventure, which he recognizes with unflinching clarity and which he symbolizes."[35] Achilles' "ruthlessness and brutality" come from his *mēnis*, his "strange compassion" from his *philotēs*. He does not speak sarcastically when he addresses Lykaon as "friend" (*philos*, 21.106). Rather, he invites the Trojan youth to join him in the only solidarity and shared humanity that mean anything to him, the solidarity of their shared mortality, the solidarity of death. In effect he says, "You appeal to me as a suppliant, as one with whom you have broken bread, to show you mercy. I shall do what I can for you, I shall show you the only mercy I know, I shall treat you, *philos*, as I treat myself: I shall kill you." In Achilles' vision, human solidarity and deadly hatred have been fused in a will toward death for

Hektor and all the Trojans and for himself. As C. H. Whitman says, "There is little rancor. . . , only an engrossing vision of death, which sweeps aside what are now mere trivialities— mercy, ransom, and hope."[36] Nevertheless, the immediate objects of his fury are the Trojans. After he flings the dead Lykaon into the river for the fishes to feed on, he exclaims:

> Die on, all of you, till we reach the city of sacred Ilion,
> you fleeing and I cutting you down from behind.
> Nor will your fair-flowing, silver-eddying river
> help you, to whom you have long been sacrificing large
>   numbers of bulls,
> and for whom you drown single-hoofed horses in its eddies.
> But even so, die all an evil doom, until all of you
> pay for the slaughter of Patroklos and the devastation of the
>   Achaians,
> whom you slew by the swift ships when I was far away.
>   (21.128–35)

In Whitman's words, "Achilles speaks like the very angel of death; death only is purity."[37] In fact, Achilles is to attain to an even greater "purity" in his killing of Hektor, where he neither recalls his previous clemency nor addresses his enemy as *philos*. For all its brutality, the scene with Lykaon serves to remind us of the hero's humanity and tenderness, so that we realize not only what he has lost with the gentle Patroklos but also how much further into alienation and death he enters when he slays Hektor and, with him, himself.

Before bringing Hektor and Achilles together in their final duel, Homer modulates from the grisly reality of Achilles' slaughter of the Trojans through his battle with the river to the conflict among the gods. The transition is artful: the next human victim of Achilles, Asteropaios, boasts at length of his descent from the broad-flowing river Axios, and is strengthened for combat by Skamandros, who has been angered by Achilles' slaughter of Trojan warriors in his stream. When Achilles kills Asteropaios after being grazed in the elbow (which would again remind an audience familiar with a mythological tradition of his invulnerability that in the *Iliad* he is mortal and vulnerable), he boasts of his own descent from Zeus and of the superiority of Zeus to all rivers. Compared with other mortals,

Achilles stands out in his greatness as if he were the son of Zeus himself. But after Achilles dwells on his divine lineage, when the river god rises to oppose him in earnest as he is slaying the followers of Asteropaios, we are made aware once again of the hero's mortal limits.

At 21.213 Homer says that Skamandros spoke to Achilles "in the appearance of a man," but when he fights against him, he does so as a river, rising against him in a wave and rolling across the plain trying to drown him (21.234–71). Such a natural divine intervention is unparalleled elsewhere in the poem; the poet seems to have moved into a realm of pure symbol when he tells how at Hera's request Hephaistos kindles a great fire and defeats the river in a combat of elements that anticipates and symbolizes the Greeks' conquest of Troy.[38] As the breath of Hephaistos sweeps the fire across the plain, it burns everything in its path—corpses, trees, shrubbery along the river bank—and afflicts the eels and fish in the boiling water. The effect is elevated and reminiscent of the passages at 20.61–65 and 13.18–19, 27–29, which "Longinus" quotes as instances of the sublime.[39] After the river has surrendered to Hephaistos, conflict erupts among the other gods. Although those on the Greek side are victorious, again anticipating the ultimate triumph over the Trojans, the overall effect of the battle is comic. It stands as a moment of frivolity and humor between the terrible *aristeia* of Achilles and his killing of Hektor. As such, it emphasizes by contrast the tragic seriousness of these human conflicts, in particular of the impending climactic duel between Hektor and Achilles.

The slaying of Hektor comes as the fulfillment of the expectations raised since the beginning of the poem that Achilles would do something tremendous to justify his reputation as far and away the greatest warrior in either army.[40] By killing Hektor and thus, in effect, conquering Troy and winning the war (22.56–57, 410–11), Achilles satisfies these expectations. Furthermore, the terror he inspires in Priam and Hektor, the utter inhumanity with which he responds to Hektor's suggestion that they agree in advance to return for burial the body of whoever is killed, and the savage hatred that leads him both to spurn the dying Hektor's final plea for burial and to treat his corpse so foully, are a fitting climax to the fury that has marked his words and actions since his reentry into battle.

The imagery of fire and brightness that has been associated with the irresistible Achilles from his appearance at the ditch (18.203–25) through his *aristeia* is continued in Book 22.[41] When Priam sees him "rushing over the plain" toward the city, he is

> . . . shining, like the star
> that comes in the autumn, whose conspicuous brightness
> shines out among the many stars in the dark of night,
> the star that they call Orion's dog.
> This is the brightest star in the sky; it is established as a sign of
>   evil,
> and brings great fever for pitiful mortals.
> So brightly shone the bronze on Achilles' chest as he was
>   running.
>
> (22.26–32)

This image of the baleful Sirius is picked up by the picture of Achilles charging to kill Hektor:

> As a star comes among the other stars in the dark of night,
> the Evening Star, which stands as the most beautiful star in the
>   heaven,
> so was the shining from the sharp spear which Achilles
> shook in his right hand, intending evil toward the brilliant
>   Hektor,
> looking over his beautiful flesh to see where it would most give
>   way.
>
> (22.317–21)

Between these passages, Hektor sees Achilles approaching,

> the equal of the lord of battles, Enualios of the shining helmet,
> shaking above his right shoulder the Pelian ash spear
> which was so terrifying; the bronze shone around him like the
>   glare
> of blazing fire or of the rising sun.
>
> (22.132–35)

This deadly shining so shakes him that he can no longer await Achilles and flees before him. "The flight of Hector is the final satisfaction of what we expect of Achilles the warrior";[42] nothing could more effectively express how incomparably fearsome

and powerful Achilles is at the height of his wrath than the om-
inous brightness that even Hektor cannot endure.

It is, of course, his wrath that makes him so pitiless and inhuman. The humane detachment is absent that had led him to
call Lykaon "friend" (21.106) and in earlier days to bury Andromache's father, Eëtion, with reverence (6.417) and to take prisoners alive (11.104–6, 112; 21.100–102). When Hektor proposes
that they agree that the body of the victim be returned by the
victor for burial, Achilles replies:

> Hektor, you whose deeds I can never forget, don't talk to me of
>   agreements:
> as there are no trustworthy oaths between men and lions,
> but they always and unceasingly intend evil to one another,
> so it is not possible that you and I have solidarity [philēmenai]
>   with one another, and for us two
> there will be no oaths at all, before one of us, at least, falls
> and gluts Ares, the warrior who is steady under the shield,
>   with his blood.
>
> (22.261–67)

After the duel he refuses his dying enemy's final plea to ransom his body for burial with a climactic outburst of savagery
that is as extreme as anything in Homer:

> Dog, don't supplicate me by my knees or my parents;
> I wish that my spirit and anger would impel me
> to cut off your meat and eat it raw myself, for what you have
>   done to me,
> just as there is no one who can keep the dogs away from your
>   head. . . .
>
> (22.345–48)

Elsewhere in the *Iliad*, only when Zeus accuses Hera of wanting to eat the Trojans raw (4.34–36) and when Hecuba in her
grief and fury at Achilles wishes she could "grow into the midst
of his liver and devour it" (24.212–13) is there any mention of
cannibalism. It is clear from the Cyclops episode in the *Odyssey*
how uncivilized cannibalism is, and Hesiod (*Works and Days*
276–80) explicitly distinguishes humans, who have "justice"
(*dikē*), from "fish and wild beasts and winged birds" who "eat
one another." Just as Achilles, in rejecting agreements and
oaths, had removed himself both from ordinary civilized stan-

dards and from his own earlier humane standards of behavior, so in wishing he could devour Hektor's meat raw he puts himself outside the ways of distinctively human culture, as defined in the poetic tradition of which the *Iliad*, like the *Odyssey* and the *Works and Days*, is a product.[43]

3

Many scholars used to consider that the *Iliad* originally ended with the killing of Hektor, which, they felt, poetically completes the story of the wrath of Achilles. These scholars held that the final two books were added by a later reviser of the poem. But there are two major reasons why an ending after Book 22, though possible in another kind of heroic poem, would be impossible for Homer's *Iliad*. Firstly, the *Iliad* is not merely such a story of killing, death, and vengeance as must have been common in the poetic tradition. Rather, it consistently and critically plays against the conventional themes and values of heroic warfare, including heroic vengeance, to develop both an appreciation of the costs as well as the rewards of such warfare and a view of human life as tragic precisely because it can only be lived within the contradictions and limitations of this heroism. If the poem were to end with the killing of Hektor, this humane, distinctively Iliadic vision would be missing, and the conclusion would be untrue to the poem's own themes and values. Secondly, at an individual level, Achilles' vengeance may be complete, but Achilles is not. Even after the death of Hektor he still is disestablished from himself and isolated from others. He remains unable to express the feelings of *philotēs*, of love and solidarity, that were part of his nature until the quarrel with Agamemnon and the death of Patroklos. Homer's poem cannot end with Achilles in this inhibited and unsympathetic alienation. Furthermore, in the light of the desperate fighting over the corpses of Sarpedon and Patroklos in Books 16 and 17 and in view of the significance attached to insuring that each receives a proper burial, the poem cannot end without a funeral for Patroklos and with Hektor lying unburied. In Books 23 and 24, Achilles is restored to his humane, social self through his role in bringing about the humanly and socially necessary ritual laments and burials of his closest friend and his most hated enemy, who, in the last analysis, have more in common as mortals than had separated them as enemies.

The only *philotēs* Achilles feels as he kills Hektor is *philotēs* for the dead Patroklos. He reminds Hektor at 22.331 that he is dying because he killed Patroklos. Later he breaks off his exhortation to the Greek army to join him in an assault on Troy with the thought that

> a corpse is lying dead beside the ships, unwept and unburied,
> Patroklos; I will never forget him as long as I am among the
>   living and my knees move;
> and if they forget the dead in Hades,
> still even there I will be mindful of my beloved comrade.
>
> (22.386–90)

When the army returns to the ships, he assures Patroklos' body, "even in the house of Hades" (23.19), that he will accomplish for him everything he had promised:

> to drag Hektor here to give to the dogs to eat raw,
> and to cut the throats before your pyre
> of twelve glorious children of the Trojans, in anger that you
>   have been killed.
>
> (23.21–23)

Once again, all that Achilles can do to express his love is to express his hatred, but now it is a corpse that he is "treating foully" (*aeikea . . . erga*, 22.395, 23.24), not a live enemy. When the prophetic words of Hektor (22.358–60) and of Patroklos' dream-image (23.80–81) again emphasize that Achilles himself is virtually dead, the self-defeating quality of his mistreatment of Hektor's corpse becomes clear.

At this point, the poem's focus shifts from the ugliness of Achilles' savagery to the pathos of his suffering. As he lies on the beach groaning for Patroklos,

> sleep took hold of him, dissolving the cares of his spirit,

sweet sleep which was poured around him—for his shining
   limbs were exhausted
from chasing Hektor toward windy Ilion.

(23.62–64)

Achilles' dream, as he sleeps, illustrates the way he remains
trapped in the contradictions of conventional heroic values.
The image of Patroklos comes to him and accuses him of "for-
getting" him now that he is dead. Of course, Achilles has had
Patroklos constantly in mind; his killing of Hektor and mistreatment of his corpse have been for Patroklos' sake. But what
Patroklos wants is burial, which is required for passage over
the river of the dead and through the gates of Hades (23.71–74).
The geography and religious doctrine are vague, but the central point is clear: Achilles is acting selfishly, in accordance with
his own needs, not those of his dead comrade. Patroklos wants
burial, eventually with Achilles for the sake of their love, but
for now simply as something all the dead must have to rest
peacefully. No conclusions are drawn from Patroklos' request
about the burial of Hektor; Achilles is in no condition to think
of his enemy's human needs. Rather, Homer dwells on Achilles' agony and wonder as he tries in vain to embrace his dead
comrade's ghost.

When Achilles presides over the funeral of Patroklos on the
following day, he really is presiding over his own funeral: eventually a single urn will hold both his and Patroklos' bones, and
when he himself is dead, the Achaians will raise a gravemound
over both of them. It even has been shown that Homer uses
several motifs and perhaps specific verses which were associated in the poetic tradition with the funeral of Achilles to describe that of Patroklos.[44] Thus his audience would have recognized even more clearly than we can to what extent Achilles
is here treated as if he were already dead. They would have
been prepared for such a poetic treatment by the earlier prophecies of his death and the diction and descriptions of him in
Books 18–22 that were appropriate to a dead man.[45] The description of Patroklos' death, in Achilles' armor and as Achilles'
surrogate, would have increased their anticipation.[46] That
scene recalls the traditional death of Achilles at the hands of
Paris and Apollo as told in the *Aithiopis* (cf. 22.358).[47]

Certainly, the reality of Achilles' death for Achilles himself is conveyed in the beautiful scene where he cuts off the hair "which he was growing long and luxuriant for the river Spercheios" (23.142):

> Spercheios, in vain my father Peleus vowed to you
> that when I returned home there to my beloved native land
> I would cut off this lock for you and perform for you a sacrifice
>   of a hundred oxen.
> .   .   .   .
> So the old man vowed, but you did not accomplish what he
>   intended.
> Now, since I am not returning to my beloved native land,
> I would present this lock to the hero Patroklos to carry away.
>   (23.144–46, 149–51)

Along with the lock, Achilles ritually and definitively cuts himself off from returning home; his hair goes to the dead and to his own element of fire rather than to the life-supporting river of his native Phthia.

In the funeral games he holds in honor of Patroklos, Achilles' mood seems to change to a controlled, detached sociability. After spending so much of the previous twenty-two books in hatred and conflict, he does not compete himself but gracefully and peacefully resolves disputes between Ajax son of Oileus and Idomeneus and between Antilochos and Menelaos, as well as the wrestling match between Telamonian Ajax and Odysseus. Himself deprived of a prize and honor early in the poem, he now awards extra prizes and honor to Nestor and Eumelos, and a first prize to Agamemnon, in a courtly and considerate fashion, so as to avoid disappointment or difficulty. Homer here modulates, as it were, between the inconsolable, hateful Achilles of Books 18–23 and the humane Achilles of the scene with Priam.

For the army as a whole (and for the audience or reader who has been absorbed in the grief for Patroklos) these games not only are part of the appropriate ritual owed to the dead hero, but they serve vividly and enjoyably to restore a sense of the characters' sheer physical gusto and glory in being alive. Achilles, however, does not share in this gusto and glory. At the beginning of Book 24 he is fruitlessly still attempting to exact revenge from Hektor's corpse for the death of Patroklos, still wanting to be paid back for what he has suffered in a way that is clearly impossible. The picture of Achilles trying to sleep,

> sometimes lying on his side, sometimes again
> on his back, and at other times prone on his face,

then arising to pace along the seashore (24.10–12) and drag Hektor around Patroklos' tomb (24.15–18), is completely naturalistic. It emphasizes the dimension of human suffering that accompanies his divine *mēnis*.

When the gods meet in their final assembly of the poem to discuss what should be done about returning Hektor's body, Apollo states clearly how Achilles' fury has put him outside the bounds of common humanity. Echoing Ajax (9.628–38) and Patroklos (16.29–35) and summarizing the impression given by Achilles' savagery both in battle and in mourning for Patroklos, he addresses the other Olympians:

> No, you gods, you wish to assist accursedly destructive
>   Achilles,
> whose mind does not take into account justice and whose
>   attitude
> is inflexible; his disposition is savage, like a lion
> who, when he has yielded to his great strength and proud
>   spirit,
> goes against the flocks of men to take a meal;
> thus Achilles has destroyed pity, nor does he have in him
> any shame, which does much harm to men yet also benefits
>   them.
> A man is bound to lose someone even dearer to him,
> either a brother from the same womb or even a son,
> but when he has wept and mourned, he lets him go,
> since the Apportioners [*Moirai*] have placed in humans a spirit
>   of endurance.
> But this man, after having taken the great heart away from
>   brilliant Hektor,
> fastens him to his horses and around his beloved comrade's
>   tomb
> keeps dragging him, though this is in no way fine or better for
>   himself.
> Let him see to it that we do not become angry with him, as
>   good as he is:

> for it is dumb earth that he is treating foully in his fury.
>
> (24.39–54)

The word *oloös* (39), translated as "accursedly destructive," indicates how far outside normal humanity Achilles now is. Only here in the poem is this word used of a person rather than a destructive force of nature or some other abstract or personified element of destruction.[48] Apollo's use of the word at this point characterizes Achilles himself as such an impersonal, destructive force. The further statement that he "has destroyed pity, nor does he have in him / any shame," humane qualities par excellence, strengthens this indication. Furthermore, Achilles is compared not simply to a lion in nature but to a lion that "goes against the flocks of men," that is, to a savage force that opposes an institution and symbol of human civilization. Apollo's climactic description of Achilles' defilement of Hektor's body, now mere dust ("dumb earth"), forcefully expresses the futility of his repeated efforts at revenge.

Just as at 1.216–18 Achilles obeys Athene's request not to kill Agamemnon, so here he immediately acquiesces in Zeus' instructions to release Hektor's body for ransom (24.139–40). As in Book 1, Thetis' visit to her son reminds us of his approaching death: when Iris reaches her in her hollow cave in the sea among the sea nymphs,

> she was bewailing the doom of her faultless son,
> who was going to perish in fertile Troy, far from his native
> land.[49]
>
> (24.85–86)

When she speaks to Achilles, she asks him how long he will keep eating his heart out in sorrow and lamentation and urges him to think of positive things in life such as food and sex,

> because you will not live long, but already
> over you stand death and your overpowering portion.
>
> (24.131–32)

Homer makes it clear once again that the Achilles who receives and consoles Priam later in the book is, for all intents and purposes, already dead; that in the agony of his suffering and the intensity of his wrath, he is psychologically and ethically beyond the human pale.

Only old Priam, in whom "Nature . . . stands on the very verge / of his confine," can reach Achilles and bring about a change in his unrelenting *mēnis*. Priam, too, is virtually dead: he saw in the death of Hektor the fall of Troy, with his sons dying, his daughters and daughters-in-law being dragged away, their infants being dashed to the ground, and himself, dead in his own doorway, being savagely devoured by the very dogs which had fed from his table and guarded his house (22.62–72). When Iris comes to convey Zeus' command that he go to the ships to ransom Hektor's body, she finds Priam with his head and neck disfigured by the dung in which he has been rolling (24.163–65). Priam's utter self-abasement and his awesome gesture of

> bringing myself to do what no other mortal on the face of the
>   earth has yet done,
> to lift to my mouth the hands of the man who killed my sons,
>   (24.505–6)

along with his appeal to Achilles to look at him, think of his own father, and "have shame before the gods and take pity on me" (24.503), reach the son of Peleus and enable him to feel the generosity and humanity, the *philotēs*, that his sorrow and anger had suppressed.[50] As the two lament together, Priam curled up at the feet of Achilles weeping for Hektor, and Achilles weeping now for his father and now for Patroklos, the two enemies virtually adopt one another as father and son. Achilles finally finds a "father" whom he can accept, one with as great or greater a need than his own for consolation and elemental human solidarity, and one who, unlike Peleus, Phoinix, and Agamemnon, his other "fathers," can help restore him to himself and to the human community from which he has been alienated.

Achilles raises Priam (24.515), accepting a suppliant as he did not and could not do in Book 9 or on the battlefield in Books 20–22.[51] Then the two share a sublime vision of the human condition, as Achilles, who had been grieving so unconsolably and unceasingly, consoles and preaches to Priam with the deepest courtesy and sympathy:

> Come, be seated on this chair, and we shall even let
> our sorrows lie quiet in our hearts, although we are grieved.

> There is nothing accomplished from numbing lamentation;
> this is the way the gods have spun for wretched mortals
> to live in sorrow, while they themselves are free from cares.
>
> (24.522–26)

Achilles goes on to tell Priam the story of the two urns on the threshold of Zeus, from which he dispenses good and evil gifts to humans, giving to some a mixed life of both good and evil, to others only evil. Like Peleus, Priam has had the mixed life, and the two old men are linked in their sorrows through Achilles: Peleus is a great king and married a goddess; but he has only one son, who will die young and do him no good as he grows old, since he is busy at Troy causing woe for Priam and his children. Achilles concludes:

> Bear up, and don't grieve in your heart unceasingly,
> since you won't accomplish anything by grieving for your son,
> and you won't bring him back to life; sooner you will suffer yet
>   another evil.
>
> (24.549–51)

The detachment and clarity with which Achilles offers his hard-won, realistic wisdom and profound sympathy to Priam recall his speech to Lykaon at 21.99–113. But in Book 21 the humane qualities of Achilles had been so transformed that all he could do to express his sympathy for his suppliant was to kill him; here the unique solidarity and humanity shared with Priam surpass even the earlier *philotēs* characteristic of Achilles before his *mēnis*. When Priam momentarily resumes the grief-stricken speech and behavior that the earlier conversation between the two had transcended—when, that is, he refuses to sit down while Hector is lying uncared-for and presses Achilles to accept the ransom he has brought and to release the body—Achilles becomes angry and can barely contain himself:

> Don't stir up my spirit any more in the midst of my sorrows,
> lest I not leave you alone, old man, even in my shelter
> and even though you are a suppliant, and I trespass against the
>   commands of Zeus.
>
> (24.568–70)

He is still the same Achilles, quick to anger (cf. 11.564), rising "like a lion" (24.572), and he is fighting against his sense of loyalty to Patroklos, to whom he apologizes passionately (24.592–95), asking his forgiveness for releasing Hektor's corpse. With the greatest tact and consideration he goes to prepare the body for Priam and keeps it out of sight, in case the old man might be unable to hold down his anger and he, in turn, might lose control and kill him.

Just as the Achilles who himself has continued to grieve and mourn urges Priam not to do so, so the Achilles who refused to eat (19.209–10, 306–7), or who has eaten only reluctantly (23.48) and at his mother's urging (24.475–76), now presses Priam to join him in a meal. In doing so he modifies the traditional legend of Niobe and uses it as a mythological example to support his exhortation by reminding Priam that she ate though her loss was even greater than his.[52] Coming from Achilles, who has suffered a similar loss (cf. 23.222–25), this exhortation is successful. The two break bread together in an expression of their shared humanity; this takes precedence over their previous enmity and acknowledges the necessities of a life that goes on even after such deep losses as they have suffered. Before they go to bed, Priam and Achilles seal their reconciliation in a "brief but inestimable moment of clarity and peace":[53]

> When they had released their desire for food and drink,
> Priam the son of Dardanos gazed in wonder at Achilles,
> at his greatness and beauty, for he was like the gods to look at.
> And Achilles in turn was gazing in wonder at Priam the son of
>   Dardanos,
> viewing his noble looks and listening to his words.
>
> (24.628–32)

This sublime moment of mutual wonder is beyond explication. Achilles and Priam view one another in the way that Hephaistos promised that mortals would view the shield of Achilles—as if they were products of divine art.[54] Only "when they had taken their pleasure in viewing one another" (24.633) does Priam tell Achilles to send him to bed so that he can sleep for the first time since Hektor was killed, since which time he has been "groaning continually and nursing infinite sorrows" (24.639). The phrase "nursing infinite sorrows" had been used by Achilles of Niobe a few lines earlier (24.617), and its repetition by Priam formally signifies his acceptance of Achilles' consolation, just as his willingness to go to bed signals his acceptance of his kindness and hospitality. Achilles, in turn, addresses him as "aged sir and beloved friend" (*geron phile*, 24.650), using the word *philos*, which previously he had spoken to a Trojan only when refusing Lykaon's supplication and calling on him to join in the solidarity of death (21.106). Here Achilles is sharing with Priam in a common humanity beyond death, or rather, in a humanity conditioned by their mortality and mutual understanding of "the way the gods have spun for wretched mortals / to live in sorrow, while they themselves are free from cares" (24.525–26).

Achilles goes on to ask Priam for how long he should delay the resumption of fighting, so that the Trojans may "pay honor with funeral rites to brilliant Hektor" (24.657). Priam requests eleven days, "and on the twelfth we shall fight, if there is necessity" (24.667). The whole scene of the meeting between the two takes place under the shadow of death—not only Hektor's death and Patroklos', but the deaths of Achilles, of Priam, and of Troy. As Kakridis has said, "For a few hours the two foes will enjoy the common boon of sleep, near one another, reconciled, passionless and carefree—in twelve days fierce war will burst out again till the fall of Troy, till Achilles is killed by Priam's son and Priam is killed by Achilles' son."[55]

The meeting between Priam and Achilles forms an appropriate end to the tragedy of the wrath of Achilles; in the words of Owen, "it restores the character of the hero to harmony with itself and us to sympathy with him."[56] But Achilles is not changed into a new and different character, either because of some inward, spiritual growth or on account of his reintegration into the human community. Rather, he is reestablished as his distinctive self—as the hero with capacities for both *philotēs* and *mēnis* he was at the beginning of Book 1. The sympathy he shows Priam is the same sympathy that led him to summon the assembly at 1.54 in an attempt to find an end to the plague. But this sympathy and Achilles' capacity for *philotēs* have been deepened both by his understanding of his own sorrow and by his realization that his tragedy is not private to himself but is Priam's tragedy as well, and a "tragedy inherent in the conditions of human life."[57]

For all his divine heroism, his brief life, and his unique prowess, Achilles is but an extreme instance of every hero in the *Iliad*
who fights for the honor and glory that will grace a transient life
with significance. But Achilles' foreknowledge of his death, the
extremity of his suffering, the intensity of his fury, and his unparalleled generosity and humanity make his tragic existence
more pathetic and more moving than the lives of other more
conventional heroes. For both the original audience and the
modern reader, Achilles embodies in purest form the characteristically Homeric conception of the tragic contradictions of
warfare and heroic life, of the potential greatness and potential
horror, the inextricably linked beauty and sorrow of human existence.

Notes to Chapter 5

[1]On "daemonic," see Chapter Four, p. 121, n. 4.

[2]See J. Th. Kakridis, *Homeric Researches* (Lund, 1949), pp. 65–95.

[3]Ibid., p. 69 n. 7.

[4]11.425, 13.508 = 17.315, 13.520 = 14.452.

[5]4.175, 5.647, 13.414, 16.541, 17.92, etc.

[6]Cf. 16.776.

[7]As E. T. Owen (*The Story of the Iliad* [1946; reprint, Ann Arbor, 1966],
p. 178) observes: "The pictorial and verbal echo seems to strengthen
and yet soften the mournfulness of the former scene." Cf. the univer-
salized lament for Prometheus in *Prometheus Bound* 406–35, as sung by
the chorus of sea nymphs, whose rise from the sea to the rocks of Scy-
thia upon hearing the sound of Prometheus being nailed to the cliff
(128–34) recalls the Nereids' emergence in Book 18.

[8]Kakridis, *Homeric Researches*, pp. 68–69. Cf. M. Alexiou, *The Ritual
Lament in Greek Tradition* (Cambridge, 1974), p. 6.

[9]On Thetis' marriage to a mortal, see Chapter Four, p. 92.

[10]See Chapter Three, p. 87, n. 29; O. M. Davidson, "Indo-European
Dimensions of Herakles in *Iliad* 19.95–133," *Arethusa* 13 (1980), pp. 197–
202.

[11]On serious combats among the gods as a thing of the past, see
Chapter Two, p. 50.

[12]2.658, 666; 5.638; 11.690; 19.98. That the formulaic phrase and the
simple name really are equivalents is made clear by 11.690, in which a
masculine participle, *elthōn*, is in grammatical agreement with this
phrase. Even though the phrase is feminine in gender, it can take this
masculine participle because it is equivalent to Herakles.

[13]E.g., "the violence of Herakles" (biē Heraklēos) 18.117; "the violence of Priam" (Priamoio biēn), 3.105; "the shaggy heart of Pylaimenes" (Pulaimeneos lasion kēr), 2.851.

[14]Herakles: the five instances mentioned in n. 13 plus Od. 11.601; Eteokles: 4.386; Iphikles: Od. 11.290, 296.

R. Schmitt, Dichtung und Dichtersprache in indogermanischer Zeit (Wiesbaden, 1967), p. 110 n. 67, referred to by G. Nagy, The Best of the Achaeans: Concepts of the Hero in Archaic Greek Poetry (Baltimore and London, 1979), p. 318 §2n2, argues that periphrases combining a noun with a proper adjective are more archaic than those combining a noun with a possessive form of a name. As Nagy notes, "In this light, the preponderance of biē plus adjective of [Herakles] over biē plus [possessive form] of [Herakles] is itself significant."

[15]Nagy, Best of the Achaeans, p. 318.

[16]Cf. Chapter Four, p. 125, n. 27.

[17]Cf. 9.592–94; Od. 8.523–30.

[18]Owen, Story of the Iliad, p. 183.

[19]Eating food (and drinking wine) are defining activities of mortals in contrast to immortal gods: cf. 5.341, 6.142, 13.322, 21.465; Od. 5.197, 8.222, 9.89 = 10.101.

[20]On the significance of nektar and ambrosia, see Chapter Two, pp. 52–53 with n. 21.

[21]An ecphrasis is a literary description of a work of art. Ecphrases may describe actual works or, in the words of J. Th. Kakridis, Homer Revisited (Lund, 1971), p. 109, may be "freely conceived descriptions of works of art, which do not really exist, . . . imagined ecphrases." It is now generally agreed that Homer, though he may have had in mind contemporary decorated shields, was not describing the actual decoration on any real shield. As Kakridis says (p. 108), "Achilles' shield is a creation conceived in Homer's imagination alone." Cf. W. Schadewaldt, Von Homers Welt und Werk, 4th ed. (Stuttgart, 1965), p. 357: "Der Schild des Achilleus ist nicht in einer wirklichen Werkstatt, sondern der Gedankenwerkstatt Homers entstanden."

[22]F. M. Stawell, Homer and the Iliad (London, 1910), p. 69, quoted by Owen, Story of the Iliad, p. 187.

[23]See W. Marg, Homer über die Dichtung (Münster, 1957), p. 29, who refers to the shield as "dem Bild der Menschenwelt als ganzem."

[24]K. Reinhardt, Die Ilias und ihr Dichter (Göttingen, 1961), p. 401. Cf. Schadewaldt, Welt und Werk, p. 363.

[25]J. T. Sheppard, The Pattern of the Iliad (1922; reprint, London and New York, 1969), p. 10.

[26]See Ø. Andersen, "Some Thoughts on the Shield of Achilles,"

Symbolae Osloenses 51 (1976), pp. 5–18; O. Taplin, "The Shield of Achilles within the *Iliad*," *Greece and Rome* 27 (1980), pp. 1–21.

[27]On problems of translation and interpretation, see Andersen, "Some Thoughts," pp. 11–16; L. Muellner, *The Meaning of Homeric EUCHOMAI Through Its Formulas* (Innsbruck, 1976), pp. 105–6, followed by Nagy, *Best of the Achaeans*, p. 109.

[28]*Homer über die Dichtung*, pp. 32, 36–37.

[29]Sheppard, *Pattern of the Iliad*, pp. 8–10, 204–5.

[30]See Chapter 3, pp. 80–82.

[31]Cf. Reinhardt, *Die Ilias und ihr Dichter*, p.410.

[32]This is true with the exception perhaps of Priam after the death of Hektor. Even Andromache, after Hektor's death, anticipates the fall of Troy, her own enslavement, and the murder of her son (24.728–35), but for Achilles, after the death of Patroklos, there is nothing worse to anticipate.

[33]Owen, *Story of the Iliad*, p. 207.

[34]On the Lykaon scene, see J. Th. Kakridis, *Homerika Themata* (Athens, 1954), pp. 36–42 (in Greek); G. Strasburger, "Die kleinen Kämpfer der Ilias" (diss. Frankfurt-am-Main, 1954), p. 85; W. Marg, "Kampf und Tod in der Ilias," *Würzburger Jahrbücher für die Altertumswissenschaft*, n.s., 2 (1976), pp. 15–17.

[35]Owen, *Story of the Iliad*, p. 209.

[36]C. H. Whitman, *Homer and the Heroic Tradition* (Cambridge, Mass., 1958), p. 207.

[37]Ibid.

[38]See ibid., pp. 139–41. M. N. Nagler, *Spontaneity and Tradition: A Study in the Oral Art of Homer* (Berkeley and Los Angeles, 1974), pp. 149–51, suggests that, "The river fight is best appreciated not only as a combat myth . . . but also as a flood story of the exact type that Sumerian and Babylonian documents have made dramatically familiar to scholars. . . ." "The basic issue treated by this type of myth . . . is the life and death of the race itself, the continued evolution of humankind, in a word, destiny" (pp. 150–51). Nagler sees Skamandros as representing, on different levels, "chthonian monster, death god, and chaos demon," and his defeat as the reassertion of unity, order, and the dominance of the sky god, "the guarantor of cosmic order, whose victory is certain" (pp. 151–52). A summary cannot do justice to the subtle ways in which Nagler attempts to connect this Mesopotamian motif with the central themes and narrative patterns of the *Iliad*. See pp. 149–66 of his book.

[39]See Chapter Two, pp. 51–52.

[40]Owen, *Story of the Iliad*, p. 223.

[41]See Whitman, *Homer*, pp. 138–44.

[42]Owen, *Story of the Iliad*, p. 229.

[43]On the significance of Achilles' cannibalistic impulse, see C. P. Segal, *The Theme of the Mutilation of the Corpse in the Iliad*, Mnemosyne Supplements, no. 17 (Leiden, 1971), pp. 40–41.

[44]Some of these motifs can make sense only in the context of Achilles' death, e.g., Iris' fetching the North and West winds to fan the pyre of Patroklos, which wouldn't burn (23.192–217). In the *Aithiopis*, which contained a description of Achilles' funeral, Achilles had killed Memnon, the winds' half-brother, and it would have been perfectly appropriate for them to refuse to help burn his body. See Kakridis, *Homeric Researches*, pp. 75–83. For the *Aithiopis*, see Proclus, *Chrestomatheia* 2, in H. G. Evelyn-White, ed. and trans., *Hesiod, The Homeric Hymns and Homerica* (1936; reprint, Cambridge, Mass. and London, 1959), pp. 508–9.

[45]See above, pp. 129–32.

[46]Perhaps, too, as Nagy, *Best of the Achaeans*, p. 33 with §8n2, suggests, a Homeric audience may have felt that "The death of Patroklos is a function of his being the *therapōn* of Achilles: this word *therapōn* is a prehistoric Greek borrowing from the Anatolian languages (most likely sometime in the second millennium B.C.) where it had meant 'ritual substitute.' " Patroklos is called Achilles' *therapōn* at 16.165 = 17.388, 16.244, 653; 17.164, 271; 18.152; 23.90. The first three passages occur after Patroklos has donned Achilles' armor, the others after he has been killed in it. Although the word clearly had lost its original meaning in ordinary Homeric usage, this meaning might have remained latent, to be "triggered" by an appropriate formulaic context.

[47]See Kakridis, *Homeric Researches*, pp. 85–88.

[48]A destructive force of nature: fire (13.629, 15.605) and night (16.567, 22.102); an abstract noun signifying an element of destruction: toil (16.568), war (3.133), rout (11.71, 16.771), madness (9.305); such a noun personified: *Moira* (16.849, 21.83, 22.5) and *Kēr*, "Death Spirit" (13.665, 18.535). *Oloös* also describes Agamemnon's mind when he quarrels with Achilles (*phrenes*, 1.342), Achilles' heart (*kēr*, 14.139), and the hands of the Achaians sacking Troy as they are envisioned by Priam (22.65).

[49]Here again, death is juxtaposed with a fruitless fertility.

[50]Shame and pity, of course, are the two qualities that Apollo had said were missing in Achilles (24.44).

[51]Cf. 20.463 (Tros); 21.34–135 (Lykaon); 22.338–54 (Hektor).

[52]As usual in Homer's mythological examples, the modifications are designed to adapt the myth more closely to the circumstances of the *Iliad*. Thus, for example, the gods perform the burial of Niobe's

children as they bring about that of Hektor, and Niobe eats because Priam is to eat. See Kakridis, *Homeric Researches*, pp. 96–105; M. M. Willcock, "Mythological Paradeigma in the *Iliad*," *Classical Quarterly*, n.s., 14 (1964), pp. 141–42.

[53]Nagler, *Spontaneity*, p. 196.

[54]Cf. the use of *thaumazein*, "to wonder," in 18.467 and 24.629 and 631.

[55]Kakridis, *Homeric Researches*, p. 105.

[56]Owen, *Story of the Iliad*, p. 248.

[57]Ibid., p. 247.

6

Hektor and Troy

1

The destruction of Troy through Odysseus' ruse of the wooden horse was known to Homer and his audience from the poetic tradition, in which it was the culminating heroic achievement of the Trojan War.[1] Although the *Iliad* does not narrate the fall of Troy, it does, as I have explained in Chapter One, incorporate this event symbolically both by the general superiority of the Greek gods and heroes to those of the Trojans and, in particular, by the death of Hektor "who alone protected Ilion" (6.403). When Priam fearfully anticipates Hektor's death, he foresees as its consequence the sack of the city and his own grisly end (22.56–76); when Hektor is slain, the people of Troy

> were held in grief and wailing down along the city.
> It was most like what it would have been, if all
> beetling Ilion were being consumed utterly by fire.
>
> (22.409–11)

The destruction of the city is repeatedly stated as the collective goal of the Greek army. It is, as it were, the social correlative of the individual hero's pursuit of honor and glory. But Homer endows it with even greater meaning by his description and depiction of Troy as a socially developed community of men

and women, parents and children, younger and older generations, whose annihilation is felt as the destruction of a rich human culture and civilization by the equally human but far more
savage Greek army. When Hektor is killed by Achilles, he falls
not only as the leading Trojan warrior but as the son of Priam
and Hecuba, the husband of Andromache and father of
Astyanax, and the chief exemplar of a familial solidarity and
loyalty that in the *Iliad* are characteristically Trojan.[2] Much of
the tragic power of the *Iliad* derives from a paradox: the activity
that has the highest value, the individual and collective attain-
ment of honor and glory by both Trojans and Greeks, involves
destroying a city that represents all that is domestically and socially most humane and civilized—a city much like the home
cities the Greek warriors left behind.

This paradox would have been especially pointed for Homer's audience in the late eighth century B.C. For Troy, although in the *Iliad* it is represented as a community of the bygone heroic age of poetic tradition, is frequently called a *polis*,
or "city-state." In the eighth century, the *polis* was emerging in
Greece as the major form of independent social and political
organization; it remained so for the next four centuries.[3] At the
heart of the city-state were family and community loyalties of
the kind shown by the Trojans and especially by Hektor. Homer's eighth-century audience would have recognized in Troy,
mutatis mutandis, many of its own social forms and values, and
felt keenly the tragedy of its eventual annihilation. Insofar as
readers today are heirs to the cultural and communal values of
the city-state and consider loyalty and responsibility to family
and community as significant virtues, they too are moved by
the destruction of Hektor and Troy and by the contradictions in
the traditional heroic value system that make this destruction a
desired end.[4]

Even in merely physical terms, Troy is described in the *Iliad*
as a product of human labor and cultural achievement. This is
reflected in many of its traditional epithets: it is "broad" (*eu-
rus*), a "well-founded" (*euktimenon*) and "well-inhabited"—
that is, "populous" (*eu naiomenon*) citadel—with "wide" and
"well-founded streets" (*euruaguian, euktimenas . . . aguias*). It is
especially distinguished by its high, strong walls, which were
built by Poseidon for Priam's father Laomedon so that the city
might be unbreakable (21.446–47).[5] Many of the most memo-

rable scenes of the *Iliad* take place at these walls: from them Helen points out the Greek leaders to Priam in Book 3; here Andromache and Hektor meet in Book 6, and Priam and Hecuba watch Hektor being killed in Book 22, after Achilles prevents him from approaching the "gates" and the "well-built towers" where his people could help him (22.194–98). Troy is called "well-walled" (*euteicheon*), "steep" (*aipu*), "towering" (*aipeinē*), and "beetling" (*ophruoessa*); it has a "great tower" (*purgon . . . megan*), and is "windy" (*ēnemoessa*), an adjective apparently referring to its height. Troy also is "abounding in horses" (*eupōlē*) and the Trojans are "tamers of horses" (*hippodamoi*), which particularly suggests the efforts of human culture taming nature. Most often the city is called "sacred" (*hirē*), which probably refers to the temples of the gods established by its inhabitants in the upper part of the town, like those of Athene (6.297) and Zeus (22.172).

In Book 6 Hektor makes his way

> . . . to the very beautiful house of Priam
> made with smooth-hewn porticoes: in it
> there were fifty bedrooms of smooth-hewn stone,
> built near one another, and there the sons
> of Priam slept with the wives they had wooed;
> on the other side, opposite, within the court were his
>   daughters'
> twelve covered bedrooms of smooth-hewn stone,
> built near one another, and there the sons-in-law
> of Priam slept by their respected wives.
>
> (6.242–50)

Later Hektor reaches the house of Paris,

> beautiful, which Paris himself made with the men who at that
>   time
> were the best carpenters in fertile Troy,
> who made for him a bedroom and a home and a yard
> near Priam's and Hektor's, in the upper part of the city.
>
> (6.314–17)

The beauty and sophistication of the architecture, combined with Homer's emphasis on the sleeping arrangements of Priam's children and their spouses, show Troy to be a center of civilized refinement and domestic decorum. There is an obvious contrast to the camp of the Greeks, with its temporary shelters arranged in accordance with individual heroes' confidence in their own prowess (8.222–26 = 11.5–9) and its hastily constructed wall (7.435–41) that fails to keep the Trojan army away from the ships.

The social organization of Troy is likewise more complex than that of the Greek army. This has nothing to do with any ethnic distinction between Greeks and Trojans: each community left behind in Greece would presumably resemble Troy closely in its social forms, and, in any event, Homer is completely even-handed and unprejudiced in his depictions of Greeks and Trojans.[6] Rather, the differences between the two societies are thematically determined. The Greeks, who are away from their homes on an expedition of conquest, are all males and almost all young, and the various warrior-princes are independent of one another and equal in authority, except for the first-among-equals status of Agamemnon. The Trojan society includes not only their own youth and allied warriors, but also parents, children, and wives, old men and babies, who have the various social roles and relations appropriate to a complete human society. For example, the Greek army includes only two old men, Nestor and Phoinix, who are past the age of significant military activity. Phoinix has no real function apart from his participation in the embassy to Achilles in Book 9, and Nestor, although he is honored as a kind of "high priest" of heroism and still drives out to battle in a chariot, spends most of his time recalling his exploits when he was young, which are the reason why he should be respected and his advice should be followed. On the other hand, among the Trojans there are a number of old men, including King Priam, who "having been stopped by old age from fighting" sit at the Skaian gates as "elders of the people" and "leaders of the Trojans" and are respected for their wisdom and for the power of oratory appropriate to their age (3.146–53). These elders remark that Helen, although "she is terribly like the immortal goddesses face to face," should be sent away "lest she be left behind as suffering for ourselves and our children in the future" (3.158–60); one of them, Antenor, proposes this course of action in the Trojan assembly (7.350–53). But Helen is not sent home, and the elders have no effect on the conduct of the war. In the society of Troy, as in modern Mediterranean cultures studied by anthropologists, the knowledge and status of elders are respected, and parents retain titular authority over their adult sons and grandsons; but the actual power is held by the men who do the fighting or the other activities essential for the survival and prosperity of the family and community. Though Priam is summoned from the city to perform the sacrifices before the single combat between Paris and Menelaos, because, as Agamemnon says, "the minds of younger men always are flighty" (3.108), it is Hektor who agrees to the terms of the duel and makes the practical arrangements. When Paris, occasional fighter that he is, opposes Antenor's proposal in the Trojan assembly, the discussion is finished, although Priam formally announces the decision as his own before dismissing the gathering (7.357–78).[7]

The situation of women among the Trojans is similar to that of old men. In the Greek army, which exists solely for the sake of war, there are no women apart from prisoners of war who serve as slaves and concubines. These women are possessions, items of honor for the men who possess them; they can be transferred as gifts or prizes like other valuable possessions.[8] The women in Troy, like those in the Greek camp, are dependent on and in effect defined by the men on whom they each must rely, but they also are free and active in their own right.[9] Homer depicts them as playing a set of roles complementary to those of the male warriors and fathers in a complete human community. The men's sphere of responsibility includes the public activities of war and decision making; the women's sphere is the home, with its normal activities of housekeeping and homemaking: cleaning, weaving, child rearing, and supervision of female servants. The fragrant storage chamber of Priam's palace contains chests of elaborate robes, "the works of Sidonian women," the most beautiful of which Hecuba selects as an offering to Athene from the old women of the city (6.288–96). When Andromache is interrupted by the cry from the wall at Hektor's death, she is "weaving a web in the inner part of the high house, / a purple one in two folds, and sprinkling varied flowers into it" (22.440–41), while giving orders to her household servants to set a three-footed cauldron over the fire to prepare a hot bath for Hektor (22.442–44). As Achilles pursues Hektor around Troy, they pass the two springs of the river Skamandros:

> There beside them, nearby, were the washing pits
> made of stone, beautiful, where the wives of the Trojans
> and their beautiful daughters used to wash their shining
>   garments
> before, in peacetime, before the sons of the Achaians came.
>
> (22.152–56)

Each of these examples of "the works of women" illustrates the distinct role and sphere of women among the Trojans, in contrast to the masculine society of the Greek army. Therefore, when Paris remains at home with Helen, merely handling his armor rather than wearing it in battle, Hektor accuses him of acting strangely and slacking off (6.321–31), and Paris seems to be less than the warrior-hero he should be, given the norms of his society. When Andromache, in her concern for Hektor, rushes to the city walls to view the battle and, on meeting her husband, advises him on military tactics (6.433–39), Hektor tells her to

> go to the house and take care of your own works,
> the loom and the spindle, and give orders to the servants
> to go about their work; war will be a concern to men,
> to all men who live in Ilion, and especially to me.
>
> (6.490–93)

These instructions reflect clearly the characteristic, doubtless traditional division of responsibility according to gender in Trojan society.

Yet Homer not only represents but also at the same time plays against this traditional opposition between male and female spheres of activity, public and private roles.[10] He uses the relationship between Hektor and Andromache to clarify certain characteristically Iliadic complexities and contradictions within the conventional social arrangement. Andromache, like all women in the poem, has a primary loyalty to her immediate family; in her case, since her father, brothers, and mother are dead (6.413–30), this means to Hektor and their baby, Astyanax. Hektor, like all men, feels a primary loyalty to the community at large that he preserves by his heroic prowess. In accordance with her loyalties, Andromache urges Hektor for her sake and that of Astyanax to stay in the city and not to return to the battlefield (6.431–39), and he refuses to do so in the name of his responsibilities to the men and women of Troy and to his own heroism. Yet Homer makes it clear in the previous hundred lines that Andromache, not the Trojan people, is dearer to Hektor than anyone in the world. He conveys this through "the ascending scale of affection motif," a poetic convention whereby a hero meets or refers to various relatives and comrades in the order of his increasing love for them.[11] At 6.450–55, Hektor tells Andromache,

> But the trouble of the Trojans in the future is not so much a
>   concern to me,
> nor of Hecuba herself nor King Priam,
> nor of my brothers who, brave and numerous,
> may fall in the dust beneath men who are their enemies,
> as much as yours is, when someone of the bronze-clad
>   Achaians
> leads you away weeping, having robbed you of your day of
>   freedom.

In this passage, the ascending scale—Trojans, Hecuba and Priam, brothers, and Andromache—is obvious, and indicates to anyone familiar with the convention that Hektor's wife is dearer to him and more honored than the others. Similarly, the order in which Hektor encounters and speaks with the Trojans in Book 6—wives and daughters of the Trojans, Hecuba, Helen and Paris, and Andromache—confirms his supreme loyalty and love for his spouse. Thus, when he refuses her plea to remain with her in Troy, he is forced to go against his own feelings as well as hers. Hektor's loyalties are divided: as a traditional man and hero, he belongs outside with the other fighting men; as a husband and father, his care is for his wife and child. In Redfield's words, Homer "dramatizes the pain of the warrior's role, of the man who, in behalf of his family, must leave his family, so that his very defense of them becomes a betrayal."[12]

One of the most striking features of Homer's depiction of the relationship between Andromache and Hektor is the way in which each is made to participate in the other's sphere of activity.[13] In Book 6, Hektor enters his home—the woman's place—to seek Andromache, who, he learns, has rushed to the wall to look for him on the plain of battle. As I already have mentioned, Andromache offers Hektor military advice when she implores him to remain in the city; on the other hand, Hektor includes his love for his family in the love for Troy generally that leads him to return to battle, and he joins her in holding and kissing their son before his departure. Hektor is portrayed as torn between the claims of his role as a warrior, learned since childhood,

> . . . to be brave
> always and to fight in the front ranks of the Trojans,
> trying to win great glory for my father and my own glory,
> (6.444–46)

and his tender feelings for Andromache and Astyanax. When the baby shrinks back, frightened at the sight of Hektor's plumed helmet (6.467–70), the contradiction between Hektor's heroic values and familial loyalties comes to the fore. Astyanax is described (6.468) as "dazed [*atuchtheis*] by the sight of his own dear father." The verb *atuzomai* is normally used of warriors or their horses on the battlefield who are terrified and being stampeded in flight by their enemies (6.38, 41; 18.7; 21.4, 454).[14] Its use at 6.468 makes Hektor's heroism, symbolized by his helmet, have on the baby he loves an effect like that it has on his enemies. Though he removes his helmet to kiss and dandle his son (6.472–73) and he and Andromache laugh at Astyanax's reaction, their laughter in no way mitigates the contradiction inherent in Hektor's combination of conflicting familial and heroic loyalties—a contradiction perfectly expressed a few lines later by the description of Andromache as "laughing through her tears" (*dakruoen gelasāsa*, 6.484).

Homer connects Andromache's destiny closely with that of Hektor when, at 22.466–67, she faints as she sees Hektor's corpse being dragged by Achilles' horses. Like Astyanax at 6.468, Andromache is "dazed" (*atuzomenēn*, 22.474) by the sight. As C. Segal has shown, this is part of a pattern in which her faint is described in formulaic diction traditionally appropriate to a "stricken warrior": darkness covers her eyes as she falls backward and breathes out her "life-breath" (*psuchēn*,

22.467).[15] This description, in Segal's words, "equates her suffering with the more 'public' sufferings of the heroes themselves" and makes her "fate . . . at one with Hektor's. . . . [She comes] as close as a woman can in the *Iliad* to feeling the blow of the spear."[16] Andromache herself expresses this at 22.477–78:

> Hektor, I am wretched! after all we were born to a single
>   portion,
> both of us.

As she faints she throws from her head "the veil which golden Aphrodite had given her / on that day when Hektor of the shining helmet brought her / from the house of Eëtion, after he gave countless gifts" (22.470–72). This is a gesture which symbolizes both the end of her marriage and, to the extent that her identity is bound up with that of Hektor, the end of her life.[17] Furthermore, because the word for veil, *krēdemnon*, can denote both a woman's chastity and the tower of a city, the loss of her veil suggests both the sexual violation of Andromache and the final destruction of Troy.[18] Her violation by Achilles' slaying of her husband anticipates the rape and enslavement of the Trojan women in the eventual sack of the city. The phrase "Hektor of the shining helmet" (22.471) in the reference to her wedding day evokes an image that stands in sharp contrast to the description of his dark locks and formerly handsome head lying in the dust as he is dragged away by Achilles' horses (22.401–3). Both images, along with Andromache's loss of the veil, recall Hektor's removal of his helmet at 6.472–73 in order to calm his frightened son.[19] This reference to the earlier scene with his family reaffirms the paradox that Hektor's heroism, which results in his death, is as harmful to his family as it is to his enemies.

This paradox, like the contradiction between Hektor's familial and heroic loyalties, also is expressed by the confused alternation between resignation and hope in his reply to Andromache's entreaty that he stay in the city. After expressing both his sorrow at the slavery that awaits her after the inevitable fall of Troy and his wish that he might be dead before he witnesses it, he prays to Zeus and the other gods to make his son outstanding, like himself, as a warrior and ruler among the Trojans:

And someday may a man say, "This one is far better than his
    father,"
as he returns from war; may he bring the bloody spoils back
after he has killed an enemy man, and may his mother
rejoice in her heart.

(6.479–81)

Hektor realizes that the war will lead to the destruction of his
city and the enslavement of his wife, but the only wish that he
can make for Astyanax is that he be a preeminent warrior and
hence a joy to his mother. Even Hektor's final words (6.488–
93), meant as encouragement for Andromache, have to do with
his "portion" (*moira*), with what can't be changed. Just as
Achilles is trapped within the contradictions of a heroism he
qualitatively transcends but to which he has no alternative, so
Hektor, as the defender of his city, cannot escape the consequences of a heroic way of life that necessarily involves both
his own destruction and the abandonment and destruction of
the family he loves more than his city and more than all the
world.

In the original Greek these contradictions are particularly
clear because the same words which express Hektor's obligation as a warrior to Troy also express his responsibility to Andromache: *aidōs*, usually translated as "shame" or "respect,"
and the corresponding verb *aideomai*, "to feel shame or respect
toward others [or: toward one's sense of oneself in relation to
others]." *Aidōs* is both an individual and a social concept; it is
an internal, emotional impulse toward correct behavior in conformity with what is expected of one by others. In Redfield's
words, "*Aidōs* is . . . an emotion provoked by the perception of
one's place in the social structure and of the obligations which
accompany that place." In particular, it is "felt toward persons
in the exercise of their social roles or when they are perceived
as having a social relation to oneself."[20]

Combat is "the crucial social act" in the *Iliad*.[21] In that context, *aidōs* is the fear of disapproval or condemnation by others
that makes a man stand and fight bravely.[22] At 6.441–46 Hektor
tells Andromache,

> But most dreadfully
> I feel shame [*aideomai*] before the Trojan men and the Trojan
>   women with trailing robes,

if I should shrink far away from battle like a coward;
nor does my spirit command me [*sc.* to shrink like a coward],
    since I have learned to be brave
always and to fight in the front ranks of the Trojans,
trying to win great glory for my father and my own glory.

Hektor here defines himself as a warrior not on the basis of some innate attraction to warfare but because of his obligation to his people. But this other-directed motivation, which might be thought of merely as duty, is fully internalized in the *Iliad* as shame, and complemented by another inner drive: "nor does my spirit command me. . . ." This in turn is explained as something Hektor has learned: to act in conformity with his noble birth in a way that will win "glory" (*kleos*)—which includes immortality in heroic poetry—for himself and for his father, to whom he owes such glory. There is no distinction between individual and social, instinctual and learned behavior: the same words translated as "brave" and "coward" (*esthlos* and *kakos*) denote "noble" and "base" in terms of birth and breeding.[23] The "shame" that makes Hektor reject Andromache's plea and return to battle is a fear of what the Trojan men and women will say if he does not live up to what he knows they expect of him. This is the same "shame" that makes Hektor ignore the pleas of his parents to retreat to the safety of the city in Book 22:

> I feel shame [*aideomai*] before the Trojan men and Trojan
>   women with trailing robes,
> lest someone who is baser and more cowardly [*kakōteros*, more
>   *kakos*] than I, may say:
> "Hektor relied on his own might and destroyed the army."
> Thus they will say, but for me it would then be more
>   advantageous
> either to return when I have killed Achilles before their eyes
> or to be destroyed by him before the city in a way that is
>   glorious.
>
> (22.105–10)

Hektor, as Redfield has said, is "above all else a hero of *aidōs*," which means a hero of social obligations and responsibilities.[24] But these obligations and responsibilities are not only to "the Trojan men and Trojan women with trailing robes," that is, to the people of Troy in general. For *aidōs*, in addition to denoting the impulse toward warrior-bravery owed to comrades and community and associated with the honor and glory to be won in battle, signifies the generosity and pity owed to the weak and helpless who are directly dependent on one's kindness and mercy for their survival and welfare. These include, in the society of the *Iliad* and *Odyssey*, guests, beggars, and suppliants, and in particular the women, children, and aged parents of a hero's immediate family.[25] When Andromache entreats Hektor to remain in the city, she asks for "pity"(*eleaire*, 6.431) for herself and Astyanax, who are utterly dependent on him. When Priam urges his son to come into the city, he likewise tries to arouse pity (22.37), and in the same scene Hecuba, extending the breast that he had sucked as an infant, implores him to "have a sense of shame (*aideo*) before this and pity me (*m'eleēson*), Hektor, my child" (22.82). Hektor is forced to choose between the direct, familial plea for *aidōs* by those who are dearest to him and his sense of the *aidōs* he owes to his city and his people. These obligations are mutually contradictory, and the contradiction is never resolved; it is built into the nature and conditions of Hektor's and Troy's existence.[26] There is no more possibility of Hektor's finding a way out of these human, social limitations than there is of Achilles' replacing with a new one the social value system from which he comes to be alienated. Both heroes can only suffer and inflict sufferings on others, trapped in the contradictions of the heroism by which they live. The major consequences of their actions and sufferings are their own deaths and the fall of Troy.[27]

2

Hektor and Achilles appear or are referred to more frequently than any other figures in the *Iliad*, Hektor in all twenty-four books and Achilles in every book except Book 3.[28] Their actions are the main actions of the poem, which reaches its climax when one kills the other. They speak at greater length and more vividly and individualistically than any other characters.[29] In this way they are characterized more deeply and fully, and their behavior is made to reflect the inner "selves" expressed by their speeches. The similes in which they are compared to elements of nature represent them as victor and victim respectively. Achilles, more often than any other hero, is compared to a predatory animal on the attack: for example, a lion (20.164–75, 24.41–45), a "great-gaping dolphin" (21.22–26), a hawk (22.139–42), and a dog chasing a fawn (22.189–90). Hektor never is compared to a predator, but instead several times is a predator's potential victim: for example, a dog chasing a lion or wild boar (8.338–42), a timid dove (22.140–42), and a fawn (22.189–92). His role in the poem is best expressed by the long simile at 13.137–48, comparing him, as he charges the Greeks, to

> . . . a destructive boulder rolled from a rock-cliff,
> which a river flooded with winter snow pushes down from the edge,
> having broken the grip of the ruthless rock with its endless water;
> bounding high the boulder flies forward, and beneath it thunders
> the forest; it rushes headlong, unswervingly, until it reaches
> level ground, then it rolls not at all although it is eager to do so.
> Thus Hektor for a while was threatening easily to pass through
> the ships and shelters of the Achaians as far as the sea,
> killing; but when he encountered their dense battle-formations,
> he stopped, having been bent back hard on himself.
> The sons of the Achaians opposite him,
> stabbing with swords and spears pointed at both ends,
> pushed him away, and he was forced back and retreated.

Like the boulder, Hektor rushes forward destructively until his force is spent and, in the end, lies motionless on the plain. Achilles, on the other hand, never is compared to a passive element of nature; he is, rather, like a raging forest fire (20.490–94) or the fever-bearing dog-star (22.26–32).

Perhaps the main difference between the two heroes is that Hektor is represented as quintessentially social and human, while Achilles is inhumanly isolated and daemonic in his greatness. This difference is reflected in numerous details throughout the poem. Achilles is cut off from his parents, who dwell far off in the depths of the sea and back home in Phthia, but Hektor's parents are present and watch him from the walls. While Achilles' mother sends her son into battle and to his death, when he wishes to go, and obtains new armor for him, Hecuba and Priam try to keep Hektor out of battle in order to save his life. Even Hektor's horses evoke a picture of his and Andromache's domestic life and its contradictory relation to his heroism: he reminds them that Andromache herself gives them honey-sweet grain to feed on and mixes wine for them to drink when they wish, even before she feeds "me, who claim to be her blooming husband" (8.190); therefore they ought to repay this care by helping him win greater glory (8.186, 191–97). On the other hand, Achilles' horses, immortal, serve chiefly to emphasize Achilles' unique closeness to the gods and therefore, by contrast, his doomed mortality: Zeus wonders whether the gods gave them as a wedding present to Peleus so that they must experience the griefs of wretched mortals (17.443–45), and one of them uncannily speaks to Achilles to prophesy his imminent death (19.408–17).

Achilles' closeness to the gods contributes to his isolation from his fellow humans; Hektor's family is part of what makes him paradigmatically human. For Achilles, the main thing in life is winning honor and glory; his disillusionment and attendant alienation in Book 9, and the isolated detachment he shares with Priam in Book 24, move him to his deepest perceptions about human existence. Hektor, preeminently a familial and social hero, whose sense of shame is his main heroic virtue, is led to his deepest perceptions by the reunion with his family in Book 6.

More important than the great differences between Hektor and Achilles is the final, elemental similarity between them: both are mortal, and both move in the course of the poem inescapably toward their deaths, helpless to understand fully or to alter the tragic circumstances of their existence. Achilles knows, and the audience or reader knows, from the beginning of the *Iliad* that he is "short-lived" (1.352) and "most swiftly-doomed beyond others" (1.505). This knowledge, objective and accurate as imparted by his divine mother, Achilles confirms in Book 18 by his decision to die at once provided that he can avenge the death of Patroklos. From that point on, references to his death increase and are intensified until by the end of the poem he is virtually dead. A similar fatality shadows Hektor from the end of Book 6 onward. He tells Andomache,

> Well do I know this in my mind and my spirit:
> there will be a day when sacred Ilion shall perish,
> and Priam and the people of Priam of the good ash-tree spear,
> (6.450–52)

and he envisions his own death as coming before that day (6.464–65). He also speaks of his possible death in his challenge to the Greek leaders at 7.77–80. But stronger than Hektor's own anticipation of his death is Andromache's certainty that he will not return again from battle. As soon as

> . . . she reached the well-inhabited house
> of manslaughtering Hektor, and found within many
> servants, in all of them she aroused a lament for the dead
> [goön].
> The women lamented for Hektor in his own house while he
> was still alive,
> for they thought that he would not again, returning from
> battle,
> come back, having escaped the strength and the hands of the
> Achaians.
> (6.497–502)

Hektor does return again from battle and presumably sees Andromache again, but *poetically* the conversation between the two takes place in their last meeting before Hektor's death.[30] As a result, Homer's audience and readers are absorbed in Hektor's impending doom throughout the subsequent sixteen books (7–22), a doom explicitly prophesied by Zeus at 15.68 and 17.201–8 and referred to by Homer at 15.612–14. In these passages, the audience's knowledge of Hektor's approaching death becomes objective and certain, but Hektor himself never shares in this objective knowledge as Achilles does in the knowledge of his own death. He knows, of course, that it will come at some time and that it is unavoidable (6.487–89), but in contrast to Achilles, who seems more than human because he can accept how human he is, Hektor is merely human, and cannot—will not—accept this knowledge. He continues to hope; he never consciously foresees, chooses, or prepares himself for his death until it is inescapably upon him.[31] Even as Andromache is arousing in her servants the lament for Hektor, he is speaking to Paris about the possibility that

> . . . Zeus
> may grant that for the heavenly gods who live forever
> we set up in our halls the mixing bowl of freedom,
> when we have driven the well-greaved Achaians from Troy.
>
> (6.526–29)

Even when Patroklos in his dying breath prophesies Hektor's death in the near future at the hands of Achilles (16.853–54), Hektor continues vainly to hope against hope:

> who knows if Achilles, the son of fair-haired Thetis,
> may first lose his life, having been hit by my spear?
>
> (16.860–61)

By contrast, Achilles readily accepts the death foretold to him by the dying Hektor, whenever it may come (22.358–66).

Hektor's inability to foresee his imminent death is but one facet of his generally limited perception of himself and his circumstances. He is trapped not only by these circumstances, that is, by the external conditions of his existence, but by his own character and his limited vision of reality. In Books 12 through 17, as he reaps the victory promised to him by Zeus, his delusion that he will set the Greek ships on fire and destroy their army increases. Though Zeus assures him only of "triumphant power / to kill, until he reaches the well-benched ships / and the sun sets and sacred darkness comes on" (11.192–94, 207–9), Hektor interprets this as a promise of total victory (15.718–25).[32] In the long day of battle he breaks through the Greeks' wall with Zeus' help (12.445–66), drives their army toward the camp, sets the ship of Protesilaos on fire, and kills Patroklos and threatens to carry off his body. But as he advances in triumph, there are increasing references to the possibility of the Greeks' pushing the Trojans back toward the city and to Hektor's ignorance of what is in store for him.[33] Near the beginning of the day, Poulydamas, interpreting a bird-omen, warns him that

> even if we break through the gates and wall of the Achaians
> in great strength, and the Achaians give way,

we shall not return the same way from the ships in order,
for we shall leave behind many of the Trojans, whom the
    Achaians
will slay with the bronze as they fight in defense of the ships.

(12.223–27)

This warning provokes in Hektor an impious rejection of all bird-omens, to which he contrasts Zeus' personal assurance of victory (12.235–40); he accuses Poulydamas, whose words eventually prove correct, of cowardice and threatens to kill him if he holds himself back from battle or if he tries to turn anyone else away (12.245–50). A similar occasion arises at the end of the day, after Achilles has routed the Trojans with his daemonic shout and with the fire Athene kindled above his head (18.217–29), and after the sunset has signaled the end of Hektor's triumphant power (18.239–42).[34] At that point Poulydamas again warns Hektor to lead the army back to the city and not to camp out on the plain beside the ships:

Now night has stopped the swift-footed son of Peleus,
immortal night. But if he catches us here
tomorrow, having set upon us with weapons and armor, well
    shall a man
know him; for he will be happy to reach sacred Ilion,
whoever escapes, but the dogs and birds will devour many of
    the Trojans.

(18.267–72)

Once again Hektor rejects the sound advice, referring to Zeus' promise (18.293–94); he boasts that he will stand against Achilles "whether he carries off a great triumph, or I carry it off. / The god of war is even-handed, and kills the killer" (18.308–9). These pathetic words are cheered by the Trojans, whom Homer calls "foolish, for Pallas Athene took away their intelligence" (18.311).

The warnings of Poulydamas are parallel to and reinforce the other hints and prophecies of Hektor's impending death.[35] They are explicit occasions for Hektor's ignorant choices to press on to the Greek ships and to await Achilles on the plain. Hektor makes these choices thinking that he is living up to his heroic values and patriotic obligations, and that Zeus is behind him. He does not realize that Zeus plans only a temporary Trojan victory followed by their defeat, his own death, and the sack of Troy (15.61–71; 17.201–8).[36] Poulydamas is mentioned in the *Iliad* only in Books 11–18, which describe the long day of Hektor's triumph and delusion, and at 22.100, when the thought of Poulydamas' reproach influences Hektor's decision to remain outside the walls to face Achilles. He seems to exist solely for the sake of his contrast to Hektor.[37] Homer underlines this contrast at 18.249–52, where he describes Poulydamas as a comrade of Hektor, born on the same night, who was victorious with his words as Hektor was with his spear. He further characterizes him as "sensible"(*pepnumenos*, 18.249) and says that "he alone looked behind and before him" (18.250)— a standard formula for a prudent and intelligent man. Poulydamas' good sense makes him a counterpart of Nestor on the Trojan side.[38] When Hektor's choices have involved him in madness and delusion, he no longer follows the advice of Poulydamas as he formerly did (12.80), as Agamemnon heeds the advice of Nestor. Just as Homer opposes Paris and Achilles to Hektor in order to explore the distinctive heroic and domestic qualities of the husband of Andromache and defender of Troy, so Poulydamas is paired with Hektor in order to underscore his all-too-human ignorance and the tragic limitations of his otherwise admirable heroism and trust in Zeus.[39]

Hektor's ignorance and limitations are everywhere obvious in the final third of the poem. When he boasts over the dying Patroklos, Hektor supposes that Achilles had commanded his comrade not to return "before tearing the bloody shirt around the chest / of manslaughtering Hektor" (16.840–41), although Achilles' instructions were just the opposite (16.89–96). As already noted, he does not accept Patroklos' prophecy of his approaching death (16.852–54) any more than he heeds the advice of Poulydamas. When from Olympos Zeus sees Hektor donning the armor of Achilles he had stripped from Patroklos, Zeus remarks to himself, "Ah, poor wretch! death is not at all in your heart, / death which is near to you" (17.201–2). Hektor is similarly deceived about his own ability to oppose Achilles in battle. Although he boasts to both Patroklos and Poulydamas that he will stand and fight him (16.860–61, 18.305–9), he breaks and runs when he actually sees him approaching (22.131–37).[40] Even at the end, when he finally makes his stand, he thinks that Deïphobos is beside him. Only after Athene's departure makes the truth plain to him (22.296) can he die with a clear understanding of his real circumstances, charging Achilles in an act of bravery that will assure his future glory (22.304–11).

The single combat between Hektor and Achilles is the event toward which the poem has been moving since the death of Patroklos. These two contrasting heroes, one bent on individual vengeance and the other defending not only himself but his community and its way of life, join in an action resulting in both their deaths. The duel is not a matter of good versus evil, right versus wrong; rather, it is a climactic explosion of the brilliance and energy of two warriors trapped in the contradictions of human existence and tragically opposing one another in an archetypal conflict that, though grounded in their mortality, paradoxically makes them immortal through its depiction in Homer's poetry. Owen observes that the conquest of Hektor satisfies the expectation developed since the beginning of the poem that Achilles finally will do some deed to justify his reputation as the poem's supreme warrior, but the poem cannot end with the death of Hektor.[41] Achilles, in the act of killing him and defiling his corpse, has himself ceased to be human. Just as his mistreatment of Hektor's body is the measure of Achilles' inhumanity, so its restoration and burial serve as the means by which Achilles is reintegrated into the human community. Furthermore, the laments and burial of Hektor are a ritually appropriate conclusion to all of the poem's killing and dying, which culminates in Hektor's death. They even constitute a triumph, not of Hektor himself, of course, but of the civilized values of Troy: though defeated and destroyed militarily, they have the last word poetically. As G. K. Whitfield has said, "The ritual of burial is the social means by which death is humanized, just as marriage is the ritual means by which love is humanized."[42] When Achilles, in his conversation with Priam, appreciates the need for this humanizing ritual, he not only surrenders Hektor's corpse as the gods had instructed but he also asks of his own accord how much time the Trojans will need to mourn and bury Hektor properly and guarantees that they will be free to do so (24.656–70). The resumption of the war in twelve days and the subsequent death of Achilles and fall of Troy are certain. But by making his poem end with the funeral of Hektor, Homer places the final emphasis on death not as the necessary end for each individual (and so the reason for his heroism), but as an occasion for the affirmation of the continuity of human, social existence in the face of inevitable suffering and loss. In the end, love and solidarity seem somehow more powerful than death and destruction. In this way the *Iliad* concludes by pointing beyond conventional heroic values toward an ethic of humaneness and compassion.[43] For Homer's audience, such an ethic must have strongly affirmed the values of the newly emerging city-state. While the juxtaposition of the values of warrior-heroism and humane compassion probably was conventional in the poetic tradition, Homer developed this juxtaposition into a fundamental thematic contrast sharpened and clarified through his portrayal of Hektor and the Trojans.

From the beginning of the *Iliad*, it is clear that cremation and burial are the normal and desirable way of treating corpses. At 1.52 "the pyres of the corpses [killed by Apollo's plague] burned frequently," and at 7.375–77 Priam instructs Idaios to request from the Greeks a truce "until we burn the corpses," to which Agamemnon consents: "For there is no sparing of the dead corpses / whenever they die, to appease them quickly with fire" (7.409–10). Elsewhere, in the cases of Sarpedon and Patroklos, it is said that burial and lamentation are "the special honor of the dead" (16.457, 675; 23.9). The emphasis placed on assuring these heroes a proper funeral at the hands of those who care for them is itself one indication that the poem will not end with Hektor's corpse lying unburied and at the mercy of its enemies.[44]

Yet along with the emphasis on cremation and burial as normal and desirable, there also is a pattern of threats on the part of heroes in both armies to throw their victims—both enemies and cowards on their own side—to the birds or dogs. Homer states in the opening lines of the poem that the wrath of Achilles "hurled forth to Hades many strong souls / of heroes, and made them [*sc.* their bodies] prey for dogs / and all the birds" (1.3–5). Though no warrior on either side is said to have been eaten by scavengers in this way, the threats are continual.[45] Sometimes they expressly contrast such defilement to a proper burial, as when Odysseus vaunts over Sokos, whom he has just killed:

> Ah, poor wretch! not for you will your father and the lady your
>   mother
> close your eyes, although you are dead, but birds
> who eat raw flesh will pull at you, beating their dense feathers
>   around you.
> But as for me, if I die, the shining Achaians will bury me with
>   full honors.
>
> (11.452–55)

C. Segal has shown that references to the mutilation of corpses, especially by feeding them to animals, become more and more frequent from Book 16 onward.[46] They are represented in action when Achilles hurls the body of Lykaon into the river and leaves the dead Asteropaios for eels and fish to feed on (21.120–27, 201–4); they are further intensified when Achilles assures Hektor that dogs and birds will devour him, while the Achaians will bury Patroklos with full honors (22.335–36). Finally, the peak of savagery is reached when Achilles wishes that he himself could cut off Hektor's flesh and eat it raw, promising that Hecuba never will lament over his bier but dogs and birds will divide all of him among themselves (22.346–54). Like Odysseus speaking to Sokos, Achilles contrasts his intended mutilation of Hektor's corpse with the normal social ritual he will provide for Patroklos and refuse to Hektor.

Achilles continues vainly to try to punish Hektor even after he is dead for the death of Patroklos but, as Apollo tells the other Olympians (24.54), all he can do is furiously mutilate and mistreat "dumb earth"—the material remains of Hektor. Achilles' real offense in venting his hatred and sorrow on Hektor's corpse is not against Hektor but against the family and community who wish to mourn and bury him. He is violating the social need on the part of the living to bury the dead with formal, ritual propriety in order to humanize the fact of death and make it more tolerable. This communal need eventually is satisfied by the burial described in 24.782–804. The Trojans spend nine days gathering wood for Hektor's pyre and cremate his body on the tenth day. On the eleventh day they place his bones, wrapped in soft, purple robes, in a golden urn, which in turn they put into a grave beneath a pile of stones and a funeral mound. Then they gather at Priam's house for a "glorious feast" (24.801–3), which symbolically marks the end of the period of mourning and helps prepare them for the resumption of the war—that is, of life—on the following day. Before this communal burial, the members of Hektor's family join professional singers of dirges in ritual laments; significantly, these laments are spoken by the women of the family, whom Hektor especially protected and whom he visited earlier in the poem.[47] As Priam and Idaios are returning with the body, Hektor's sister Kassandra sees them from the citadel and calls on the men and women of Troy to "come and see Hektor, / if ever when he was alive and returned from battle / you rejoiced, since he was a great joy to the city and the whole people" (24.704–6). In the traditional mythology, reflected in such later dramas as Aeschylus' *Agamemnon* and Euripides' *Trojan Women*, Kassandra is the first Trojan to foresee the destruction of the city.[48] Characteristically, Homer transforms this mythology to make her the first to catch sight of the body of Hektor, whose death symbolizes this destruction. Her words about the Trojans rejoicing when Hektor returned alive from battle recall Andromache's arousing her servants to lamentation at the end of Book 6, when they did not think Hektor would return again from the war (6.500–502). Kassandra prepares the way for the formal lamentation by the three women with whom Hektor spoke during that earlier visit to Troy: Andromache, Hecuba, and Helen.

Before this formal lamentation begins, the Trojans bring Hektor's corpse into Priam's house and place it "on a perforated bier" (*trētois en lecheëssi*, 24.720). This detail is especially charged, as earlier Achilles had threatened that Hektor's mother would never place him "on a bier" (*en lecheëssi*) and lament over him (22.353).[49] When, near the end of her lament, Andromache regrets that "you did not reach out your hands from the bed [*lecheōn*] as you were dying / nor speak some sound word which always / I would remember all my nights and days as I pour down tears" (24.743–45), the contrast between the bier on which Hektor's body is lying and the bed Andromache futilely wishes he could have died in is made particularly clear and moving by Homer's use of the same word for

"bed" as had been used for "bier" a few lines earlier. Andromache's lament, like her plea to Hektor in Book 6, centers on
her own and Astyanax's future: she refers explicitly to the inevitable fall of the city, her own enslavement, and Astyanax's
traditional mythological death—namely, by being flung from
the city walls (24.728–35). Significantly, however, she does not
attribute this infanticide to a fear on the part of the Greeks that
he may grow up to avenge his father and city, which is the motive for his murder in *The Trojan Women*, but to anger on the part
of some Greek whose brother or father or son Hektor killed,
"for very many of the Achaians / took the endless dust in their
teeth by the hands of Hektor" (24.737–38). The effect is to emphasize once again the fatal nature of Hektor's heroism for his
own family as well as for his enemies. Andromache, even in the
midst of grief, expresses her unsentimental, realistic understanding that Hektor's (and her own) death is a concomitant of
his way of life. As in Book 6, Homer sustains what Segal has
called the "characteristic tonality of everything which sur-
rounds Hector and Andromache: potential peace and happi-
ness negated by a harsher reality; the tranquil, natural unfold-
ing of normal domestic life abruptly cut off."[50] As we have
seen, however, from Homer's descriptions of the deaths of
Simoeisios and other Trojan youths, this "tonality" might be
considered generally and characteristically Trojan, and Hektor
and Andromache merely its main exemplars.[51]

The lament of Hecuba for Hektor is consistent with her pride
in her son and with the savage, unrelenting hatred for Achilles she exhibited earlier in Book 24, when she wished she
"could grow into the midst of his liver and have it / to devour
raw; then there would be compensatory works of vengeance /
for my son . . . "(24.212–14). Although she finds satisfaction
in the "fresh and dewy," lifelike appearance of Hektor, whom
the gods care for and preserve from harm even when he lies
dead (24.750, 757), Hecuba recalls how Achilles kept dragging
him around the tomb "of Patroklos, whom you killed; but he
did not raise him up, all the same" (24.756). For Hecuba, unlike
Priam, there can be no reconciliation with Achilles, and she
continues to be gratified by the pain and frustration Hektor
caused for his killer.[52] She maintains her harshness and hatred
for her enemy, and this hatred, like Andromache's vision of

what is in store for her and Astyanax, keeps present in the mind of a listener or reader the impending resumption of hostilities and the future fall of Troy. Hecuba's final words about Hektor lying in the house "fresh and dewy," as if he had been killed by the gentle shafts of Apollo (24.757–59), contrast strongly with the actual manner of his death outside on the plain and also with her own continuing hatred. This contrast resembles that between the two aspects of Hektor: his gentleness to his family and his heroic fierceness toward his enemies.

Helen's lament for Hektor is in the same tone as the end of Hecuba's. She focuses on his unique gentleness and kindness: "for to me no one else in broad Troy is any longer / mild and friendly, but they all shudder at me" (24.774–75). Helen's speech recalls Briseis' lament over the dead Patroklos at 19.287–300; each speaker emphasizes the gentleness and kindness of the dead warrior toward herself as a stranger in the community, which contrasts strongly with the savage heroism that led to his destruction.[53] Thus Helen, in the final comment on Hektor by anyone in the poem, reinforces the double perspective Andromache and Hecuba have presented. When the Trojans, whose most common epithet is "tamers of horses," bury "Hektor, tamer of horses" (24.804), they celebrate the funeral not only of the preeminent representative of their culture and civilization but of the city itself, whose destruction is inextricably bound up with that of Hektor.

Notes to Chapter 6

[1]Part of the story of the sack of Troy is sung by Demodokos, at Odysseus' request, at *Odyssey* 8.499–520; it was told fully in the Epic Cycle in *The Sack of Ilium*, which was based on traditional mythology and which, in turn, left its mark on Vergil's description of the event in *Aeneid* 2.

[2]Cf. W. Schadewaldt, *Iliasstudien*, 3d ed. (Darmstadt, 1966), p. 108, who refers to "das Heldentum Hektors" as "das Heldentum des gebundenen Menschen."

[3]On the rise of the *polis* as an eighth-century phenomenon, see V. Ehrenberg, *The Greek State*, 2d ed. (1960; reprint, New York, 1964), cited by G. K. Whitfield, "The Restored Relation: The Supplication Theme in the *Iliad*" (Ph.D. diss., Columbia, 1967), p. 82; A. M. Snodgrass, *Archaic Greece* (Berkeley and Los Angeles, 1980), pp. 15–84.

[4]Cf. J. M. Redfield, *Nature and Culture in the Iliad: The Tragedy of Hector* (Chicago and London, 1975), pp. 109–10. It is a major theme of Redfield's book that we today can identify with, and therefore be tragically moved by, the human heroism of Hektor, "a hero of responsibilities" (p. 110), more readily than we can comprehend and be affected by that of Achilles.

[5]Strong walls, with wide and numerous gates, are the sign *par excellence* of a major city in the *Iliad* and in the poetic tradition generally, and many Greek myths celebrate heroes who built and walled cities. The *Iliad* mentions "seven-gated Thebes," which the Greek army sacked before coming to Troy, although it had withstood their fathers' expedition (4.406–10), and Egyptian Thebes, with one hundred gates, to which Achilles refers at 9.381–84. It is possible that the word *polis* originally denoted a walled and therefore protected area, where inhabitants of a region could be safe from wild animals and human enemies. At various Bronze Age sites in Greece, notably Tiryns and Mycenae, the remains of huge, "Cyclopean" walls surrounding royal "palaces" have been discovered, and anthropologists and archaeologists have linked the development of walls in various Mesopotamian locations with the rise of the state. In this connection it is notable that the *Epic of Gilgamesh* refers to the walls of Uruk which the hero built.

[6]See J. Th. Kakridis, *Homer Revisited* (Lund, 1971), pp. 54–67.

[7]For an instructive discussion of "age-grading" in the *Iliad* from a different perspective than my own, see Redfield, *Nature and Culture*, pp. 110–12.

[8]Agamemnon includes seven women among the gifts he promises to Achilles if he rejoins the army (9.128–30, 270–72), and Achilles offers two as prizes in the funeral games of Patroklos (23.261, 263, 704–5). For the Greeks, women exist only for their literal and symbolic use and exchange value. Both Nestor (2.354–55) and Agamemnon (3.301) envision the sexual possession of the Trojan wives by the Greeks as part of the eventual victory in the war, and Agamemnon (4.238–39) speaks of taking away the wives and children of the Trojans in the Greek ships, when the city has been captured.

[9]Redfield, *Nature and Culture*, pp. 119–23.

[10]For a somewhat different formulation, see M. B. Arthur, "The Divided World of *Iliad* VI," in H. Foley, ed., *Aspects of Women in Antiquity* (London and New York, 1982), pp. 19–41, especially p. 19.

[11]On "the ascending scale of affection" motif, see J. Th. Kakridis, *Homeric Researches* (Lund, 1949), pp. 21–25, 49–51.

[12]Redfield, *Nature and Culture*, p. 123.

[13]See W. Schadewaldt, *Von Homers Welt und Werk*, 4th ed. (Stuttgart, 1965), p. 216; Arthur, "Divided World," pp. 30–31.

[14]Cf. 15.90, where Themis compares Hera, who has, in effect, just been threatened and routed by Zeus, to "one who is dazed" (*atuzomenēi*).

[15]C. Segal, "Andromache's *Anagnorisis*," *Harvard Studies in Classical Philology* 75 (1971), pp. 33–57, especially pp. 43–55.

[16]Ibid., pp. 55, 56.

[17]Cf. Schadewaldt, *Welt und Werk*, p. 331.

[18]M. N. Nagler, *Spontaneity and Tradition: A Study in the Oral Art of Homer* (Berkeley and Los Angeles, 1974), pp. 48–51.

[19]Cf. Segal, "Andromache's *Anagnorisis*," p. 49.

[20]Redfield, *Nature and Culture*, p. 118.

[21]Ibid., p. 119.

[22]See, e.g., 5.530; 8.228; 13.95, 122; 15.502, 561–63, 657; 16.422.

[23]Cf. Schadewaldt, *Welt und Werk*, p. 220: "Aber diese Pflicht: immer Bester zu sein, im vordersten Feld zu kämpfen, dem Ruf des Vaters nicht Schande zu machen, den eigenen Ruf zu wahren, ist eben das, was er als Edler 'gelernt' hat. Was einst Vorschrift und Beispiel war, ist ihm durch Zucht längst zur zweiten Natur geworden. Keine Fiber seines Inneres regt sich dagegen."

[24]Redfield, *Nature and Culture*, p. 119.

[25]On this sense of *aidōs*, see Whitfield, "Restored Relation," pp. 56–58.

[26]Redfield, *Nature and Culture*, p. 126.

[27]Cf. C. H. Whitman, *Homer and the Heroic Tradition* (Cambridge, Mass., 1958), p. 208.

[28]J. A. Scott, *The Unity of Homer* (Berkeley, 1921), p. 218.

[29]S. E. Bassett, *The Poetry of Homer* (Berkeley and Los Angeles, 1938), p. 78, notes that Hektor speaks more, and more picturesquely, than any other character except Achilles.

[30]Hektor presumably sees Andromache during the nights indicated at 7.282, 288–380; 7.429–31; and 7.476–77. Analytic critics of Homer have made much of this narrative inconsistency, e.g., U. von Wilamowitz-Moellendorff, *Die Ilias und Homer* (Berlin, 1920), p. 28, and G. Jachmann, "Homerische Einzellieder," in *Symbola Coloniensia* (Cologne, 1949), p. 23, for whom it is an "atrocious ugliness" (*Abscheulichkeit*). These critics misapply logic and realism in their reading of the *Iliad*. In the words of W. Schadewaldt, in "Hektor in der Ilias," *Hellas und Hesperien*, 2d ed., 2 vols. (Zurich and Stuttgart, 1970), vol. 1, p. 24, they fail to appreciate that, especially in oral poetry, "only that is poetically existent, which the poet calls forth through his words and through the images and ideas forcibly awakened by these words in the hearer's imagination." Cf. pp. 22–24 of Schadewaldt's essay, and Scott, *Unity of Homer*, pp. 210–15.

[31]Cf. Schadewaldt, *Iliasstudien*, p. 108.

[32]On Zeus' support of Hektor as perceived both by Hektor himself and by the Greeks, see Schadewaldt, *Iliasstudien*, p. 104 n. 3.

[33]Ibid., pp. 105–8.

[34]Cf. E. T. Owen, *The Story of the Iliad* (1946; reprint, Ann Arbor, 1966), pp. 182–83.

[35]Schadewaldt, "Hektor in der Ilias," pp. 33–34.

[36]Cf. K. Reinhardt, *Die Ilias und ihr Dichter* (Göttingen, 1961), p. 274; Redfield, *Nature and Culture*, p. 145.

[37]In this way Poulydamas resembles Phoinix, who exists in the *Iliad* exclusively in relation to Achilles. See Reinhardt, *Die Ilias und ihr Dichter*, p. 276.

[38]Cf. F. Robert, *Homère* (Paris, 1949), pp. 251–55.

[39]Redfield, *Nature and Culture*, pp. 146–47. Redfield's whole discussion of Hektor and Poulydamas, pp. 144–47, is enlightening.

[40]Perhaps the form of these boasts is meant to show Hektor's real lack of confidence. To Patroklos he offers a rhetorical question: "Who knows if Achilles, the son of fair-haired Thetis, / may not lose his life, having first been struck by my spear?" (16.860–61). To Poulydamas he says, in effect, "I won't flee, but I'll stand and face him. Either he'll kill me or I'll kill him. Anything can happen in war" (18.306–9). Neither of these vaunts expresses the confidence characteristic of warriors elsewhere in the poem or reflects any real certainty in Hektor's mind of his ability to handle Achilles.

[41]Cf. Owen, *Story of the Iliad*, pp. 223, 232–35.

[42]Whitfield, "Restored Relation," p. 151.

[43]Ibid., pp. 152–53.

[44]See Owen, *Story of the Iliad*, p. 234. Perhaps the fact that Sarpedon and Patroklos are the only heroes of whom the formula, "for this is the special honor of the dead," is used, is in some way related to details of their respective funerals that suggest that Homer is drawing on traditional descriptions of hero cult. On Sarpedon, see Chapter 2, p. 48. In the case of Patroklos, the sacrifice of horses, dogs, and humans at his pyre (23.166–76) is unparalleled and out of place in the *Iliad*; it may imply Chthonic religious assumptions about the survival of a hero after death. Homer, of course, makes nothing of such implications. These allusions to a Chthonic religious perspective, if they are such allusions, only serve to emphasize more strongly that in the *Iliad* there is no such posthumous heroic immortality.

[45]E.g., 2.393, 4.237, 13.831–32.

[46]C. Segal, *The Theme of the Mutilation of the Corpse in the Iliad*, Mnemosyne Supplements, no. 17 (Leiden, 1971), pp. 18–47.

[47]See M. Alexiou, *The Ritual Lament in Greek Tradition* (Cambridge, 1974), pp. 12, 21, and 212 n. 107 on women's role as mourners.

[48]I assume here and below that the sufferings and destinies of the women of Troy and of Astyanax portrayed in extant fifth-century tragedies are derived from the same mythological tradition of which the *Iliad* is a product, and that Homer repeatedly alludes to this mythology and transforms it in accordance with the themes and purposes of his poem. See Chapter 1, pp. 14–15.

[49]Segal, *Mutilation of the Corpse*, p. 68, suggests that the adjective "perforated" (*trētois*) has a further ironic point at the "moment of resolution," because the only other occasion it (and the whole phrase *trētois en lecheëssi*) are used in the *Iliad* is at 3.448, to describe the bed in which Paris and Helen make love.

[50]Ibid.

[51]Cf. Chapter 3, pp. 75–76.

[52]Segal, *Mutilation of the Corpse*, p. 69.

[53]Hektor and Patroklos are associated with one another both by their tenderness to victims of Achilles, who destroyed the families and cities of Briseis and Andromache on the same expedition (2.691, 6.414–24, 19.291–99), and because, after each is killed in Achilles' armor, "the life [*psuchē*] went flying to Hades', / lamenting its doom, leaving behind its manliness and youthful prime" (16.856–57 = 22.362–63).

Bibliography

This list includes all works referred to in the text and notes, as well as several others which may be of interest to readers of the *Iliad*.

Editions, Commentaries, and Translations

Allen, T. W., ed. *Homeri Opera*, 2d ed. Vols. 3 and 4, *Odyssey*. Oxford: 1917 and 1919.

Allen, T. W., ed. *Homeri Opera*. Vol. 5, *Hymns, Epic Cycle*. Oxford: 1912.

Evelyn-White, H. G., ed. and trans. *Hesiod, The Homeric Hymns and Homerica*. Loeb Classical Library. Cambridge, Mass. and London: 1936.

Frazer, J. G., ed. and trans. *Apollodorus, The Library*. Vols. 1 and 2. Loeb Classical Library. London and New York: 1921.

Lattimore, R., trans. *The Iliad of Homer*. Chicago: 1951.

————, trans. *The Odyssey of Homer*. New York: 1965.

Leaf, W., ed. *The Iliad*. 2d ed. Vols. 1 and 2. 1900 and 1902. Reprint. Amsterdam: 1960.

Macleod, C. W., ed. *Homer: Iliad, Book XXIV*. Cambridge: 1982.

Monro, D. B., ed. *Homer's Odyssey, Books XIII–XXIV*. Oxford: 1901.

Monro, D. B., and T. W. Allen, eds. *Homeri Opera*. 3d ed. Vols. 1 and 2, *Iliad*. Oxford: 1920.

Solmsen, F., ed. *Hesiodi Theogonia, Opera et Dies, Scutum*, with Merkelbach, R., and M. L. West, eds., *Fragmenta Selecta*. Oxford: 1970.

Willcock, M., ed. *The Iliad of Homer, Books I–XII*. London: 1978.

Works on Language

Benveniste, E. *Indo-European Language and Society*. Translated by E. Palmer. Miami Linguistics Series, no. 12. Coral Gables: 1973.

Bergren, A. L. T. *The Etymology and Usage of PEIRAR in Early Greek Poetry*. American Classical Studies, no. 2. New York: 1975.

Chantraine, P. *Dictionnaire étymologique de la langue grecque. Histoire des mots*. 4 vols. Paris: 1968–1980.

Householder, F. W. and G. Nagy. *Greek: A Survey of Recent Work*. The Hague and Paris: 1972.

Muellner, L. *The Meaning of Homeric EUCHOMAI Through Its Formulas*. Innsbruck: 1976.

Pötscher, W. "Hera und Heros." *Rheinisches Museum für Philologie* 104 (1961): pp. 302–55.

Schmitt, R. *Dichtung und Dichtersprache in indogermanischer Zeit*. Wiesbaden: 1967.

Watkins, C. "A propos de MENIS." *Bulletin de la Société de linguistique de Paris* 72 (1977): pp. 187–209.

Works on Mythology and Religion

Barnes, H. E. *The Meddling Gods*. Lincoln: 1974.

Boedeker, D. D. *Aphrodite's Entry into Greek Epic*. Mnemosyne Supplements, no. 32. Leiden: 1974.

Farnell, L. R. *Greek Hero Cults and Ideas of Immortality*. Oxford: 1921.

Nagy, G. Review of *Griechische Religion der archaischen und klassischen Epoche*, by W. Burkert. *Classical Philology* 77 (1982): pp. 70–73.

Nilsson, M. P. *The Mycenaean Origin of Greek Mythology*. 1932. Reprint. New York: 1962.

Otto, W. *The Homeric Gods: The Spiritual Significance of Greek Religion*. Translated by M. Hadas. 1954. Reprint. Boston: 1964.

Rohde, E. *Psyche*. Translated by W. B. Hillis. 2 vols. 1925. Reprint. New York: 1966.

Works on Art, Archaeology, History, and Society

Beazley, J. D. "The Rosi Krater." *Journal of Hellenic Studies* 67 (1947): pp. 1–9.

Coldstream, J. N. "Hero-Cults in the Age of Homer." *Journal of Hellenic Studies* 96 (1976): pp. 8–17.

Ehrenberg, V. *The Greek State*. 2d ed. 1960. Reprint. New York: 1964.

Finley, M. I. *The World of Odysseus*. 2d ed. New York: 1977.

Gouldner, A. W. *Enter Plato: Classical Greece and the Origins of Social Theory*. New York: 1965.

———. *The Hellenic World*. New York: 1965.

Gray, J. G. *The Warriors: Reflections on Men in Battle*. New York: 1967.

Johansen, K. F. *The Iliad in Early Greek Art*. Copenhagen: 1967.

Nilsson, M. P. *Homer and Mycenae*. 1933. Reprint. Philadelphia: 1972.

Pfuhl, E. *Masterpieces of Greek Drawing and Painting*. Translated by J. D. Beazley. London: 1955.

Schefold, K. *Myth and Legend in Early Greek Art*. London: 1966.

Snodgrass, A. M. *The Dark Age of Greece: An Archaeological Survey of the Eleventh to the Eighth Centuries*. Edinburgh: 1971.

———. *Archaic Greece*. Berkeley and Los Angeles: 1980.

Vermeule, E. *Aspects of Death in Early Greek Art and Poetry*. Berkeley and Los Angeles: 1979.

Works on the Iliad, Homer, Greek Literature and Thought

Alexiou, M. *The Ritual Lament in Greek Tradition*. Cambridge: 1974.

Andersen, Ø. "Some Thoughts on the Shield of Achilles." *Symbolae Osloenses* 51 (1976): pp. 5–18.

Arend, W. *Die typische Szenen bei Homer*. Berlin: 1933.

Arthur, M. B. "The Divided World of *Iliad* VI." In *Aspects of Women in Antiquity*, edited by H. P. Foley, pp. 19–41. London and New York: 1982.

Austin, N. *Archery at the Dark of the Moon: Poetic Problems in the Odyssey*. Berkeley and Los Angeles: 1975.

Bassett, S. E. *The Poetry of Homer*. Berkeley and Los Angeles: 1938.

Benardete, S. "Achilles and the *Iliad*." *Hermes* 91 (1963): pp. 1–16.

Bespaloff, R. *On the Iliad*. Translated by M. McCarthy. 1947. Reprint. New York: 1962.

Bowra, C. M. "The Meaning of a Heroic Age." In *The Language and Background of Homer*, edited by G. S. Kirk, pp. 22–47. Cambridge and New York: 1964.

Claus, D. B. "*Aidōs* in the Language of Achilles." *Transactions of the American Philological Association* 105 (1975): pp. 13–28.

Davidson, O. M. "Indo-European Dimensions of Herakles in *Iliad* 19.95–133." *Arethusa* 13 (1980): pp. 197–202.

Davison, J. A. "The Homeric Question." In *A Companion to Homer*, edited by A. J. B. Wace and F. Stubbings, pp. 234–65. London: 1962.

Dihle, A. *Homer-Probleme*. Opladen, 1970.

Dodds, E. R. *The Greeks and the Irrational*. Berkeley and Los Angeles: 1951.

Dunbar, H. *A Complete Concordance to the Odyssey of Homer*. Revised by B. Marzullo. Hildesheim: 1962.

Ebel, H. "The Killing of Lykaon: Homer and Literary 'Structure'." *College English* 29 (1968): pp. 503–29.

Fenik, B. *Typical Battle Scenes in the Iliad: Studies in the Narrative Technique of Homeric Battle Description*. Hermes Einzelschriften, no. 21. Wiesbaden, 1968.

Fränkel, H. *Early Greek Poetry and Philosophy*. Translated by M. Hadas and J. Willis. Oxford, 1973.

———. *Die homerischen Gleichnisse*. 2d ed. Göttingen: 1977.

Friedrich, P. and J. M. Redfield. "Speech as a Personality Symbol: The Case of Achilles." *Language* 54 (1978): pp. 263–88.

Friedrich, W.-H. *Verwundung und Tod in der Ilias*. Abh. der Akad. Wiss. Göttingen (Phil.-Hist. Kl.), Ser. 3, no. 38. Göttingen: 1956.

Goold, G. P. "Homer and the Alphabet." *Transactions of the American Philological Association* 91 (1960): pp. 272-91.

Griffin, J. "The Epic Cycle and the Uniqueness of Homer." *Journal of Hellenic Studies* 97 (1977): pp. 39–53.

———. *Homer on Life and Death*. Oxford: 1980.

Griffith, M. "Man and the Leaves: A Study of Mimnermus fr. 2." *California Studies in Classical Antiquity* 8 (1975): pp. 73–88.

Heubeck, A. "Studien zur Struktur der Ilias (Retardation-Motivübertragung)." In *Gymnasium Fridericianum. Festschrift zur Feier des 200-jährigen Bestehens des Hum. Gymnasiums Erlangen, 1745–1945*, pp. 17–36. Erlangen: 1950.

———. "Zur inneren Form der Ilias." *Gymnasium* 65 (1958): pp. 37–47.

Howald, E. *Der Dichter der Ilias*. Erlenbach-Zurich: 1946.

Jachmann, G. "Homerische Einzellieder." In *Symbola Coloniensia I. Kroll sexagenario oblata*, pp. 1–70. Cologne: 1949.

Kakridis, J. Th. *Homeric Researches*. Lund: 1949.

———. *Homerika Themata*. Athens: 1954. [In Greek.]

———. *Homer Revisited*. Lund: 1971.

———. *Prohomerika, Homerika, Hesiodeia*. Athens: 1980. [In Greek.]

Kirk, G. S., ed. *The Language and Background of Homer*. Cambridge and New York: 1964.

Knox, B. M. W. *The Heroic Temper: Studies in Sophoclean Tragedy*. Berkeley and Los Angeles: 1964.

Komnenou-Kakridis, O. *Schedio kai Techniki tis Iliadis*. Athens: 1947. [In Greek.]

Krischer, T. *Formale Konventionen der homerischen Epik*. Zetemata, no. 56. Munich: 1971.

Kullmann, W. *Das Wirken der Götter in der Ilias. Untersuchungen zur Frage der Entstehung des homerischen "Götterapparats."* Berlin: 1956.

————. *Die Quellen der Ilias (Troischer Sagenkreis)*. Hermes Einzelschriften, no. 14. Wiesbaden: 1960.

————. "Vergangenheit und Zukunft in der Ilias." *Poetica* 2 (1968): pp. 15–37.

Lang, M. L. "Reverberation and Mythology in the Iliad." In *Approaches to Homer*, edited by C. A. Rubino and C. W. Shelmerdine, pp. 140–163. Austin: 1983.

Lesky, A. *Göttliche und menschliche Motivation im homerischen Epos*. Heidelberg: 1961.

Lohmann, D. *Die Komposition der Reden in der Ilias*. Untersuchungen zur antiken Literatur und Geschichte, no. 6. Berlin: 1970.

Lord, A. B. "Composition by Theme in Homer and Southslavic Epos." *Transactions of the American Philological Association* 82 (1951): pp. 71–80.

————. *The Singer of Tales*. 1960. Reprint. New York: 1965.

MacCary, W. T. *Childlike Achilles: Ontogeny and Phylogeny in the Iliad*. New York: 1982.

Marg, W. "Kampf und Tod in der Ilias." *Die Antike* 18 (1942): pp. 167–79. (Revised and expanded in *Würzburger Jahrbücher für die Altertumswissenschaft*, n.s., 2 (1976): pp. 7–19.)

————. *Homer über die Dichtung*. Münster: 1957.

Mülder, D. *Die Ilias und ihre Quellen*. Berlin: 1910.

Myres, J. L. "The Last Book of the *Iliad*." *Journal of Hellenic Studies* 52 (1932): pp. 264–96.

Nagler, M. N. "Towards a Generative View of the Oral Formula." *Transactions of the American Philological Association* 98 (1967): pp. 269–311.

————. *Spontaneity and Tradition: A Study in the Oral Art of Homer*. Berkeley and Los Angeles: 1974.

Nagy, G. *Comparative Studies in Greek and Indic Metrics*. Cambridge, Mass.: 1974.

————. *The Best of the Achaeans: Concepts of the Hero in Archaic Greek Poetry*. Baltimore and London: 1979.

————. "On the Death of Sarpedon." In *Approaches to Homer*, edited by C. A. Rubino and C. W. Shelmerdine, pp. 189–217. Austin: 1983.

Nietzsche, F. "Homer und die klassische Philologie." In *Friedrich Nietzsche. Werke in drei Bände*, edited by K. Schlechta, vol. 3, pp. 155–74. Munich: 1966.

Otterlo, W. A. A. van. *De ringkompositie als opbouwprincipe in de epische gedichten van Homerus*. Verhandelingen der koninklijke Nederlandse

Akademie van Wetenschappen, Afd. Letterkunde, no. 51.1. Amsterdam: 1948.

Owen, E. T. *The Story of the Iliad*. 1946. Reprint. Ann Arbor: 1966.

Page, D. *History and the Homeric Iliad*. Berkeley and Los Angeles: 1959.

Parry, A. "The Language of Achilles." *Transactions of the American Philological Association* 87 (1956): pp. 1–7. (Reprinted in *The Language and Background of Homer*, edited by G. S. Kirk, pp. 48–54. Cambridge and New York: 1964.)

———. "Have We Homer's *Iliad*?," *Yale Classical Studies* 20 (1966): pp. 175–216. (Reprinted in *Essays on the Iliad. Selected Modern Criticism*, edited by J. Wright, pp. 1–27, 128–34. Bloomington and London: 1978.)

———. "Introduction." In *The Making of Homeric Verse: The Collected Papers of Milman Parry*, pp. ix–lxii. Oxford: 1971.

———. "Language and Characterization in Homer." *Harvard Studies in Classical Philology* 76 (1972): pp. 1–22.

Parry, M. *The Making of Homeric Verse: The Collected Papers of Milman Parry*. Edited by A. Parry. Oxford: 1971.

Pestalozzi, H. *Die Achilleis als Quelle der Ilias*. Erlenbach-Zurich: 1945.

Prendergast, G. L. *A Complete Concordance to the Iliad of Homer*. Revised by B. Marzullo. Hildesheim: 1962.

Redfield, J. M. *Nature and Culture in the Iliad: The Tragedy of Hector*. Chicago and London: 1975.

———. "The Proem of the *Iliad*: Homer's Art." *Classical Philology* 74 (1979): pp. 105–8.

Reeve, M. D. "The Language of Achilles." *Classical Quarterly*, n.s., 23 (1973): pp. 93–95.

Reinhardt, K. *Tradition und Geist: Gesammelte Essays zur Dichtung*. Göttingen: 1960.

———. *Die Ilias und ihr Dichter*. Göttingen: 1961.

Robert, F. *Homère*. Paris: 1949.

Rubino, C. A. and C. W. Shelmerdine, eds. *Approaches to Homer*. Austin: 1983.

Rutherford, R. B. "Tragic Form and Feeling in the *Iliad*." *Journal of Hellenic Studies* 102 (1982): pp. 145–60.

Sacks, R. "Hupo Keuthesi Gaiēs: Two Studies of the Art of the Phrase in Homer." Ph.D. diss., Harvard University, 1978.

Schadewaldt, W. *Von Homers Welt und Werk*. 4th ed. Stuttgart: 1965.

———. *Iliasstudien*. 3d ed. Darmstadt: 1966.

———. "Hektor in der Ilias." *Wiener Studien* 69 (1956): pp. 5–25. (Reprinted in *Hellas und Hesperien*, 2d ed., vol. 1, pp. 21–38. Zurich and Stuttgart: 1970.)

Scheliha, R. von. *Patroklos: Gedanken über Homers Dichtung und Gestalten*. Basel: 1943.

Schnapp-Gourbeillon, A. *Lions, héros, masques: Les représentations de l'animal chez Homère*. Paris: 1981.

Scott, J. A. *The Unity of Homer*. Berkeley: 1921.

Segal, C. "Andromache's *Anagnorisis*." *Harvard Studies in Classical Philology* 75 (1971): pp. 33–57.

———. *The Theme of the Mutilation of the Corpse in the Iliad*. Mnemosyne Supplements, no. 17. Leiden: 1971.

———. "Le structuralisme et Homère: sauvagerie, bestialité, et le problème d'Achille dans les derniers livres de l'Iliade." *Didactica Classica Gandensia* 17–18 (1977–78): pp. 191–203.

Sheppard, J. T. *The Pattern of the Iliad*. 1922. Reprint. London and New York: 1969.

Slatkin, L. "Thetis, Achilles, and the *Iliad*." Ph.D. diss., Harvard University, 1979.

Snell, B. *The Discovery of the Mind: The Greek Origins of European Thought*. Translated by T. Rosenmeyer. Cambridge, Mass.: 1953.

———. *Scenes from Greek Drama*. Berkeley and Los Angeles: 1964.

Stawell, F. M. *Homer and the Iliad*. London, 1910.

Strasburger, G. "Die kleinen Kämpfer der Ilias." Diss., Johann Wolfgang Goethe Universität, Frankfurt-am-Main, 1954.

Taplin, O. "The Shield of Achilles Within the *Iliad*." *Greece and Rome* 27 (1980): pp. 1–21.

Vernant, J.-P. *Mythe et pensée chez les Grecs: Etudes de psychologie historique*. 2d ed. Paris: 1969.

———. "*PANTA KALA* d'Homère à Simonide." *Annali della Scuola Normale Superiore di Pisa*, ser. 3, 9 (1979): pp. 1365–74.

———. "La belle mort et le cadavre outragé." *Journal de psychologie normale et pathologique* 77 (1980): pp. 209–41.

Vivante, P. *The Epithets in Homer: A Study in Poetic Values*. New Haven and London: 1982.

Wace, A. J. B. and F. Stubbings, eds. *A Companion to Homer*. London: 1962.

Wade-Gery, H. T. *The Poet of the Iliad*. Cambridge: 1952.

Webster, T. B. L. *From Mycenae to Homer*. 1958. Reprint. New York: 1964.

Weil, S. *The ILIAD or the Poem of Force*. Translated by M. McCarthy. Pendle Hill Pamphlets, no. 91. Wallingford, Pennsylvania: 1957.

Whallon, W. "The Homeric Epithets." *Yale Classical Studies* 17 (1961): pp. 97–142.

———. *Formula, Character, and Context: Studies in Homeric, Old English, and Old Testament Poetry*. Washington, D.C.: 1969.

Whitfield, G. K. "The Restored Relation: The Supplication Theme in the *Iliad*." Ph.D. diss., Columbia University, 1967.

Whitman, C. H. *Homer and the Heroic Tradition*. Cambridge, Mass.: 1958.

Wilamowitz-Moellendorf, U. von. *Die Ilias und Homer*. Berlin: 1920.

Willcock, M. M. "Mythological Paradeigma in the *Iliad*." *Classical Quarterly*, n.s., 14 (1964): pp. 141–54.

―――. "Some Aspects of the Gods in the *Iliad*." *Bulletin of the Institute of Classical Studies in London* 17 (1970): pp. 1–10. (Reprinted in *Essays on the Iliad. Selected Modern Criticism*, edited by J. Wright, pp. 58–69, 139–42. Bloomington and London: 1978.)

Woodhouse, W. J. *The Composition of Homer's Odyssey*. 1930. Reprint. Oxford: 1969.

Wright, J., ed. *Essays on the Iliad. Selected Modern Criticism*. Bloomington and London: 1978.

General Index

Achilleis, hypothesized, 28
Achilles: and Agamemnon, 19, 31, 57, 94, 98, 99, 107–8, 109, 124–25n26; in *Aithiopis*, 25–26, 95; and Ajax, 115; alienation and isolation of, 25, 27, 34, 99, 107, 110, 115–16, 140, 144, 149, 153, 180–81; *aristeia* of, 35, 81–82, 143, 145–46; armor of, 92, 93; and Athene, 57, 58, 94, 95, 137–38, 158; battle of, with Skamandros, 150; and Briseis, 108; burial of, 26, 28, 155, 166n44; and burial of Hektor, 162, 186; choice of destiny of, 90, 101, 110; and conventional heroism, 128, 136–37, 155; as daemonic, 35, 91, 128, 137–40, 145, 180–81, 184; death of. *See* Achilles, death of; disillusionment of, 71, 106, 110, 181; dislocation of, from self, 27, 129, 132, 136, 149, 152–53; and Eëtion, 103, 137, 152; embassy to, 104–16; emotions of, in speeches, 107–8, 109, 118–20, 133–34; evolves during poem, 1, 90; fathers of, surrogate, 98, 107, 159; and fire, 138, 151; foreknowledge of, of destiny, 90, 121n1, 163, 181; formulas for, 6–7, 8; and friends, 112; and gods, 35, 93–94, 95, 137–40, 181; and Hektor, 32, 90, 139, 149, 150–52, 176, 179–83, 186; Hektor's corpse, mistreated by, 31, 99, 103, 150–52, 154, 186, 187, 188; Hektor's corpse, return of by, 161, 186; and Hera, 94, 137; and Herakles, 134, 136; and heroism, tragic contradictions of, 89–90, 101, 163; as hero of *Iliad*, 1, 81, 89; and honor, 100, 101, 102, 105–6, 113, 118, 132; horses of, 54, 59, 92, 93, 144, 181; humanity of, 103–4, 137, 152, 160; illogicality of, 108–9; immortality and invulnerability of, outside *Iliad*, 91, 95, 121n3; kills Memnon, 25–26; language of, 105–6, 108, 110; and lions, 158, 160; and Lykaon, 98–99, 147–49, 160, 162; *mēnis* of. *See* Achilles, *mēnis* of; mortality of, 91, 93, 95, 96, 121n3, 132, 149; as "most-swiftly doomed," 90, 92, 101, 132, 181; nihilism of, 120; and Odysseus, 48, 56, 116; and parent-child relationships, 107; and parents, 92, 180–81; and Patroklos, 27, 98, 113, 117, 118, 120, 143, 154, 155, 161; and Peleus, 93, 160; *philotēs* of. *See*

Index of Passages Cited

Compositor:	Wilsted & Taylor
Printer:	Vail-Ballou Press
Binder:	Vail-Ballou Press
Text:	Palatino
Display:	Palatino